CREATIVE CRAFTS

For camps, schools, and groups

by **Catherine T. Hammett** and **Carol M. Horrocks**

Illustrations by Carol M. Horrocks

AMERICAN CAMPING ASSOCIATION
BRADFORD WOODS
5000 STATE ROAD 67 NORTH
MARTINSVILLE, IN 46151-7902

ISBN #0-87603-106-8

Copyright 1987 by American Camping Association

Graphics Design by *Tom Dougherty*
Typesetting by *Jennifer Cassens*

TO CAMPERS EVERYWHERE

who find beauty in the world around them
who respect the creatures and the things of nature
whose imaginations and ingenuity help them
    to enjoy the out-of-doors

Contents

Preface

In *Creative Crafts* we have attempted to present arts and crafts activities which grow from the outdoor living setting, using basic arts and crafts media to develop good crafts for campers.

Many camp leaders throughout the country shared in the development of the various projects. Campers, too, helped, especially those who responded beyond the usual desire to make something, and who worked at projects with imagination and enthusiasm for the craft and for the out-of-doors. All the projects were developed by some individual or group; many were tested by campers and leaders-in-training at Derrybrook in Vermont. The book is an expression of appreciation to all the campers, young and old, who contributed ideas, suggestions and testing to the working out of the projects.

We express appreciation to these persons who helped in writing and in the production of the first edition: Miss Norma Lord, Mrs. Louise Nixon, Mrs. Ruth Richardson, Miss Margaret Rodewig, and Mrs. Virginia Stockman. For this edition we are grateful to Mrs. Corinne Murphy and Miss Marion Roberts for helpful suggestions. Mrs. Beverly Ball has helped with her camping experience and her editing skills.

CATHERINE T. HAMMETT
CAROL M. HORROCKS

Rhode Island
APRIL 1987

Camp Progamming

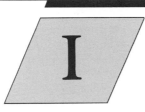

Part I: Camp Programming

The program that is carried on in the organized camp has many facets, all of them designed to help young people develop into healthy, happy individuals. Because the setting of a camp is in the out-of-doors, the major activities are those related to living in the out-of-doors, learning to know, to enjoy, and to appreciate the natural surroundings, and to make good use of the resources found there. The activities include learning to live happily with others, learning and using skills such as fire building, cooking, and lashing which make living out-of-doors simple and fun, and activities that make use of the out-of-doors such as swimming, hiking, boating, and campfires. In general, those activities that are not available in town during the rest of the year are the foundation of the camp program.

An organized camp program is everything that affects the lives of the campers. Many kinds of activities take place in camp; these are what campers think of as program. But, the daily routine, the give and take of living in a tent or cabin group, the making and carrying out of plans, health and safety, the guidance of campers in their living together, and in their progression in interests and skills are important parts of a good camp program from the adult leaders' points of view.

Reynold Carlson, former president of the American Camping Association, has stated it in this way: "The term 'program' includes everything the camper does in camp, planned and unplanned. The program is not an end in itself, but a means whereby the camper develops those personal qualities, attitudes, skills and interests that are the primary values of camp life. Through the program the counselor and the camper (we hope cooperatively and democratically) work out their camp projects."[1]

WHAT IS CAMPING?

Camping is a general term used to describe living places for armies, gypsy bands, tourists, and many other groups. Camping, or organized camping, is also the term used by individuals, organizations, churches, schools, and similar groups for the vacation programs carried on in the out-of-doors by youth leaders and groups of young people. This is the interpretation of the term *camping* in this book. Within this definition there is a great diversity, for camps are organized for two, four, or eight-week sessions in the summer, some for weekend and vacation periods year-round, some for day periods only, and some for trip or travel groups. Individuals, organizations, foundations, or churches may operate organized camps for boys and girls of all ages, for family groups, for young adults, and for senior adults.

The American Camping Association defines organized camping as: "A sustained experience which provides a creative educational opportunity in group living in the out-of-doors. It utilizes trained leadership and the resource of natural surroundings to contribute to each camper's mental, physical, social, and spiritual growth."[2]

Objectives for specific camps are expressed for each camp, but, in general, most camps have some such aims as these:

—Development of the camper as an individual and as a member of his own small living group and of the wider camp community.
—Development of appreciation and enjoyment of the out-of-doors with a growing sense of responsibility for the wise use of natural resources for that enjoyment.
—Growth in initiative, resourcefulness, and self-reliance.
—Gain in total health.
—Fun and adventure, especially that which cannot be enjoyed in town, or at other times of the year.

Camps present a unique part in the total education of young people. The influences of the home, school, church, and year-round affiliations are supplemented by a camping experience. Because camp is different, the experience adds something unique to the growth of the individual camper. How is it different?

—The *setting* is different because camps are established in the out-of-doors.
—The *activities* are different because of the possibilities offered by this setting.
—The *group experience* is different, for campers live in a camper-community with opportunities to govern themselves, to plan and act by themselves, under the guidance of leaders, in small living groups or in the wider camp community.
—*More time for guidance of individuals* is available because of the closeness of the living groups and leaders; there is more time for growth in physical skills, for the planning and carrying out of activities, and for the practice of democracy.
—The *camp is isolated from other influences;* the camper is away from home and on his own in his own peer group for twenty-four hours of the day, week in and week out. There is isolation from the hustle and bustle of city life and the year-round school and home situation.
—The *leader-camper relationship* is very close in this living situation; leaders in camp are guides in an informal situation, free from curriculum and pressures of the town situation. In general, camp leaders enjoy being out-of-doors themselves and set a happy, healthy example of good fun and living.
—There is a *readiness* on the part of the campers for camp life for it is fun, it is different—full of adventures found in the out-of-doors with experts to guide and companions with whom to share. It is vacation time, and therefore a time for enjoyment, new learnings, new experiences.

FACTORS THAT DETERMINE PROGRAM

Camp programs in specific camps are determined by certain factors that extend or limit the programming, such as:

—*Aims, objectives, and emphases of the camp, the director, and of the sponsoring organization,* if there is one: Stated reasons for establishing and maintaining the camp should be known to parents of campers, staff members, sponsoring boards.
—*Camper group*(s): Girls, boys, co-ed, adults, families; varying ages, outdoor experiences, backgrounds (national, geographic, racial, religious, economic); physical condition.
—*Staff:* Number, ages, experience, general and specific skills in leadership and program areas, interests, liking for young people, enjoyment of outdoor living and activities; pre-camp and in-camp training and supervision.
—*The Camping Place:* Site possibilities, organization into living groups, outposts and surrounding country, special natural features, hazards.
—*Facilities, Equipment and Materials:* For living, for general and specific activities such as small camp groupings, waterfront, campcraft, arts and crafts.
—*Climate, Weather:* General climate and expected weather, emergencies, provision for extremes, health considerations.
—*Seasons:* Primarily summer; year-round use of facilities for weekends and holidays.
—*Length of the Camping Period(s):* Short or long term resident periods, day camp sessions, weekends.
—*Budget:* Provision for program staff, facilities, equipment, materials, transportation.

Planning *for* the variety of program activities that will evolve in a camp is the responsibility of the director, the camp committee (if there is one) and some of the staff before the camp sessions begin. The factors listed above are part of that planning. The camp that has equipment, facilities, and materials on hand for camper-counselor planning, and leadership that is willing to let the campers make their specific plans, based on the program possibilities, will most nearly achieve the objectives listed earlier in this chapter. Planning day-by-day, week-by-week program is accomplished by the campers and the staff together; through good planning, discussion, stimulation, and guidance each camper develops his own camping fun, sometimes as an individual, sometimes in the small living group, sometimes as part of the large camp group.

TESTS FOR A GOOD CAMP ACTIVITY

What, then, are the best types of activity for a camp program? Those, of course, that contribute to the development of the camper and that carry out the objectives of the camp. If objectives similar to those listed are used as a guide, some such criteria as these will be used to determine what activities are good for camp program and which may better be left for in-town, year-round programs:

—Does the activity develop enjoyment and appreciation of the out-of-doors?
—Does the activity grow from the outdoor living situation or contribute to it?
—Does the activity aid in the development of the camper as an individual and as a member of a group?
—Does the activity develop self-reliance, resourcefulness, initiative?
—Is there an element of fun and adventure in it?
—Is there opportunity for self-expression, self-determination?

Basically, it will be seen that there are two major elements in an organized camping experience—people and the out-of-doors. Both of these elements are present in a good camping activity.

Part II: Arts and Crafts in the Camp Program

In many camp activities there are opportunities to employ arts and crafts media and techniques for enjoyment, appreciation, and usefulness. Because arts and crafts can play such an important part in the organized camp program, this book is written to help the small group counselor as well as the specialist in arts and crafts to relate these craft areas to the program of living in the out-of-doors.

Innumerable opportunities will be found for campers to use their hands and their heads to create projects in camps. In almost every camp activity area there are needs for equipment, chances to use materials at hand, opportunities for individual expression. Often arts and crafts are so correlated with nature or the waterfront or campcraft skills that it is impossible to separate the activities, if indeed there is a desire to do so.

Arts and crafts present good activity possibilities in themselves, also; and many fields of arts and crafts will meet the criteria suggested above.

Just as there are good camp activities, there are good arts and crafts activities. The objectives of any arts and crafts program in school or in camp will be the same, and standards of performance will be the same in any craft situation. When the activity is carried out as part of the camp program, these objectives and standards of arts and crafts that specifically aid in the achievement of camping aims and emphases will help determine the suitable projects to be offered.

Arts and crafts should help an individual to explore and experiment with media and techniques and should present opportunities for creativity and for individual expression. Such criteria as these will measure the worth of an arts and crafts project.

—There should be opportunity for the individual to get acquainted with craft media and techniques and to explore and experiment with these.
—These media should be in the accepted fields of arts and crafts.
—There should be development of respect for tools and materials and experience in care and use of them.
—There should be development of honest work habits.
—There should be opportunities to solve problems by one's own efforts.
—There should be development of appreciation of beauty, materials, craftsmanship, and of artistry.

In addition, arts and crafts for camp activities should:

—Develop appreciation and enjoyment of the out-of-doors.
—Make use of designs from nature and/or materials found in nature—used with good conservation practices.
—Extend basic camping skills.
—Develop objects for use in camp living.

From the camper's point of view, the satisfactions of making something, of expressing himself in some familiar or new media, and of increasing his ability and his appreciation will spell the success of the projects undertaken. From the leader's point of view, this is not enough, for it is not the object or the project that is most important, but what happens to the camper in the making or the experiencing of the activity. Opportunities to awaken interest, to challenge, to guide, to suggest, to encourage, to stimulate exploration of materials, individual expression and work, and enjoyment and appreciation—these are the goal of the arts and crafts leader in camp.

Competition that selects the best or the most has little place in a creative arts and crafts program. Progress is to be measured in relation to the individual camper's development and expression, rather than by adult standards of skill and performance. For each camper there is a starting point of his own, and counselors must recognize and honor that starting point.

LEADERSHIP OF ARTS AND CRAFTS IN CAMPS

In organized camps every staff member takes some part in most camp activities, and often it is the hobbyist rather than the specialist who encourages or stimulates a camper to try some new venture. So it is that when a camp has a staff that likes to "do things with their hands" and is to be found whittling or sketching or exploring a clay bank discovered on a hike, it will follow that most of the campers will also be doing things with *their* hands. Stimulation of good arts and crafts is a responsibility of all staff members, just as good singing or interest in nature may be. There will, however, be some staff members who are specialized in arts and crafts and who have specific responsibilities for this phase of the camp program.

Camp staffs usually have two categories of counselors: those who serve the entire camp in administrative or program capacities, and those who are counselors for living groups. In the first group will be found the director, dietitian, nurse, and waterfront, craft, music, nature, trip, and similar counselors. The second group consists of the counselors of tent, cabin, unit and small camp groups whose major responsibility is the minute-by-minute, day-by-day living of the campers in their specified groups. Some of the first group may also be counselors for living, and some of the second group may assist in various programs or administrative areas. These staff members get acquainted with each other, with the camp's way of work, emphases, facilities, and so forth, through a period of pre-camp training before the camping season begins.

Because arts and crafts activities call for the help of qualified staff members, because the managing of tools, materials, and equipment requires a special storage place, and because the activities may need a special craft workshop or center, usually one or more counselors are the arts and crafts specialists or consultants.

The crafts counselor or staff member in charge of arts and crafts activities may have a job that encompasses such activities as these:

—Has charge of the craft workshop or center, equipment, materials.
—Gives general help to all staff in craft activities.
—Sets standards of performance, outlines progressive steps.
—Stimulates, motivates, introduces possibilities for activities.
—Conducts activities at craft center for groups or individuals.
—Supplements other staff as needed.
—Correlates crafts with other program activities.
—Keeps inventories of supplies, purchases equipment and supplies; signs out supplies and equipment to small groups.
—Makes reports on individuals and on the craft program as required; makes recommendations for the next year with suggested purchasing list.

Assistants in crafts may do the following:

—Help in craft workshop or center.
—Help in small camp groups.
—Help with general camp activities.
—May maintain a small craft center in some subsection of the camp.
—May live in a living group and act as counselor there.

All staff members may have these responsibilities in the arts and crafts areas:

—Be interested in and enthusiastic about campers' projects.
—Be encouraging in all camper efforts.
—Maintain standards set by crafts staff.
—Set example in own craft activities.

General qualifications of camp staff members vary with camps and with camp responsibilities, but usually these may be expected of each camp staff member:

—Enjoys working with boys and girls.
—Is interested in the out-of-doors and enjoys living there.
—Has ability to work with other adults.
—Is emotionally mature.
—Has good health and energy.
—Is enthusiastic about many phases of camp activities, not just one.
—Accepts the policies and ways of work of the specific camp.
—Has ability to help campers do it themselves.

In addition, qualifications for craft counselors would include:

—Experience and skill in arts and crafts fields.
—Adaptability to camp situation and to wide use of crafts in camp living.

PLACES WHERE ARTS AND CRAFTS ARE CARRIED OUT

A camp may have a craft center or workshop; there may be centers in units, junior or senior camp, or other subdivisions of the camp where there are craft corners; and, the camper's pocket or knapsack may be the storage place for projects that can be worked upon wherever the camper may be.

The Craft Workshop or Center

The craft center may be a corner of a general activity center, a special building or shelter, or a special room in which arts and crafts activities are carried out. The center may be mainly a storeroom for supplies and equipment, the activity taking place under trees, on a porch, or in outdoor areas. Facilities and equipment should include:

—Working spaces such as tables, benches, stumps, that are sturdy and firm, with tops that may be used roughly.
—Vises, bench pins, and similar working devices.
—Benches, stools, or logs.

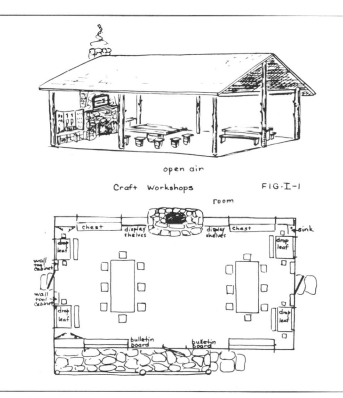

open air
Craft Workshops   FIG·I-I

—Tool racks with marked places for tools.
—Boxes, cupboards, and chests for supplies, materials; large shelves or drawers for paper, leather, and similar flat sheets.
—Shelves for books and files for pictures and clippings.
—Shelves or cupboards for unfinished articles.
—Water supply with sink for washing hands, etc. (running water, if possible).
—Bulletin boards and places for exhibits and display; adequate lighting.

Tools and equipment for the workshop will be governed by the types of craft projects that are proposed for the summer's program. In the following chapters specific tools and equipment for each craft field are

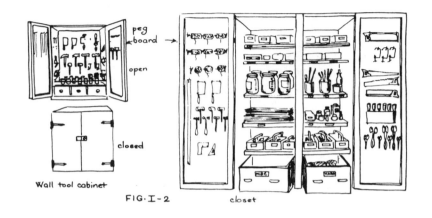

peg board →

open

closed

Wall tool cabinet

FIG. I-2

closet

listed. In general, the materials and equipment needed for any craft area should be provided rather than kits or packets of ready-cut or to-be-assembled projects which not only do not challenge the camper to originality, creativity, or exploration, but also are more expensive than material bought in bulk.

Tools and material should be arranged so that there is easy access to them, so that the camper can know how and where to put them after using them. Care and respect for tools and equipment should be part of the learning process for beginners and advanced craftsmen.

Peg boards and hooks, or pine board with wooden pegs or nails and marked areas for tools, help to keep the tools in place, ready for the next craftsman to use.

The craft library can be limited to a dozen or so books or expanded to include many of the thousands of crafts books available today. A camp may be able to borrow a set of books from a public library for use during the camp season; this is a splendid way of supplementing the camp library.

Films, filmstrips, and sets of slides may be valuable additions to a camp library if projecting equipment is available. These are especially good to use on rainy or cold days. The photography enthusiasts may cooperate in

making a set of slides that show step-by-step processes or that show completed projects.

Equipment stocked in the craft workshop supply cabinets might well consist of the following items:

—Paper—newsprint, rolls of white, unglazed shelf paper, mimeograph or typing paper, drawing and watercolor paper, construction paper in many colors, 12 inches by 18 inches, and a roll of brown wrapping paper 30 inches or 36 inches wide.
—Paints, crayons—poster, watercolor and enamel paints, charcoal, wax and pastel crayons, brushes, lettering ink and pens, pencils.
—Rulers, T-squares, yardsticks.
—Paste, rubber and household cement, wood glue, twine, cord, string.
—Shears, tin snips, scissors (all-purpose kitchen shears are good)
—Clamps and vises.
—Sandpaper, emery cloth, steel wool, wax for polishing.
—Knives, sharpeners, machine oil.
—Hammers, pliers, saws (hand and coping), screwdriver, drill and bits, files.
—Can openers—rotary and punch types.
—Work gloves.
—Rags, newspapers, plastic for covers.
—Denim, unbleached muslin, cheesecloth.
—Plywood and other wood.
—Shellac, varnish, turpentine, kerosene, alcohol, and brushes.
—Grommets, pin-backs.
—Thumbtacks, masking tape, Scotch tape.
—Stapler and staples.
—Assorted nails and screws.

Quantities of materials and the number of tools will vary with the number of campers expected to use the materials and tools, the emphases and types of projects offered, the length of the camping season, the length of time campers will be in camp. The availability of supplies and the ease of reordering will be factors in the stocking of the general supplies.

Craft supply houses in all parts of the country have such equipment and materials for sale. Many items can be purchased in hardware or department stores.

Crafts in the Living Areas

Arts and crafts in camp should not be confined to those projects that are carried out in the craft workshop or center. Some projects may, of necessity, be worked upon in the center where there may be special equipment or tools; but most camp handcraft projects are best carried out wherever activities go on, and the living place of tent or cabin is just such a place. It is important that counselors in tents, cabins, or units be aware of possibilities for good crafts and be ready to encourage or stimulate creativity on the part of campers. Having some equipment and materials on hand in the unit hut, the junior camp center, or near tents and cabins

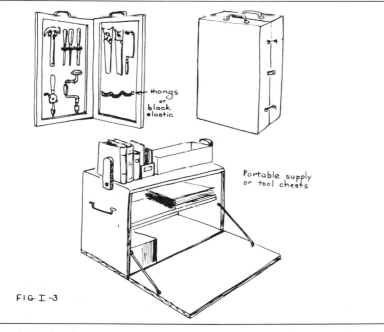

thongs or black elastic

Portable supply or tool chests

FIG. I -3

will make it simple to start and carry out craft projects. Articles started in the craft workshop may be worked on or completed in the living unit if there are general tools and some materials there for the campers' use.

The craft counselor may, as part of the planning for arts and crafts, supply each unit or section with a portable craft supply chest, or there may be a cupboard or chest in a lodge or gathering center which may be kept supplied. Some staff member in the living unit should be responsible for issuing such materials and supplies, for keeping the chest in order, and for requisitioning replacements.

The contents of such a chest will be similar to those listed above for the general supply chest, though the supply will be much more limited, and will, to a certain extent, depend upon the emphases for the particular season. Thus, if the craft counselor hopes to stimulate sketching, the unit supply chest should have paper, crayons, pencils, paints, brushes, and boards for group use. General contents may include:

Paper for various projects	Twine and cord
Paints, crayons, etc.	Thumbtacks, masking tape
Paste, rubber and household cement	Scissors
	Nails, screws
Sharpening stones, oil, wax, sandpaper	Hammer, screwdriver
	Stapler and staples
Multipurpose saw	Can openers
At least one general reference book	Work gloves

Pocket or Knapsack Crafts

Pocket or knapsack crafts are those projects than can be easily carried by the camper and worked on at any moment—while waiting one's turn at the camp shop, while singing outside the dining hall before a meal, while sitting around on tent floor or cabin step, during rest periods or quiet moments anywhere.

Braided belts, whittling, sketching, equipment, and leather projects all lend themselves to this mobility. When counselors and campers alike have such handwork in evidence at all times, surely a good atmosphere of creativity exists in the camp. The conversations about what one is making, how one is doing, how each individual is working out a design or symbol or special pattern—all these make for good talk and good crafts. Counselors will find that the quiet moments they share with the shy or awkward camper in such pocket crafts will be rewarded with new opportunities for knowing the camper, for discovering needs and for chances for leadership.

INITIATING AND STIMULATING ACTIVITIES

Not all campers know the enjoyment to be found in creating some craft article, but once introduced to the possibilities they find adventure and satisfactions that open new horizons to them. Those campers who do not know some of the possibilities will welcome suggestions for new steps and new ventures. Beginners need to be helped to start simply, so that they understand the medium and know some of the possibilities in its use before they can create an article. They should be encouraged to explore and experiment on their own to get the feel of the medium.

Program starts at the point of desire and interest of individuals, and the job of the staff is to help campers branch out from that point to new and interesting activities that will satisfy their desires, but also meet needs. Safety in the use of tools and materials will be a consideration of the counselor in the teaching of how to use and how to handle the specific equipment.

Of the many ways of motivating or stimulating activities, some have already been mentioned, such as the example set by interested staff members who have projects of their own. Here are a few suggestions, in brief:

—Have exhibits of several types of finished articles in any field (not just one to copy). Have step-by-step exhibits of simple activities, so campers can follow without instruction.
—Have bulletin boards that tell a story in colorful, pictorial fashion.
—Have progressive steps to help measure progress.
—Recognize each camper's work for what it is rather than having awards.
—Make it the accepted thing to participate in arts and crafts and to individualize each project.

Above all, in stimulating and encouraging camper participation in arts and crafts activities, remember that what happens to the camper in the doing is what is important. Once having helped him to know the possibilities of the medium and the basic techniques in the field, let him explore, experiment, use his own ideas. Judge each camper's efforts in relation to his own level of skill and experience, not by an adult level or the level of other campers. Encourage individual expression and achievement in performance.

MECHANICS, RECORDS, AND REPORTS

Arts and crafts counselors will be expected to keep some records, to use others, and to make reports. The extent of this recording and reporting will depend upon the camp. In most camps forms for records and reports have been developed, and these are explained to counselors in the pre-camp training period.

Mechanics

Signing up for counselor help, for tools, for supplies. If it is possible for the craft counselor to work away from the craft center with a tent or unit or small camp group, there must be some way in which the appointment is made. This may be by a personal checking of the staff members concerned, or it may be by signing on a special calendar developed for the purpose.

The same may be true of special tools; for instance, sketching boards and charcoal and paper may be available for groups of eight or ten. A group may sign up for the equipment for one or more afternoons. This may be arranged by consultation or by some sign-up method.

Use of the craft workshop. A schedule should be planned and times posted when the craft center is open for instruction and help in the use of equipment and materials. Then it may be desirable to allow campers to drop in whenever the workshop is open, or it may be necessary for individuals or groups to sign up or to attend by a rotating plan.

It is good to have some time when crafts counselors are on hand for informal activity, especially so that individuals can get help for projects already under way. Rainy days will bring about a shift in scheduling, as more campers will wish to make use of the workshop and the equipment or will want to carry out some group plan in the unit hut or center.

Sometimes when a group goes to the workshop, a counselor from that living group goes along to help the crafts counselors, as extra hands and heads will serve to keep projects going with larger groups. It is difficult for one counselor to help more than ten or twelve individuals at one time, though this varies somewhat with the type of activity. If campers are to be encouraged to develop their own individual projects and are not to be herded through a set course, a number of staff members should be on hand to help and encourage.

Requisitions for supplies and equipment. The camp will undoubtedly have a form for requesting supplies. One such list will be made by the crafts counselor well before the beginning of the camp season, and periodic requisitions may be used during the season. The crafts counselors should understand the financial arrangements in the crafts program; some materials may be available to campers as part of the program, without cost, and some may be paid for by the individual using other types of materials. Tools, equipment, and such general supplies as construction paper, sandpaper, crayons, etc., are usually provided by the camp. Leather for a special project or cord for a belt may be paid for by the camper. Such expenditures should be kept to a minimum; the more resourcefulness used in getting materials from the out-of-doors, the less the need for exchange of money for projects, especially at the beginner's level.

Requisition forms may be used for the tent, cabin, unit, or small camp counselors to use in replenishing craft chest supplies or for special events. The crafts counselor works out some plan for getting such material and equipment to the living units.

All staff must understand what can be requisitioned, what must be paid for by campers, and what is provided by the camp. A sheet in the counselors' workbook or manual (usually provided by the camp at the beginning of the season) will make this clear. The system is usually worked out by the crafts counselor and the business manager. Information on prices should be posted so that campers will know the possibilities and the cost, and so there will be no misunderstandings and disappointments.

Records and Reports

Inventories and reports from the previous summer, indicating what was done in the department, what was packed away at the end of the season, and what will be needed by way of supplies or equipment for the following summer, should be in the hands of the counselor before the beginning of the season.

At precamp training time the craft center is set up, ready for use in training the general staff and for use later by campers.

If there are unit or small camp supply chests, these are also inventoried and are made ready for use before the first day of camp.

Weekly or monthly or terminal reports will be expected of the crafts counselor, stating accomplishments, problems, needs, and so forth. The terminal report is an evaluation of the summer's program and serves as a basis for the following summer's work. It should contain recommendations, suggested purchasing lists, requests for repairs or replacements or new equipment. Such a report is usually talked over with the camp director before the crafts counselor leaves the camp.

Records of campers may be kept to show attendance, progress, or payment for materials. When the camper must pay for some of the materials used, it must be clear to him what the cost will be and how the money will be collected. Sometimes the crafts counselor presents a list to the business manager who charges the amount to the camper's account; sometimes the camper signs a camp store check for the amount and pays at the end of the session.

In some camps an annotated record of individual campers is encouraged; such records may be shared with the tent or cabin counselor. Sometimes the crafts counselor is able to pass along information on the good participation or performance of a shy camper so that the tent counselor can know how to use that camper in some other activity which calls for some craft skill. There is not much time for this sort of recording, but when it can be done the results will prove of great assistance to other staff members.

Sometimes progress and attendance records are required in the camp. All records serve as an aid in the compilation of terminal reports of the work of the arts and crafts department.

FOOTNOTES

1. Hammett, Catherine T. and Musselman, Virginia. *The Camp Program Book*. New York, NY: Association Press, 1951.
2. American Camping Association. *Standards with Interpretations*. Martinsville, IN: American Camping Association, 1984.

Braiding and Knotting

II

—*Cord* of various kinds may be used. A *hand-twist small cord* for lanyards and belts comes under such trade names as Belfast cord, Derrycord, Dreadnaught cord; it may be obtained in many colors, usually in 250-foot balls, from craft supply houses. *Seine twine,* a softer, heavier cord, suitable for belts and bags, is good for beginners for braiding and knotting; obtainable in many colors, from some craft supply houses. *Chalk line* or *mason's twine* is heavier,

Sailors, cowboys, horsemen, and homemakers all make use of knots in their daily work. The necessary skills of knotting, braiding, and thonging were widely used by those who lived in the pioneer days of our country. The best known craftsmen with rope and cord were sailors who spent idle hours on sailing vessels making intricate articles of rope or cord for use on shipboard or gifts for those at home.

Macrame, a knotting and fringing craft dating from ancient times, burgeoned into a worldwide hobby in the sixties and seventies of this century. Popularity for this craft has lessened in recent years, but there are still enthusiasts who enjoy the hobby, and knotting and braiding projects are excellent crafts for campers, growing out of one of the first campcraft skills beginners learn.

A knotted belt, a turk's head scarf or tie slide, a lashed tripod, or a hanging shelf will make wide use of basic knots. Macrame projects may include plant hangers, wall hangings, owls, or necklaces. Knotted articles often make use of other craft techniques, such as a whittled buckle or toggle for a belt. Rope craft is a good pocket craft, as it is easily carried about in knapsack or pocket. Braiding and knotting call for few tools and for relatively inexpensive materials: cord and small rope are the usual materials; leather or gimp strips are also used for braided and knotted projects.

MATERIALS USED

Various materials are used for projects in braiding and knotting, depending on the type, the size, and the general use for the article to be made.

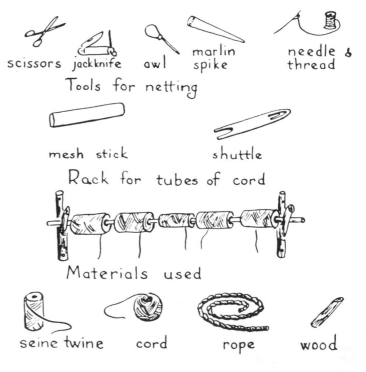

TOOLS USED in BRAIDING and KNOTTING

scissors   jackknife   awl   marlin spike   needle & thread

Tools for netting

mesh stick   shuttle

Rack for tubes of cord

Materials used

seine twine   cord   rope   wood

PLATE II

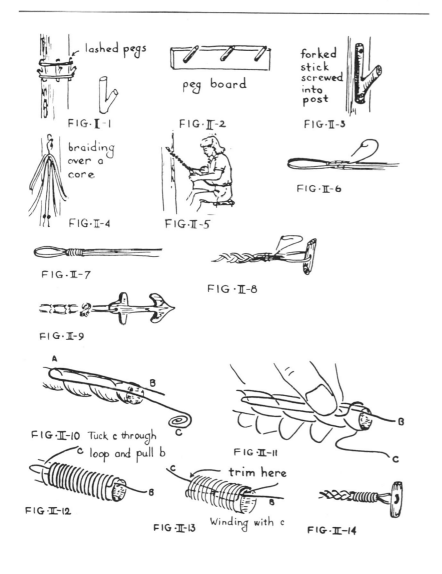

FIG·I-1

lashed pegs

peg board

FIG·II-2

forked
stick
screwed
into
post

FIG·II-3

braiding
over a
core

FIG·II-4

FIG·II-5

FIG·II-6

FIG·II-7

FIG·II-8

FIG·II-9

A

B

FIG·II-10 Tuck c through
c loop and pull b

FIG·II-11

B

C

FIG·II-12

B

c

FIG·II-13 Winding with c

trim here

B

FIG·II-14

somewhat harder than seine twine, and is used for bags and belts. It comes in white or yellow and is easily obtained at hardware stores. *Small rope* is also obtainable in many sizes at any hardware store. *Binder twine* is a shaggy, relatively inexpensive twine used for lashed articles and for making rope.

—*Leather and gimp* strips are used for lanyards, belts, etc. Plastic braiding cords in many colors and sizes may also be obtained for various projects.

—*Rope,* available in many types and sizes, is made of cotton, hemp, manila, nylon, or plastic. Woven cotton rope is easiest for use in learning to tie knots, but hemp or manila rope is generally used on waterfronts. Plastic rope is not usually considered satisfactory for rope work; nylon rope is used in boating and near salt water because it will not rot or mildew, is very strong, and will not kink or swell when wet. Twisted rope of cotton, hemp, or nylon is used for splicing.

—*Fishing line,* nylon or plastic (not monofilament), is used in some braiding and knotting projects.

TECHNIQUES

Few special techniques are used in braiding and knotting.

Practice Pieces

Braiding and knotting call for skill in producing an even braid or an even pull on the knots. A few practice pieces hung on pegs around the craft shop or outdoors (Figures II-1, 2, 3) will give campers a chance to see pieces before launching out on specific projects. Make these pieces of short cords, so they are easily tied and untied for the next person to use.

Braiding Over a Core

When strands are braided over a core, it is important to keep the core taut. This may be done on a post or tree by thumbtacking end (Figure II-4), or the core may be tied to a hook or to the camper's belt or leg (Figure II-5).

Attaching Toggles and Buckles

Loops are needed on both ends for fastening a braided or knotted belt. One end is a loop, double or single, and the other end is a loop fastened to toggle or buckle.

One or more strands should be at least 14 inches longer than other strands and are used for the fastening loops (Figures II-6 and 7). The loop is made and, with other strands, stitched in place with needle and thread, and the ends tapered. The stitching is covered with a whipping or a turk's head (Figures II-19-14 and II-59-64).

The toggle or buckle is attached by passing one (or more) strands through holes drilled in the wood; the strand is then carried back to the other strands, all are stitched together, and the stitching covered with whipping or a turk's head (Figures II-8 and 9). Ends are tapered off as they are stitched in place to make as small a joining place as possible. A drop of clear glue will help secure a knot or ends of strands.

Whipping a Rope

Whipping is a method of binding the end of a rope or cord to keep it from raveling; it also serves as trimming in some projects—in covering rough ends of cord on a belt or trimming the ends of cord on a knapsack. Sometimes, as in splicing, it is a temporary measure to keep strands in order while working.

Equipment: Knife or scissors.
Materials: Rope to be whipped; 12-inch piece of smaller cord or string for whipping.

Steps

1. Make loop *A* 1 to 2 inches at one end of string and lay it along one end of rope (on top), so that both ends of string (*B* and *C*) hang off end of rope (Figure II-10).
2. Hold with thumb at end of rope; begin to wind with long end *C* around end, toward loop *A*. End *B* stays hanging at end of rope (Figure II-11).
3. Keep winding, neatly and firmly, covering string until within 1/2 inch of loop *A* (Figure II-12).

4. Tuck end *C*, with which you have been winding, into loop *A*, and pull end *C* taut (Figure II-12).
5. Shift to end *B*; pull *B*, making loop *A* grow smaller; as it reaches the edge of winding, give a tug and pull loop *A* under the winding, carrying end *C* with it. Pull until you judge loop *A*, with *C*, is about half way under winding (Figure II-13).
6. Trim ends *B* and *C* close to winding; ends will stay under the winding. Test by trying to push whipping off with thumb and finger; if it stays, the whipping is good.
7. Trim end of rope to about 1/4 inch from whipping (Figure II-14).

Knots Commonly Used in Craft Projects

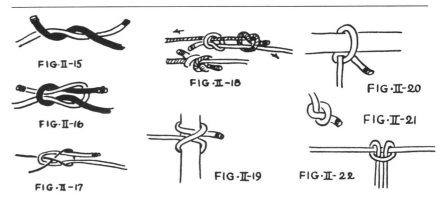

FIG·II-15
FIG·II-18
FIG·II-20
FIG·II-16
FIG·II-21
FIG·II-19
FIG·II-22
FIG·II-17

—*Half knot:* A simple knot, used as beginning of other knots (Figure II-15)
—*Square knot:* Joins two ends of similar sized rope (Figure II-16)
—*Sheet bend:* Joins two ends of different size; sometimes called the weaver's or triangle knot (Figure II-17)
—*Fisherman's knot:* Joins two ends; will not become loose (Figure II-18)
—*Clove hitch:* Used to fasten one end to a bar, pole, etc. (Figure II-19)
—*Half hitch:* Used to make an end fast, temporarily (Figure II-20)
—*Overhand knot:* Used as a stopper knot (Figure II-21)
—*Lark's head:* Used for fastening strands to a buckle, etc. (Figure II-22)

Monkey's fists (page 18), Turk's head knots (page 19), and crown knots (page 24) are shown later in this chapter.

PROJECTS

Three-strand Braided Belt

This is a simple project for beginners. It may be made with cord in single, double, or triple strands.

Equipment: Knife; peg or nail; sandpaper and wax for toggle.
Materials: Small cord or rope, chalk line, mason's twine, or seine twine; 12-inch piece of smaller cord or twine for whipping; toggle.

Steps

1. To measure: the length of one strand is equal to waist measure plus six inches. Cut two strands this length and a third strand equal to the others, plus fourteen inches.

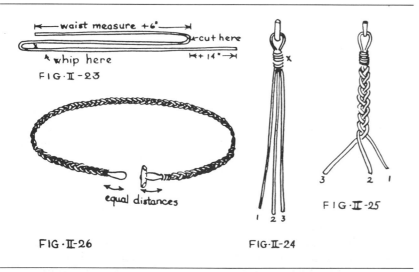

FIG·II-23

FIG·II-26

FIG·II-24

FIG·II-25

2. Pull longest strand so there is a loop (about two inches) at one end (Figure II-23 *x*); gather loop and two other strands together; stitch and cover with whipping (see Figures II-6, 7, 23 *x*). Cut loop at opposite end (Figure II-23).

3. To braid: hang loop on peg and braid evenly to end (Figure II-25). Cross left strand over center strand; cross right strand over center strand (*1* over *2, 3* over *1, 2* over *3, 1* over *2*). Repeat.
4. Braid to desired length, allowing for equal distance at toggle end, to correspond with loop end (Figure II-26).
5. Attach toggle with longest cord, putting through hole, and back to other ends of cord; stitch all together, cut off extra ends; cover with whipping (Figure II-26).

Variation: Use seine twine with double or triple strands of varying colors.

Belt of Five-strand Braiding Over Stationary Core

This is a more advanced braiding project; it offers a wide range of color combinations. The braiding should be practiced on a practice strip before attempting the project.

Equipment: Knife; sandpaper and wax for toggle or buckle.
Materials: Seine twine in one, two, or three colors; 12-inch piece of smaller string for whipping; wooden toggle or buckle.

Steps

1. To measure and cut: twelve strands, in three colors as follows—two strands of color *A* for core; four strands of color *B;* six strands of color *C*. The length of each strand is the waist measure plus six inches. Add fourteen inches on end of any one or two strands for buckle loops (color *A* strands shown here (Figure II-27).
2. Lay lengths of twine on table so that one loop (one or two strands) extends desired length, and all other loops are together (Figure II-27). Fasten these together by stitching and covering with whipping (see preceding pages). Cut loops at other end (Figure II-27 *Z*).
3. Arrange strands so *A* strands make center core. Put loop over peg and fasten core strands (*A*) so that they are taut (Figure II-28). Arrange other strands so that there are two strands of color *B* and three strands of color *C* on each side. Keep strands lying side by side—never twisted.

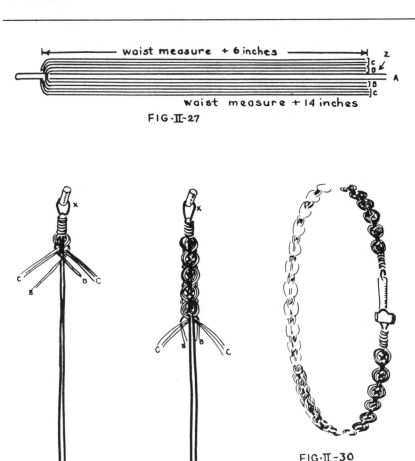

waist measure + 6 inches

waist measure + 14 inches

FIG·II-27

FIG·II-28

FIG·II-29

FIG·II-30

4. To braid: take three strands of C in each hand, bring over B strand, cross them in back of core A; pick up two strands of B, bring around under C strands and cross on top of core (Figure II-28). Repeat throughout length of core to desired length.

Make the braiding firm by pulling the strands *outward* rather than down, thus giving a rounded look to this particular braiding (Figure II-29). The braiding follows a simple formula: Cs over Bs and cross in back, and Bs under Cs and cross in front.

At end of belt use the long strands to attach to buckle (see preceding pages (Figure II-30).

Carrick Bend Knotted Belt

This is a beginner's project using a fancy knot. Single cord may be used, but ordinarily double strands of seine twine in interesting color combinations are used.

Equipment: equipment to make toggle or buckle (see Chapter X on Woodworking).
Materials: Seine twine in two colors, or small cord; 12-inch piece of string to whip ends, in appropriate color; toggle or buckle.

Steps

Read directions for measuring belt first. Practice on a short practice piece of single cord. (Figures II-31 and 32 show the knot.) Directions for the belt are given for double strands of seine twine.

1. To make carrick bend: use a practice piece of a small cord hung over a peg. Make a loop of right-hand cord A, with long end of cord on top of loop (Figure II-31); hold this loop in place, on top of left-hand cord B, with left hand.

   Take left-hand cord in right hand; bring end over long strand formed by loop of A, then up on right, in back of A, over A, under B and out to left, over A, weaving under and over from right to left (Figure II-32).

   Pull cord through and adjust strands at loops in middle of knot making the loops even. A and B strands will hang down, ready for next knot. Ease strands into place and pull evenly (Figure II-36). Knot need not be untied to adjust.

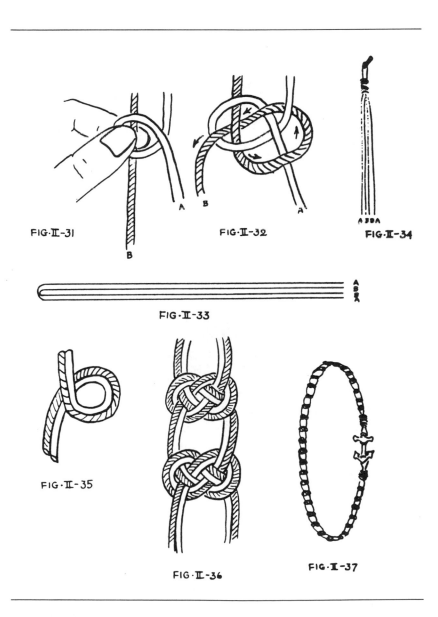

FIG·II-31

FIG·II-32

FIG·II-34

FIG·II-33

FIG·II-35

FIG·II-36

FIG·II-37

2. To measure for belt: the length of one strand is equal to four times the waist measure, with the knots approximately 1½ inch apart. When double strands are used the strand to be on the outside of knots should be 3 to 4 inches longer than the inside strand. (Figure II-34—outside strands *A*, inside strands *B*). If knots are to be closer together, make strands longer as desired. Measure and cut one strand each of *A* and *B* colors; divide in half so there are loops at one end, ends at the other (Figure II-33); arrange colors as desired. (Illustrations shown *A* strands on outside, *B* strands on inside; they might be arranged with double strands of one color on right, double strands of other color on left.)

3. To make belt: fasten loops with whipping (Figure II-34) and hang on peg.

Use the two right-hand strands *A-B* as one and the two left-hand strands as the other working strand; make a carrick bend, as above, spacing about 1½ inch from the whipping.

Pull knot evenly, not too tight; adjust by pulling loops at sides.

Repeat knots to end being sure the knots are pulled evenly and spaced the same distance apart; take care to keep the outside strands on the outside of knots (Figures II-35 and 36).

Put one (or two) strands through buckle or toggle and loop back to end of knotting (Figure II-37); stitch ends together, trim and cover with whipping (see Figures II-6-9).

Square Knot Belt

A square knot belt is a good step in progression. This type of knotting is basic in many macrame projects. Once mastered, many intricate objects may be made. The simplest square knot belts are made with four or eight strands, but any combination of four strands may be used depending on desired width of belt, size of cord, and size of buckle. The project illustrated here is for a twelve-strand belt of small cord, using lark's heads, square knots, and half hitches.

Equipment: Peg or nail; knife; large-eyed needle.
Materials: Small hard cord (Belfast, Derry, or Dreadnaught, etc.) in desired colors; metal or wooden buckle.

Steps

1. To make knot: practice on practice piece of four strands of small cord. Hang practice piece on peg; fasten two inside strands to belt for core (Figures II-4 and 5) to keep taut.

   Lay left-hand strand *A* over core; bring right-hand strand *B* down over *A* at right of core, under in back of core and up through space between left side of core and *A* (Figure II-38). Pull *A* and *B* out to right (*A*) and left (*B*), make knot even and tight at top of core.

   Reverse, laying *A* across core from right to left; bring *B* down over *A* at left of core, under core, and up through space between right side of core and *A*, and out to right (Figure II-39). Pull out to left (*A*) and to right (*B*), close against frist part of knot.

   Repeat as desired for flat knots.

   To make spiral knots: repeat first step for square knot (Figure II-38), always beginning with strand on same side (Figure II-40).

2. To measure strands: one strand is equal to seven times waist measure; cut as many strands as desired; six such strands will be required for the twelve-strand belt illustrated. Plan colors before measuring and cutting.

   Divide strands in half so the loops are at one end and the cut ends at the other.

3. To make belt: plan design for combining colors in strands. Attach strands to buckle, fastening at center of strands with lark's head knot (see Figures II-22 and 41).

   Hang buckle on peg, and arrange some way of keeping the core strands taut by tying to belt, etc. (See Figures II-4 and 5).

   Knot as desired, according to plan. Sometimes join the strands in the middle, dropping outside strands and picking up later (Figure II-42).

   To make a solid section of knots: make one row of double knots all across belt; next row, drop the two outside strands on each edge and make two knots in center; next row, repeat the first. Pull knots tight to get a solid effect (Figure II-43).

   To end belt: taper knots off so there is a point in center (Figure II-44); with a needle run ends back into belt, trim off excess cord. Or, take left-hand strand and hold it diagonally across the belt to lowest point in center (Figure II-44). Make a series of half hitches (Figure II-45) with every strand the diagonal crosses, to center. Start with extreme right-hand strand and repeat half hitch process. Tie square knot in center. Cut off excess cord. Use a drop of glue to secure ends, or run ends back as above.

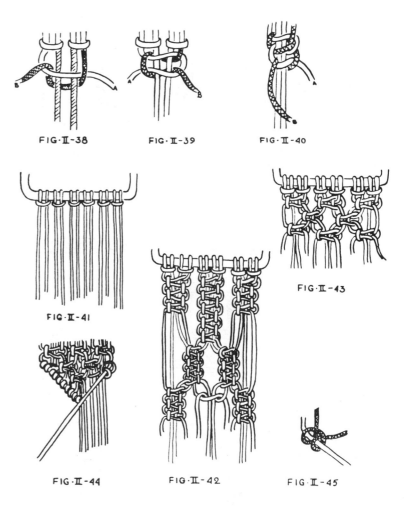

FIG·II-38   FIG·II-39   FIG·II-40

FIG·II-43

FIG·II-41

FIG·II-44   FIG·II-42   FIG·II-45

Four-strand Flat Braided Leather Belt

Flat braiding is done with flat strands of some flexible material such as leather. It is a good project for beginners in leather work. The strips may be cut; but for beginners, the ready-cut belt strips, obtainable from leather craft supply houses, will prove most satisfactory. Greatest satisfaction, of course, comes when the craftsman is able to cut his own. See Chapter Five on Leatherwork for cutting leather.

Equipment: Ruler; leather punching and fastening tools; leather cement.

Materials: Strip of cowhide or similar leather, desired width and length, cut in narrow strips to within 6 inches of one end; 6-inch strip for finishing; metal or wooden buckle; small piece of lacing.

Steps

1. Braid as follows: bring strand *1* over *2* so it is next to *3* (Figure II-46). Bring strand *4* under *3* and over *1*. Continue these two steps, bringing outer strand at left over the strand at its right, and the outer right strand under strand at its left.

   Use both hands simultaneously, keeping the same tension throughout length of belt. Be sure smooth side of leather is kept on top (Figure II-47). Braid until belt is required length. Hold with elastic band.

2. To finish: cut solid end of belt into point (Figure II-48) and punch three or more holes, making middle hold the correct belt measure, allowing for buckle strip.

   Punch slot in extra piece of leather by making two holes, and joining, for the tongue of buckle (Figure II-49).

   Cut off any surplus strands on braided belt to make belt desired length (Figure II-50), allowing 2 inches. Place buckle and strands in place inside the folded strip and cement (Figure II-50). Clamp and allow to dry. Punch holes around edge, and lace, tucking ends of lacing underneath (Figure II-51).

   Hammer with rawhide mallet; polish with shoe polish or wax.

Variation: Five-strand flat braiding differs only slightly from braiding with four strands. Start with strand **1** at left, and bring over **2**, next to **3**. Bring **5** at outer right *over* **4**, under **3**, and over **1** (Figure II-52). To con-

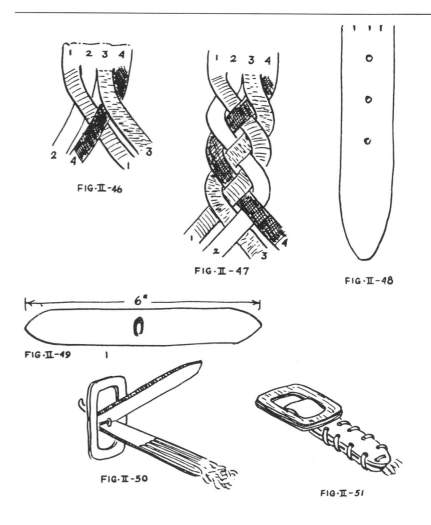

FIG·II-46

FIG·II-47

FIG·II-48

FIG·II-49

FIG·II-50

FIG·II-51

tinue, repeat these two steps, bringing outer left strand over strand at its right, then outer right strand over strand at its left, under next, over next (Figure II-53).

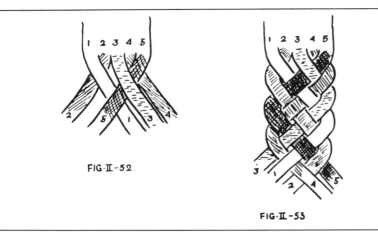

FIG·II-52

FIG·II-53

Decorative Knots

Decorative knots are used to finish articles, to make buttons, to cover ragged ends of cord, and as sliding knots for a kerchief or lanyard. Such knots give an extra "finish" to knotted and braided projects and are good progressive steps. Two of the most useful are given here; there are hundreds of variations or similar knots found in any encyclopedia of knots.

Monkey's Fist

This is a decorative knot used at the end of a strand for a button or as a "stopper" knot to keep the cord from slipping through a hole or ring as on a buckle.

Equipment: None.
Materials: Cord or leather strip—about 18 inches of seine twine or leather, to 30 inches for ¼-inch rope.

Steps

1. Make three complete turns around fingers of left hand (Figure II-54).
2. Bring cord up to center and make three horizontal turns to left, behind

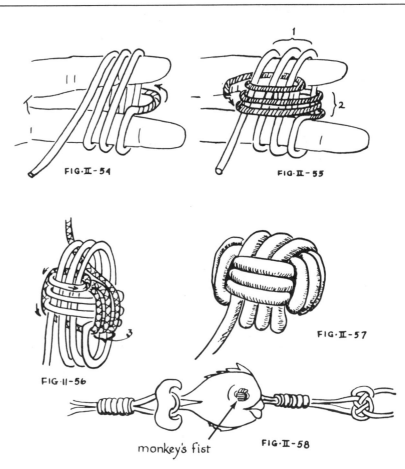

FIG·II-54

FIG·II-55

FIG·II-56

FIG·II-57

monkey's fist

FIG·II-58

and around first turns (Figures II-54 and 55).
3. Pass end through center of first loops (Figure II-55) and around second group of loops three times (Figure II-56). End in center of knot.
4. Tighten by pulling all loops in the order in which they were made; end with the two ends coming out from center (Figure II-57). Put both ends through opening and join as needed (Figure II-58).

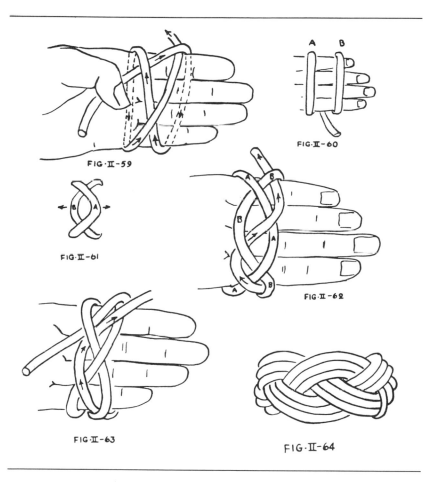

FIG·II-59

FIG·II-60

FIG·II-61

FIG·II-62

FIG·II-63

FIG·II-64

Materials: Any cord or leather strip, as desired; for practice a ¼-inch soft cord or rope 3 feet long is good; 18 inches of seine twine for tie slide.

Steps

1. Start with the cord over fingers of left hand, holding end down with thumb.
2. Go around hand, cross end in palm, around back of hand, up in palm again, crossing second strand, and ending at top of fingers, parallel with the first strand (Figure II-59).
3. Tuck end under first strand, and turn hand over. Back of knot shows to parallel lines (Figure II-60). Cross left-hand strand *A* over right-hand strand *B* (Figure II-61), and tuck working end up, over *A* and under *B*, through center of loops, over *A* and under *B* at top of hand (Figure II-62).
4. Turn hand back, and tuck working end which is in middle over strand in left, and on beside, and to the right of, the first strand (Figure II-63). One complete turn is now finished.
5. Follow the course taken by the first strand, keeping working end parallel to first strand, always at the *right*.
6. Continue complete turn, two, three, or four times. Tighten as desired by taking up slack in all turns.
7. Fasten ends inside by gluing.

This knot may be made over a cylinder as a decorative knot; to finish, pull tight and tuck ends underneath.

For small turk's head work on two fingers or pencil with threaded needle.

Knotted Twine Bag

This is a bag of many uses; it is a good general "tote" bag, and if lined with plastic or cotton, may be used for small as well as large articles. In some camps, especially in pioneer units and on trips, a "dunking" bag is used for dish washing. Small bags of knotted twine are excellent for individual dish-kits; larger bags are excellent for group use.

Equipment: Knife.
Materials: Small cord or twine such as mason's or seine twine; heavier cord or twine for handle.

Turk's Head Knot

This is a decorative knot used to cover ends as a whipping is used in previous projects, or as a sliding knot for a lanyard or kerchief.

Equipment: Spike or big nail, or awl, or large-eyed needle for small cord.

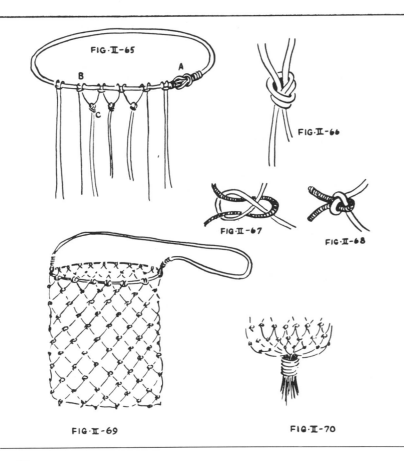

FIG·II-65

FIG·II-66

FIG·II-67

FIG·II-68

FIG·II-69

FIG·II-70

Steps

1. To measure and cut: cut twenty-four strands 72 feet long; double in half to make forty-eight working strands. Cut one 24-inch piece for top. Cut 18 inches for a short handle and 36 inches for a shoulder handle.
2. Tie single strand in circle with square knot, whipping loose ends to strand (Figure II-65 *A*). (See earlier pages in this chapter for knot and whipping.)

3. Attach the center loops of the twenty-four strands with lark's head knots to the circle (Figure II-65 *B*); place 1 inch apart.
4. Tie either overhand or triangle knots.

   To tie overhand knot (Figure II-66): hold both strands between thumb and finger of left hand; with right hand make a loop loosely around left foreginger, crossing over from right to left; put end down through loop, from back to center, and out in front and down. Tighten with a downward pull; move into place before tightening.

   To tie triangle knot (Figures II-67 and 68): make loop of left-hand strand, to right. Bring right-hand strand over top of loop, carry to left, under both parts of left-hand loop, up and back to right, over first right-hand strand, crossing over, and down under loop (Figure II-67). Pull evenly to tighten (Figure II-68).
5. Tie one strand from one set to adjacent strand of next set, and continue around bag until all strands are joined to next strands.
6. Start next row, keeping knots evenly spaced; continue to within 2 inches of bottom of bag. Tie ends across, making squared bottoms (Figure II-69).
7. Gather all ends together in a tassel (Figure II-70). Tie around and cover with a whipping.
8. Make a handle of twisted seine twine or braided twine or cord and attach at top on opposite sites (Figure II-69).

Three-strand Braided Lanyard

This is a beginner's project which may lead to many progressive steps. Lanyards are used to carry knives, whistles, small hand lenses for nature study, or similar small articles.

Equipment: Peg or nail; knife.
Materials: Seine twine or hard cord, braided fish line or flat plastic strips in desired colors; swivel, if desired (from craft supply house); small piece for whipping.

Steps

1. To measure and cut; seine twine—three strands 2 yards each; Belfast (or similar) cord: use triple lengths to make each working

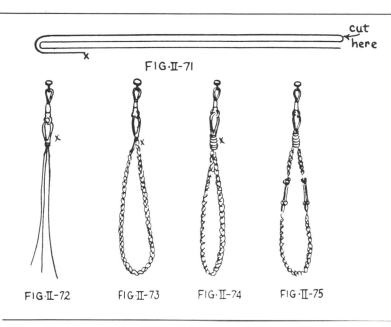

FIG·II-71

FIG·II-72   FIG·II-73   FIG·II-74   FIG·II-75

strand—nine lengths in all, each 2 yards in length.

2. Arrange strands as in Figure II-71; cut loop(s) at one end.
3. If swivel is used, thread loop end through swivel ring, making a 2-inch loop (Figure II71 x); sew this loop and end to working strands (Figure II-72 x). If no swivel is used, make the loop and sew in same manner.
4. Hang loop on peg; braid (see Three-Strand Braided Belt earlier in chapter) evenly until desired length is reached. Measure around neck, making long enough to go in pocket, if desired.
5. Stitch loose ends of braiding to same spot where loop ends were stitched (Figure II-73 x).
6. Cover stitching with whipping or turk's head knot (see earlier in chapter).

For Belfast cord: make loop at swivel of three strands, rather than all nine; be careful to keep the groups of three strands flat as you braid.

Lanyards often combine a number of knots and braids; square knotting, round and square braiding, crown or turk's head knots, etc. (Figure II-75). See following pages for variations.

Four-strand Round or Spiral Braided Lanyard

This project uses either seine twine or flat strips of leather or gimp lacing. A good step in progression is made with the sliding knot to finish off the lanyard.

Equipment: Peg or nail; knife; awl.
Materials: Leather lacing, flat gimp or seine twine or similar small cord; swivel (from craft supply house).

Steps

1. To measure and cut: cut two lengths of six times the desired length of finished lanyard. *Do not cut loops.* If two colors are used, cut one length of each color and arrange alternately. Draw strands through ring of swivel so it is in center of strands (Figure II-76).

2. To braid: hang swivel on peg. With strand *1,* go around back, come through between strands *3* and *4,* cross over *3* to left (Figure II-77) and hold at left center. Strands are now *2, 1, 3, 4* (Figure II-78).

   With strand *4,* go in back, come up between strands *2* and *1* on left, cross over strand *1,* to center right (Figure II-79). Strands are now *2, 1, 4, 3.*

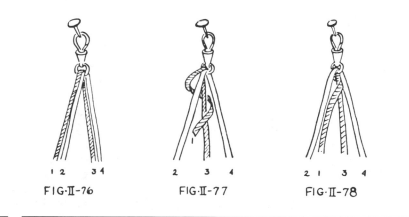

1 2   3 4   2   3   4   2 1   3   4

FIG·II-76   FIG·II-77   FIG·II-78

With strand *2,* go in back, come through between *4* and *3;* cross over *4* to left (Figure II-80). Grasp strands in both hands (Figure II-81), and pull sideways to tighten braiding.

Continue with strand *3,* as for *4* above.

Repeat, continuing to within twelve inches of ends of strands, and finish off with sliding knot (below).

3. To make sliding knot; make loop in lanyard, with swivel at top; hold

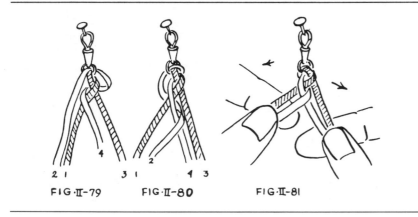

FIG·II-79   FIG·II-80   FIG·II-81

between left thumb and forefinger (Figure II-82). Arrange strands so colors are alternate—*1* and *3* of one color, *2* and *4* of the other (Figure II-82).

Working counterclockwise, follow this procedure: strands are pointing in four directions (Figure II-82); take strand *1* and fold it over between strands *2* and *3* (Figure II-83); take strand *2* and fold it over strand *1,* laying it between strands *3* and *4* (Figure II-84); bring strand *3* toward you, over strand *2* (Figure II-85); fold strand *4* over strand *3* and thread end of *4* through loop of *1* (Figure II-86).

Pull strands tight, but allow enough to play so that knot will slide up and down on braided lanyard as a core.

Work next row clockwise in similar manner, starting with strand *4* over *3;* alternate rows counterclockwise then clockwise for as long as desired (Figure II-87).

End knot weaving ends back, using awl to loosen knots, to allow strands to work through.

Or make a lock knot: starting as in Figure II-87, bring end *1* around, under end *2,* under cross strand which is on top, and out at center of square (Figure II-88). Do this to other three ends in order (Figures II-89 and 90). Twist knot toward you so the end with which you are working is in original position of end *1.* Pull ends until all loops have disappeared; pull ends tight; cut off evenly about one inch from knot (Figure II-91).

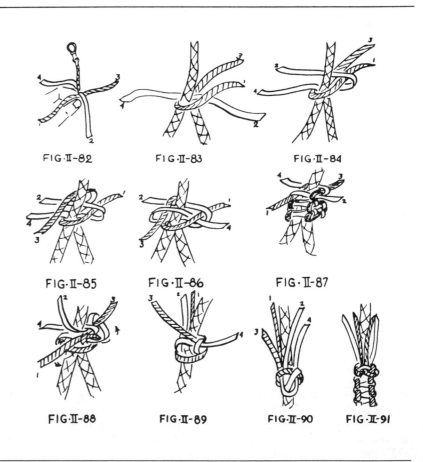

FIG·II-82   FIG·II-83   FIG·II-84

FIG·II-85   FIG·II-86   FIG·II-87

FIG·II-88   FIG·II-89   FIG·II-90   FIG·II-91

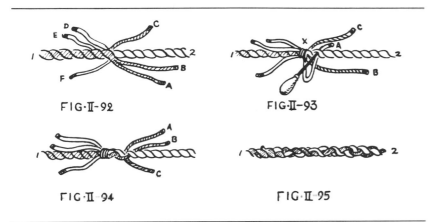

FIG·II-92

FIG·II-93

FIG·II·94

FIG·II·95

Splicing Rope

Splicing is a method of joining rope ends, of making an eye or loop in the end of rope, of finishing the end of a rope, or of making a continuous ring or grommet. Correctly made, a splice is stronger than a knot and is preferred for use with loads and strains when a rope is to slide through a pulley, or for a neat end. Splicing is a skill that shows good workmanship. It is used in craft work to give an extra finish to the project.

Equipment: Awl or large spike or marlin spike.
Material: Three-strand twisted rope—cotton rope is easiest for practice, hemp rope is generally used for lasting projects.

The four usual types of splicing are: short, eye, end, and long. The first three are described here.

For practice in splicing it is helpful to whip the ends of the strands of rope, and also to color them three different colors with ink or crayon.

Short Splice

This joins two pieces of similar rope, making just a slight bulge at the joining point.

Steps

1. Unlay (unwind) ends of each piece of rope for about a foot; whip ends, and color, if desired.
2. Place strands of one end of rope in between strands of other end (like fingers clasped together) (Figure II-92). Tie, temporarily, one set of strands to opposite rope (Figure II-93 x). Work with other three strands A-B-C.
3. Using awl or spike to pry up twisted strands, take end A and tuck it over and under one strand of the rope, loosening strand with awl (Figure II-93). Tuck against twist or "lay" of rope, pulling down length of rope. End will go over one strand, under second, out between second and third.
4. Twist a little in hand and repeat with end B, being sure you go over and under different strands from step 1, coming out at a different point on the rope. Repeat with end C. To test, be sure that each end comes out at a different place on rope, evenly distributed around rope (Figure II-94).
5. Repeat for two more tucks around, tapering by cutting away half of each end before the last tuck. Trim off ends.
6. Untie other side, and do the same with other three ends (Figure II-95).
7. Roll under foot on flat surface to even the splice.

Eye Splice

This makes a loop at end of rope (Figure II-99).

Steps

1. Unlay (unwind) strands of one end about 6 to 3 inches, and whip ends. Color, if desired.
2. Bend rope back on itself, forming an eye or loop of desired size.
3. Loosen one strand on standing part of rope, and tuck end **A** under it (Figure II-96).
4. Tuck end B under next strand of rope (Figure II-97).
5. Turn rope to back, and tuck end C under strand as in Figure II-98.
6. Pull ends tight into rope, checking to have them spaced evenly, and pulling down the rope, away from the eye or loop.

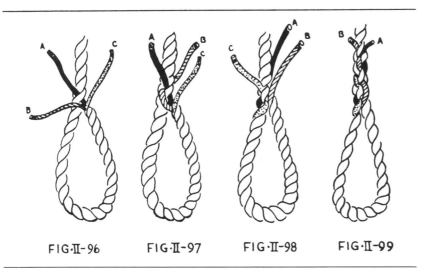

FIG·II-96   FIG·II-97   FIG·II-98   FIG·II-99

7. Repeat the three tuckings, taper as in short splice, and cut off ends (Figure II-99).

Crown Knot and End or Back Splice

This knot is used on ends of ropes to keep them from untwisting; it is usually followed by end splicing into the standing part.

Steps

1. To make crown knot: unlay strands for about 6 to 8 inches, and arrange as in Figure II-100. Cross end *A* over *B*, leaving a loop (Figure II-100). Bring end *B* over end *A*, and over toward right (Figure II-101). Take end *c* and cross over end *b* and go through loop of *A*. Pull all ends evenly (Figure II-103), each end emerging at a different spot, evenly spaced in twist of rope and pointing down rope. Work ends down rope as follows:
2. To make end or back splice: going *against* the lay (or twist) of rope, take strands in order and tuck them under one, over the next (as in other splicing); first one goes under itself. Repeat twice (Figure II-104). Taper; cut off ends, and roll under foot on a flat surface.

Ring Splice or Rope Grommet

This is one form of splicing, making a complete circle; it may be used for handles, as on a wooden chest, or for games such as ring toss.

Equipment: Awl or marlin spike.
Materials: Piece of three-strand twisted rope—hemp or cotton—four times the circumference of desired ring; string to whip ends.

Steps

1. Unlay (untwist) the rope, making three pieces.
2. With one of the pieces, make a ring approximately one-third of length of strand; then follow the "lay" or grooves in the rope with the longer end until the starting point is reached (Figure II-105).
3. Follow through once more around the ring. Join ends with a half knot (see Figure II-15), and tuck ends under nearest strands; it is good to trim half the thickness of the rope away, to taper the ending (Figure II-106). Trim ends.
4. Keep a firm twist on the strand as you make the ring. Ring should be smooth when finished (Figure II-107).

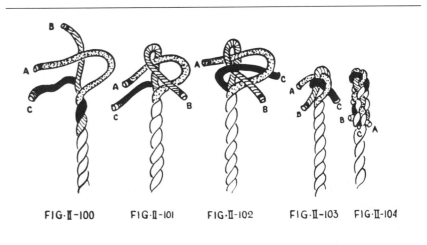

FIG·II-100   FIG·II-101   FIG·II-102   FIG·II-103   FIG·II-104

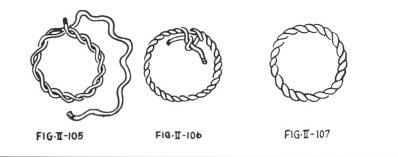

FIG·II-105   FIG·II-106   FIG·II-107

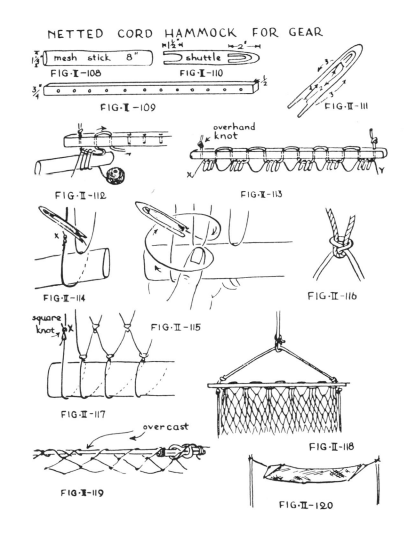

Netted Cord Hammock for Gear

This is a small hammock to be slung between tent poles or trees, to hold clothes or small articles. The process is *netting,* done with a wooden shuttle and a mesh stick. A larger, heavier hammock for reclining may be made by the same method, using larger sticks and heavier rope; such a hammock would be a good group project.

Equipment: Knife; drill—¼-inch; coping saw; sandpaper; peg.
Materials: One piece soft wood for shuttle—1/8-inch or 3/16-inch thick, 1-inch wide, 6 inches long; one piece soft wood for mesh stick—¼-inch thick, 1¼-inch wide, 8 inches long (cheese box wood or similar); two sticks hardwood ½-inch thick, ¾-inch wide 15½ inches long. Cord: 150 feet of string, cord, or fishline; two pieces clothesline (or similar)—1/12-foot piece 3/16-inch rope and two 18-inch pieces 3/16-inch rope for ends.

Steps

1. To make wooden pieces:

Mesh stick (Figure II-108): round edges and ends with knife, and sand smooth.
Two hardwood end sticks (Figure II-109): round ends with knife, sand smooth; mark off centers for ¼-inch from end. Bore hole with drill, and sand smooth. Make first and last holes big enough for the 12-foot rope to pass through (Figure II-109).
Shuttle: cut out spaces at end (Figure II-110) with coping saw and sand smooth.

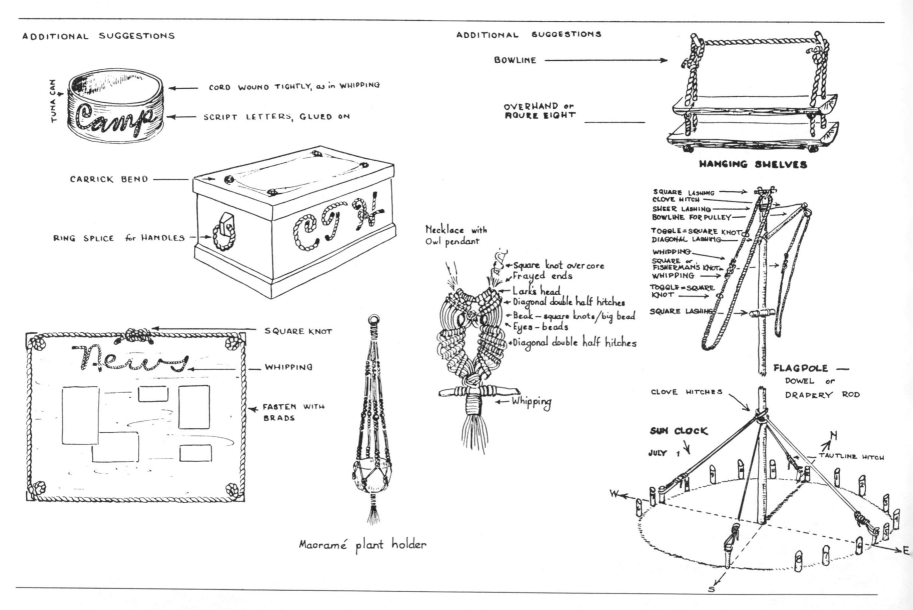

ADDITIONAL SUGGESTIONS

TUNA CAN

Camp

CORD WOUND TIGHTLY, as in WHIPPING

SCRIPT LETTERS, GLUED ON

CARRICK BEND

RING SPLICE for HANDLES

SQUARE KNOT

News

WHIPPING

FASTEN WITH BRADS

Macramé plant holder

Necklace with Owl pendant

Square knot over core
Frayed ends
Larks head
Diagonal double half hitches
Beak — square knots/big bead
Eyes — beads
Diagonal double half hitches

Whipping

ADDITIONAL SUGGESTIONS

BOWLINE

OVERHAND or FIGURE EIGHT

HANGING SHELVES

SQUARE LASHING
CLOVE HITCH
SHEER LASHING
BOWLINE FOR PULLEY
TOGGLE = SQUARE KNOT
DIAGONAL LASHING
WHIPPING
SQUARE or FISHERMAN'S KNOT
WHIPPING
TOGGLE = SQUARE KNOT
SQUARE LASHING

FLAGPOLE —
DOWEL or DRAPERY ROD

CLOVE HITCHES

SUN CLOCK

JULY 1

TAUTLINE HITCH

N

W

E

S

2. To prepare for netting: Thread one hardwood stick with one 18-inch piece of rope, as in Figure II-112. Thread one end through first hold of end stick, fasten with an overand knot, and pull through. With a 60-inch piece of the string or cord for netting, make four loops around mesh stick, and in first loop of rope; thread rope into hole *1*, across top of end stick, and down hole *3*; continue looping four loops of string around mesh stick, and rope, and threading end stick—to end. Finish rope in end stick holes with overhand knot. (The mesh stick makes loops all same size). There are now 24 loops of the netting string in the rope threaded through end stick. Cut off any extra cord (Figure II-113).

To wind shuttle (Figure II-111); start with loop around tongue, then down to forked end and up other side, around tongue and down to forked end on same side, then up front again; repeat until shuttle is filled. Tie a temporary cord to both ends of the stick (clove hitch—see Figure II-19) and hook it to a peg at a comfortable height to work.

3. To net: tie shuttle string to string *x* on left end of loops (Figure II-114). Hold mesh stick in left hand at edge of loops; bring string down in front of mesh stick, up in back, and through first loop (Figure II-114). Hold left thumb on this loop and throw string in a large loop to left over thumb (Figure II-115).

Pass shuttle behind first loop, up on left of it, over the loop, and pull tight, sometimes pulling to side rather than down, to tighten knot. Keep thumb on knot until it is completed (Figure II-116).

Continue by bringing string down in front of mesh stick, up in back, through next loop, etc. (Figure II-117).

When the end of the twenty-four loops is reached, bring cord over mesh stick, up in back and tie to loose end *y* (Figure II-113). Turn work over, so you always work from left to right. Slip meshes off stick as stick becomes full, or at end of line.

Turn work at end of each row, alternating left and right, to keep work from twisting.

When hammock is desired length (36 to 40 inches) thread the other end stock with the second 18-inch piece of rope, as in Figure II-112, with four loops between holes.

To reinforce edges, and to make loop for hanging hammock, use the 12-foot piece of rope. Start in the middle of one long side, leaving enough for a knot, and overcast the rope to edge of mesh, with a piece of netting string (Fiugre II-118). Put an overhand knot at the lower side of the end stick, thread rope through, secure with another overhand knot. Leave a loop of about 13 inches and secure to other end of stick in same manner. These four knots will keep the stick in place (Figure II-118).

Overcast rope down other side, fasten to other end stick with the four knots and loop, and continue up first side to beginning of overcasting (Figure II-118).

Join ends of rope with square knot or fisherman's knot, cutting off any unused rope. Whip ends of rope to main part of rope for neatness (Figure II-119).

4. Tie short ropes to hardwood sticks with clove hitches and hang hammock between poles or trees or bushes (Figure II-120).

Basketry III

Basket making is a craft that is ageless, one that is found in every part of the world. It is a popular camp craft because so many natural materials for basketry are found in camps, and because the articles made—from sit-upons to pack baskets—can be used in outdoor living. Tea baskets, fish baskets, flower baskets, market baskets, potato baskets—these are but a few of the fascinating array of baskets that those who have lived close to the land have used for generations. The word *basket* comes from the old English, and means a vessel made of vegetable fibers. Thus, reeds, vines, splints, rushes, sweet grass, lauhaula and palmetto leaves, long needles of pine, straw, or cornhusks may be woven into baskets of many shapes and uses. For color and variety, try weaving in colored yarns or bits of natural materials. A wastebasket for tent or cabin, a mat for the tent floor, a screen for the primitive bath shelter, a market basket for the food shoppers, a mail basket for outgoing letters, or sit-upons for campfire use—these may be the result and rewards of basketry.

Because in most camps it is possible to get materials for basketry in the natural form, it is very important to be wise conservationists in the gathering of materials. Here, as in all use of natural materials, only those leaves, vines, stalks, or grasses that grow in abundance should be gathered, and these should be harvested with restraint, so that more of the material is left than is taken, and what is taken is cut carefully so that it is not missed. There is no point in denuding the swamp of cattail leaves and stalks for this year's campers to use with the result that future generations of campers as well as future generations of red-winged blackbirds will find nothing where the cattails used to grow. Here again, the need for linking nature lore and good outdoor citizenship is a vital part of craft activities.

MATERIALS USED

There are three general types of materials used in basketry:

—Round materials: reed and vines, such as *rattan,* a plant from the Far East; *reed,* the pith of rattan; *vines* such as honeysuckle; *supple shoots* of willow, etc.
—Flexible materials: *grasses*—sweet, grass, rye, broom straw, etc.; *pine needles,* especially from the long needle pine; *husks*—cornhusks, etc.
—Flat materials: *splints*—long narrow strips pounded and cut from ash, maple, oak; *rushes*—cattail, etc.; *strips of large leaves,* such as palmetto, lauhaula.

Preparation of natural materials varies with the type of material used, and generally calls for some experimentation. Good conservation practices are essential in using natural materials; use only what is in abundance, and use only a portion of the supply. The establishing and caring for willow groves and cattail plantings will provide interesting projects for campers, and will teach outdoor citizenship and an appreciation of nature as well as ensuring supplies of materials for future groups of campers.

In general, pick materials while still green. Dry *slowly,* turning often. Most materials will need to be moistened or soaked before they are used in making baskets.

—*Willow shoots* should be gathered in the spring, as the shoots are brittle in the fall.
—*Splints* are obtained from logs that have soaked for a month or more so that the layers are loosened. The bark is stripped off, and the log pounded lengthwise with a mallet, to separate the layers. The width of the strip may be guided by lengthwise cuts down the log. An ax edge is used to pry layers apart as the work proceeds. The heart or core is used for handles, rims, and so forth.
—*Cattails and rushes* are gathered before they mature, usually in the summer. They should be dried slowly, otherwise they are brittle.

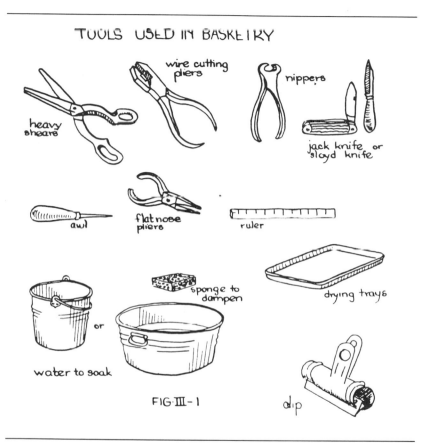

TOOLS USED IN BASKETRY

wire cutting pliers

nippers

heavy shears

jack knife or sloyd knife

awl

flat nose pliers

ruler

sponge to dampen

drying trays

or

water to soak

FIG.III-1

clip

—*Cornhusks* should be dried slowly in the shade. They may be dyed with natural or commercial dyes. The inner pieces are softest, and are used for fine weaving. Sometimes the husks have natural colors, and these are used to make color designs.

—*Grasses* are dried in the sun, slowly, being turned often.

—*Pine needles* may be used green or dried. If dried in the sun, they turn a warm brown; if dried indoors, they retain a soft green.

—*Vines* are used as weavers; they should be dried for a long time.

TECHNIQUES

There are three techniques used in making baskets: weaving, coiling, and plaiting or braiding. The primary steps in these three methods are described below.

Weaving

This is a method of weaving a long, supple strand, or weaver, over and under a series of spokes which form the framework.

Steps

1. Cut eight spokes from reeds or similar materials. Arrange them in a cross. With awl or pointed knife, make a slit in the center sections of four spokes. Point one end of each of the other four spokes, and insert in slits, pulling them through to make the cross (Figure III-2).

2. Take a long, well-soaked weaver of willow or vine, and double it back for about 10 inches. Wrap the fold around one set of four spokes, so that there is a short and a long weaver, one on top of the four spokes, one underneath (Figure III-2). Weave over and under the sets of spokes, using both weavers. If the short one starts *under* the first set, it will go *over* the second set, under the third set, over the fourth, etc. At the same time, the long weaver is going *over* the first set, *under* the second, over the third, and under the fourth (Figure III-3). Continue for three rows, or until short end is woven in place.

3. Spread spokes evenly, and continue weaving with the long weaver, going under the first and over the second and third spokes, under the fourth, and over the fifth and sixth (Figure III-4). Continue until base is desired size. Keep base wet, so that spokes are pliable.

4. To turn up side: be sure base is wet, so spokes will not crack. Turn spokes up at right angles, continuing weaving as in step 3. Pull weaver tight to make basket turn in; hold spokes at angle to make basket wider.

5. To add new weavers: turn end of old weaver (*a*) toward outside of basket, and insert end of new weaver (*b*) about three spokes back. Continue with new weaver (Figure III-5).

6. To end weaver: cut end of weaver on a slant, with stick end down beside a spoke (Figure III-6).

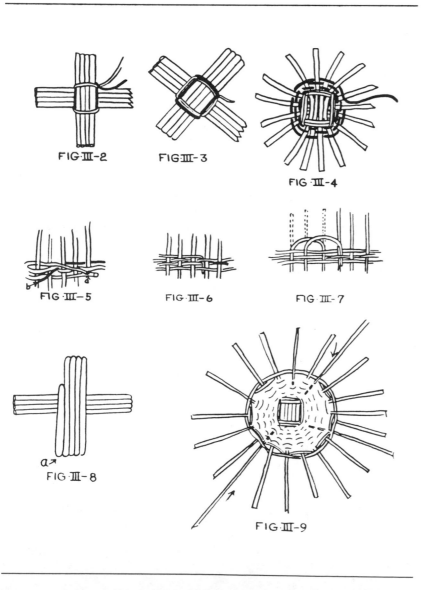

FIG·III-2

FIG·III-3

FIG·III-4

FIG·III-5

FIG·III-6

FIG·III-7

FIG·III-8

a↗

FIG·III-9

7. To finish spokes: start with any spoke; carry it toward inside of basket, behind two spokes at the right, and tuck down into the weaving beside spoke (Figure III-7). Repeat this step with each spoke in turn, until all have been tucked into weaving. Press down evenly, and trim ends of spokes inside the basket.

Variations: Add a ninth spoke just a little longer than half the length of the first spokes. Stick this extra spoke in anywhere after step 2, when the original spokes are spread evenly. Now the weaver can be woven over and under single spokes for the entire basket, as there will be an uneven number of spokes (Figure III-8 *a*).

For a larger base and basket, spokes will need to be added to the base (Figure III-9), as the original set of spokes will spread too far for firm weaving. Add a set of pointed spokes between the original spokes, pushing them down hard into the core weaving of step 2. Continue weaving by either method described above.

Coiling

This method is used with reeds or vines, or with short lengths of grasses, pine needles, rushes, etc. These are wound into a coil or core, and stitched together with raffia, grass, thread, or twine, using a large-eyed needle. The materials should be prepared (as indicated earlier in this chapter) before starting the project.

Steps

1. Using the core material of reed or vine, make a center by coiling the end into a tight button or circle, using the winding material to hold fast (Figure III-10).
2. Thread the winding material into a needle with a large eye. Use this to bind the coils together, winding raffia (or other material) twice around the reed or grass bundle, and then stitching into coil above, working out from the center (Figure III-10). This stitch is known as the Lazy Squaw stitch.
3. Continue in this manner until base is formed.
4. To shape the basket: place the core reed directly *over* the previous row, rather than beside it. Make sides curved or straight, as desired. If

flared, each row should project a little on outside; if curved, stitch rows in or out as desired. Continue stitching on side rows as on base.

5. To add new material: stretch out old end (Figure III-12 (*a*) along the reed or grass coil. Place new raffia (Figure III-12 (*b*) with end at left, under coil. Wrap with new raffia from right to left, covering ends until stitching is reached, then proceed with new pieces.

   Grasses: add new bunches of grass, staggering the ends so the coil remains the same thickness continuously (Figure III-13).

   Reeds: splice end of old reed with end of new reed by cutting a slanting cut on each end, fitting ends together to make the thickness of one (Figure III-14). Bind the joint together with winding material.

6. When using pine needles, hold several groups of needles together with sheath ends together, and smooth sides outside, to make a bundle for a coil. Add groups of pine needles so the ends are staggered (similar to adding grasses), and the same thickness is continued throughout the coiling.

Variations: The open *poma* stitch is used for pine needles and may be adapted on a larger scale for making an archery target (see Chapter Eighteen on Games and Sports Equipment). After making a center button and starting the base, carry raffia or twine or thread around coil, inserting needle into previous stitch in other coil, from right to left and from back to front (Figure III-15).

Plaiting

This method is a braiding method, used with rushes, cornhusks, and other broadleafed, soft materials. Materials should be soaked when being used so they are not brittle. Larger husks are torn into strips of even widths for narrow braiding for table mats, etc. Groups of wide husks are used for larger braid, as for floor mats or wood baskets.

Plaiting is done in a manner similar to three-strand braiding of cord (see Chapter Two on Braiding and Knotting). Use groups of materials, and divide into three strands. Tie or loop at end, and hang on peg to braid into a plaiting strand (Figure III-16). When a sufficient length of braid has been made, it is ready to be stitched into a mat or basket base. Use heavy cotton button thread for a small mat, string or twine for a heavier mat.

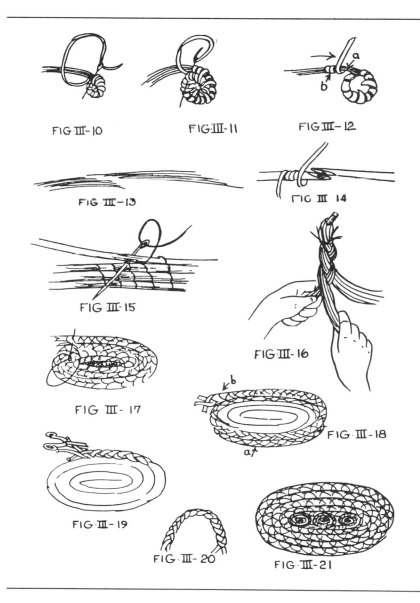

FIG·III-10   FIG·III-11   FIG·III-12

FIG·III-13   FIG·III·14

FIG·III-15   FIG·III-16

FIG·III-17   FIG·III-18

FIG·III-19   FIG·III-20   FIG·III-21

Steps

1. Start with a button of the braided strand.
2. Wind strand around and around the coil, sewing succeeding rounds to the button, being sure to keep the braided strands flat. Sew through the husk, or pass needle under a loop, making a cross stitch. (Figure III-17). Keep mat on flat surface, rather than holding in hand or lap.
3. Build sides by turning up braid, sewing a layer on the outside edge of the base, rather than beside it. Turn the side of the braided strand on edge; in Figure III-18, *a* is the bottom outside edge; *b* is the side braid, on edge.
4. End strand by stitching flatly in place. Trim off some of the under parts of the strand to taper the strand (Figure III-19).
5. Handles may be made by a small length of braid, sewed into the body of the basket near the top row. Ends of the braid may be whipped (see Figures II-10-13); or the handles may be inserted into braid of basket with an awl. Take a few stitches to make the handles secure.

Variation: To make an oval mat or base, make two or three circles and join them side by side. With a long plait, sew around outside edges of the center made of the circles (Figure III-21). Continue as for round mat or for base.

PROJECTS

Adirondack Pack Basket

The Indians of the Northeast used a basket with thongs to carry their equipment on their backs. Perhaps this was inspired by the baskets used by the Indian squaws to carry their papooses. This type of basket, known as an Adirondack Pack Basket, is used by many campers and hikers today. It has the advantage of being light but sturdy and of standing on the ground or table for easy use when cooking or when packing gear, since it will not collapse as a softer pack may do.

Splints for such a basket may be purchased ready-cut from craft supply houses or may be pounded from natural material. Use of a kit may be the first step in making this type of camping equipment, and a progression would be to procure the natural materials.

Equipment needed: Knife; awl; hammer and small nails; firm working surface; pail of water; two wooden blocks, size of bottom of basket; nails or string; brush for varnish.

Materials needed: Seventeen splints (4 feet long, 1 inch wide, or desired sizes); 1/2-inch or 3/8-inch weaving splints—each about 10 feet long; one splint for top—4½ inches wide, 10 feet long; two reinforcing splints for bottom; piece of wood for handle; 1½-inch webbing for harnesds; split rivets; varnish.

Steps

1. Lay splints on table, ten going one way, and seven woven over and under in the opposite directions to make base (Figure III-22).
2. Split the center splint on one long side with a jackknife to make an uneven number of splints for weaving (Figure III-22). This splint should be in the center of the back of basket.
3. Use two blocks the size of the bottom of basket. Nail or tie the base between these blocks (Figure III-23).
4. Tie splints loosely together at top, with board inside, and soak in pail for at least an hour (Figure III-24).
5. Soak weaving splints at same time; keep extra weavers in water throughout project.
6. Bend up sides of base, around inside board. Start weaving with a narrow weaver, under one and over one (Figure III-25).
7. Continue with the weavers. After several times around the basket, remove blocks, and turn the basket upside down to continue weaving. Keep the back of basket flat, but make the sides and front bulge slightly (Figure III-26).
8. When sides are about 12 to 15 inches tall (or desired size), stop weaving, and cut off extra splints 4 inches above last row of weaving. Using jackknife, point the splints (Figure III-26).
9. Soak to be sure the splints are supple, and fold down inside or outside the basket, tucking into weaving to fasten (Figure III-26).
10. Whittle and bend handle from a supple stick, pointing ends (Figure III-27). Tuck pointed ends down into basket at top of back.
11. Bend a splint (or a half-round supple stick) to fit inside the basket for rim. Tack to inside of basket. With a narrow weaver, fasten the rim to the basket with an over and under stitch (Figure III-27). Make a cross stitch by weaving back the opposite way, or by starting in the middle of the weaver and using both ends to make the cross.

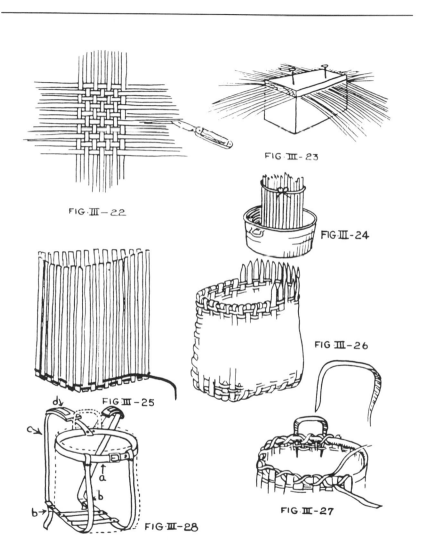

FIG·III—22

FIG·III—23

FIG·III—24

FIG·III—25

FIG·III—26

FIG·III—27

FIG·III—28

12. Reinforce the bottom with two extra splints, weaving them under the outside splints. Start at front, about two splints above bottom, turn at base, weave under bottom splints, turn at other edge, and up two splints at back. Repeat at other corner (Figure III-26).

13. Soak basket, and press into desired shape—then let dry.

14. Cover with coat of clear spar varnish, if desired.

15. To make harness: harness should be made to fit the basket. Measure completed basket with string before cutting webbing or attaching buckles. Use webbing 1¼ inch or 1½ inch wide.

Throat strap: fasten around neck of basket, just below the rim, with buckle and end in front (Figure III-28 a).

Two sling straps: make loops in one end of each strap with two split rivets (see Chapter XVI on Equipment Making). The throat strap goes through these loops. Straps go from throat strap in front down under a splint or two on bottom of basket and out to back, with 3 inches leeway. Buckles are on these ends (Figure III-28 b).

Two shoulder straps: these are fastened at the middle of the back to the throat strap with split rivets. The straps should be long enough to go over shoulders and down to buckle of sling strap at bottom of back of basket. There should be some leeway so tha the stages can

Two shoulder straps: these are fastened at the middle of the back to the throat strap with split rivets. The straps should be long enough to go over shoulders and down to buckle of sling strap at bottom of back of basket. There should be some leeway so that the straps can be adusted to fit the wearer (Figure III-28 c). A wider piece of webbing, or a pad, may be stitched in place underneath strap at shoulder to ease the pressure of the straps (Figure III-28 d).

Two short straps may be riveted to the sling straps on underneath of basket to keep straps in place, to strengthen bottom, and to help support load.

ADDITIONAL SUGGESTIONS

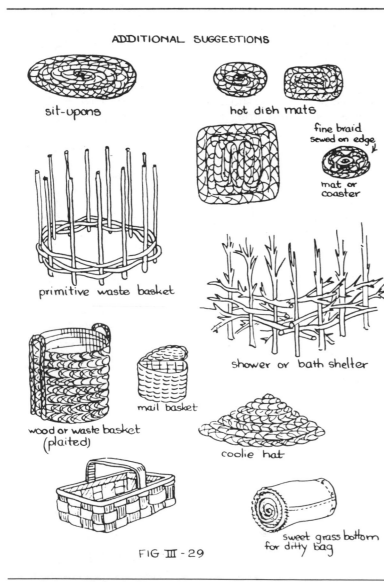

sit-upons

hot dish mats

fine braid
sewed on edge

mat or
coaster

primitive waste basket

shower or bath shelter

mail basket

wood or waste basket
(plaited)

coolie hat

sweet grass bottom
for ditty bag

FIG III - 29

Ceramics

IV

Pottery was made and used by people of ancient civilizations, and pottery making is still one of the most interesting and satisfying of crafts. Some camps are fortunate enough to have natural deposits of clay for camper use; others must import any material that is used for this activity. The making of camp symbols, utensils, and figures of animals, the use of designs from nature, and the making and using of a primitive kiln will all contribute to a good craft program.

In camps which have a natural deposit of clay, the processing of the clay will be an interesting and profitable activity, especially for older campers, but since it is an activity that takes time and effort, it is not a beginner's project. Some clay should be processed before the camp begins, so there will be a supply on hand; and then, from time to time, the supply can be replenished for succeeding groups.

Articles that have lasting value will need to be fired to make them durable. Beginners will be happy working with clay to get the feel of it, with no particular project in mind. Such articles need not be fired, and the clay may be used again and again. As the campers progress in skill and in interest, they will want to preserve their clay articles by the use of a kiln, either primitive or commercial.

TERMS USED

These are some of the terms used in ceramics:

—*Bisque or biscuit ware:* ware that has been fired once.
—*Bat:* a flat slab of plaster used to absorb moisture from clay.

—*Bone-dry:* clay that has dried completely.
—*Ceramics:* another term for articles made of clay and fired; also the name of the craft of clay making.
—*Clay:* a type of soil material of putty consistency that may be molded into desired shapes, and that hardens when exposed to heat.
—*Coil:* a rope of clay used in building forms.
—*Glaze:* a thin coat of glass which makes the clay surface non-porous and improves the appearance with color and finish.
—*Glaze firing:* the second firing, after glazing.
—*Green ware:* unfired clay articles.
—*Kiln* (pronounced *kill*): a furnace or oven for firing clay articles (Figure IV-1).
—*Leather-hard:* partly moist clay that has been exposed to air for several hours so that it is firm and stiff, but not dry.
—*Mold:* a plaster or wooden form in which clay is pressed or cast to achieve a specific shape.

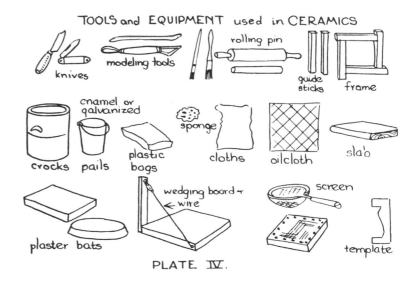

TOOLS and EQUIPMENT used in CERAMICS

knives, modeling tools, rolling pin, guide sticks, frame, enamel or galvanized, sponge, crocks, pails, plastic bags, cloths, oilcloth, slab, plaster bats, wedging board + wire, screen, template

PLATE IV.

—*Plastic:* impressionable, workable.
—*Potter's wheel:* a revolving surface used to spin clay mass as it is shaped by hand.
—*Pottery:* articles fashioned from clay and hardened by heat.
—*Slab:* a wooden form used for rolling out flat pieces of clay.
—*Slip:* diluted clay, the consistency of heavy cream, used for casting, for smoothing, for painting, for attaching two pieces of clay together.
—*To fire:* to bake in a kiln to harden clay.
—*To throw:* to form ware on the potter's wheel.
—*To wedge:* to make clay ready for use, free of air bubbles.

Methods used in ceramics and methods of decorating clay are presented later in this chapter.

Some Camp-made Tools and Equipment

—*A rolling pin* can be made from a broom handle, or from a sturdy dry stick that is shaved and cut to desired size, then sanded.
—*Guide sticks* should be square cut and sanded. A number of sets of varying sizes will facilitate activity. Small holes drilled in the sticks will make them readily usable as frames for tiles, etc.

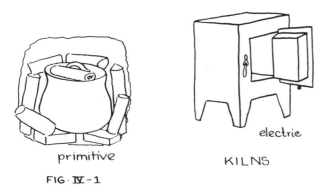

primitive

electric

KILNS

FIG·IV-1

—*Screen* for sifting clay can be made from wooden frame nailed together, with window screening tacked on top.
—*Plaster bats* are made by mixing plaster of paris with water to pouring consistency, then pouring into greased mold, such as cookie sheet or pie pan (Figure IV-2).
—*Wire for wedging board* is made by stretching wire from about one foot above table to front edge (Figure IV-3). A turn buckle helps keep the wire taut.
—*A potter's wheel* is not usually found in a camp for the simple projects described here. However, the making of a primitive wheel would be an excellent project for older campers.
—*Primitive kilns* are described on following pages, Figures IV-17-19.

TECHNIQUES

Securing Clay from Land

When a handful of earth or soil sticks together when squeezed and holds the finger imprints, it will have clay content. Experimentation will soon prove whether the clay is of high enough quality to use in making articles. The refining of clay is a rather long and tedious (but very satisfying) process, and should be undertaken by older campers to create a supply for others to use. A supply that has been refined as a service by one group can be used at the beginning of camp, and replenishments made by expeditions and groups organized for that purpose throughout the summer. Natural clay may have interesting hues that will make the articles developed in the specific camp very distinctive.

Steps

1. Dig several pails full of the earth, and break it up into small pieces, allowing it to dry thoroughly.
2. Pulverize the earth by pounding with a mallet, through a canvas or burlap bag, or in a box.
3. Put through a 1/8-inch sieve.
4. Fill a pail half full of water, then drop the sieved earth on the water, stirring thoroughly with hands. Let soak for an hour, to make slip, stirring often.

5. Let sand settle to the bottom of pail, and pour off rest into another pail, pouring it through the sieve again. Let this mixture stand overnight.
6. Pour or siphon off water on top.
7. Repeat these last two steps until the mixture is the consistency of thick cream—or slip.
8. For modeling, repeat until clay is the consistency and feel of fresh putty.
9. Store in earthenware crocks, plastic pails, or nonrusting metal containers.
10. Cover with damp cloths while storing and when a piece of work has been started. A good storing place is made by using a big container, with a platform of wood or stones on which the crock rests. Water is put in the bottom of the container, and cloths spread over the crock, with the ends dipping in the water below. The cloths will stay wet, and keep the clay moist (Figure IV-4).

Using Commercial Clay

Clay in powdered or moist form may be purchased from craft supply houses and from many local outlets. Commercial clay has been refined and is ready for use. One form of clay that is good for craft use is a clay used in making flower pots; this is a relatively inexpensive clay, and one that lends itself to camp ware because of its earthy, red-brown color.

There are also forms of self-hardening clay that do not need to be fired. Craft supply houses list such clay in catalogs. This is clay to which dextrin has been added. The air hardens the clay after it has been modeled. It may then be decorated with poster paint and painted with a transparent liquid glaze or shellac. This clay is more expensive than untreated clay.

Powdered commercial clay is prepared and used as is natural clay, starting at step 4 above, and repeating until clay is of desired consistency.

To Store Clay

Store large amounts of processed clay in earthenware, zinc-lined or enamel containers with tight covers, or with dampened cloths to cover (see Figure IV-4). Small amounts or pieces that are in the process of being worked may be stored in plastic bags, or covered with damp cloths.

When the clay has dried out and is too stiff to use, it may be made plastic by poking holes in it almost to the bottom of the mass, then filling

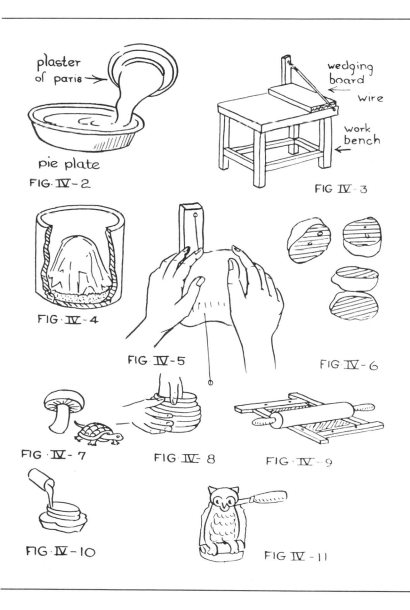

plaster of paris

pie plate

FIG. IV-2

wedging board

wire

work bench

FIG IV-3

FIG. IV-4

FIG. IV-5

FIG. IV-6

FIG. IV-7

FIG. IV-8

FIG. IV-9

FIG. IV-10

FIG. IV-11

the holes with water. Keep holes filled, and clay should be workable in a day or two.

If clay is too moist to work, wedge it on a plaster slab, or place the work on a plaster bat, and leave until moisture has been absorbed (see Figure IV-2 for plaster bat).

Wedging Clay

Clay is full of small air bubbles which must be removed before the piece is fired, or the heated air in the pockets will cause the piece to explode in the kiln. This working of the clay to remove the air is called *wedging*. It takes time, but is worth the effort. It should be done *thoroughly*. A hard working surface and a taut wire to cut the clay are necessary for wedging (see Figure IV-5).

Steps

1. Make a lump or ball of clay, and cut it in two with the wire (Figure IV-5).
2. Forcibly blend the outer surfaces of the ball together by throwing or pounding the mass on the flat surface. Knead the clay with fingers, and form new ball.
3. Repeat this process until the clay seems perfectly smooth, showing no air pockets or bubbles when cut in two (Figure IV-6).
4. Use in this form, or store for future use.

Methods of Working Clay

There are a number of methods of working in clay. The simplest are described here, and projects using some of the methods are given in this chapter.

Modeling Method

This method is the shaping of figures and other small articles from a mass of clay. This provides great freedom of activity and creativity, and is one of the steps most enjoyed by beginners. Something as simple as a snake or a toadstool or a roly-poly man may be the first figure, leading up to figurines of animals or people (Figure IV-7).

Coil Method

This method consists of building sides on a base by adding coils of clay joined together by smoothing while the clay is soft. The making of a bowl may call for a template to use as a guide in keeping the shape uniform (Figure IV-8).

Slab Method

This method employs a wooden slab, rolling pin, and guide sticks to roll out the clay in a flat piece. The guide sticks are used to obtain a piece of clay of the desired thickness. Sometimes a wooden frame is used to make a base or tile of desired proportions (Figure IV-9).

Casting

This method makes use of a mold of plaster to make specific shapes or design or to repeat designs. The mold is carved from plaster with improvised tools. This method is often used in making camp pins or symbols (Figure IV-10).

Sculpturing

This is a method of carving a piece of clay in a free standing form. It is related to modeling, but the clay is drier when worked, and the work is done with modeling tools or knives (Figure IV-11). Plaster of Paris blocks are sometimes used as the carving material.

Decorating Clay

Articles made of clay may be decorated by a number of processes, such as these:

Incising

By this method some of the clay is removed from the surface, either leaving the design raised, or cutting the design into the clay, leaving the background raised (Figure IV-12). This is done when the clay is leather-hard, but not bone-dry, before the piece is fired.

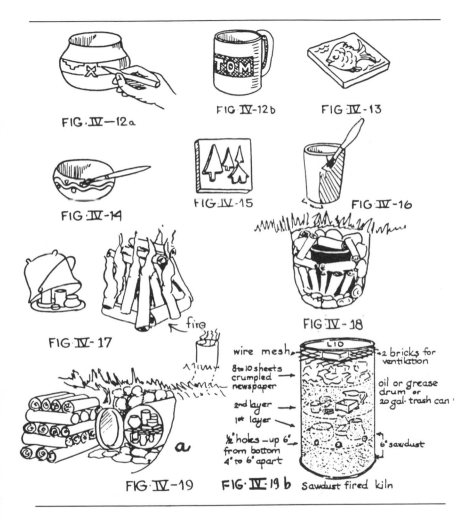

FIG. IV—12a

FIG. IV—12b

FIG. IV—13

FIG. IV—14

FIG. IV—15

FIG. IV—16

FIG. IV—17

fire

FIG. IV—18

FIG. IV—19

FIG. IV—19b Sawdust fired kiln

wire mesh

8 to 10 sheets crumpled newspaper

2nd layer

1st layer

½" holes—up 6" from bottom 4" to 6" apart

LID

2 bricks for ventilation

oil or grease drum or 20 gal. trash can

6" sawdust

a

3. Place paper design on the clay, and go over lines with a hard pencil or pointed hardwood stick, inscribing the design on the clay.
4. Go over the design in the clay with a modeling tool or sharp stick or large nail, making the grooves and areas deeper in the clay (Figure IV-12 *a*).
5. If the design is to be raised, use knife to cut away background, and use modeling tool to smooth edge (Figure IV-12 *b*).

Sgraffito

This is an Italian word meaning scratch, and this method is one of scratching or inscribing a design on a coating of slip so that the design shows the original color of the clay.

Steps

1. Make the article and let it dry to leather-hard firmness.
2. Plan design on paper.
3. Cover the article with slip of desired contrasting color. Let it dry enough so that it can be scratched without running. Inscribe the design with tools as for incised design, scratching off just enough of the slip to show the basic color underneath (Figure IV-13).
4. Dry, then fire.

Slip Painting

This method consists of painting the article with slip of paint consistency. The slip is applied to an article at the leather-hard stage; the article is then bisque fired, glazed with light or transparent glaze, and fired again (Figure IV-14).

Embossing

Embossed designs are those in which clay has been added to the original piece so that the design appears raised on the surface.

Steps

1. Make the article ready for decorating—leather-hard, but not bone-dry.
2. Make a design on paper, basing it on size and shape of article to be decorated.

Steps

1. Make article, and let it dry until a little softer than leather-hard.
2. Plan design, and cut pieces from 1/4-inch thick strips of clay.
3. Lay these pieces in place, then work into background surface, using slip and a little water to smooth the embossing pieces on to the surface (Figure IV-15).
4. Let dry and fire.
5. Apply glaze, as desired, and fire again.

Glazing

This is a method of coating the article with a shiny surface. The glaze may be transparent or in many varieties of single colors. A colored design may be applied. The simplest glazing is a coat of glaze which is brushed on the article after the bisque firing (Figures IV-16). With a second firing, the glaze melts and forms a glassy coating on the clay. There are many different types of glaze; each calls for a specific heat to be used in firing.

For firing in a primitive kiln, a simple formula for a low-fire glaze is used.

Decorating Self-Hardening Clay

Objects made of self-hardening clay may be painted with poster paints, then painted with a transparent liquid glaze or shellacked. Glaze or shellac may be applied directly to the object. It will then be hard and water-proofed.

Firing Clay

Articles made of clay must be dried and baked for permanence. The baking is done in an oven or furnace known as a *kiln* (pronounced *kill*). The articles to be baked are known as *green ware* before firing, and as *bisque* or *biscuit ware* after the first firing. The second firing, following glazing, is known as *glaze firing*.

Kilns may be wood burning, gas or electric. It is possible to construct a wood-burning kiln that will do an adequate job of firing.

The simplest type of primitive kiln is an iron pot turned over the objects to be fired (Figure IV-17). A fire is built around the pot, and slowly increased in intensity until the pot is covered with the fire. The fire is kept burning for several hours (up to eight) and then allowed to cool off slowly. As in all firing, the fire's heat is gradually increased, and then after prolonged heating, the kiln is cooled off. Sudden changes of temperature either of heating or cooling may cause the clay objects to crack and break.

A more permanent and more satisfactory primitive kiln is made in a pit (Figure IV-18). The pit is lined with stones or fire brick to hold the heat of the fire. The clay articles are put in an iron kettle or similar heavy container with a cover. The fire is built of hardwood and allowed to burn to coals. The kettle is lowered into the pit, with objects to be fired carefully placed inside. The cover is left slightly ajar to allow evaporation. When the kettle has warmed from the coals, the fire is rebuilt around it, and on top of it, and kept burning from five to eight hours, then allowed to die out gradually. Another type of primitive kiln is built in a bank (Figure 19). The hole is dug in a spot protected from the wind, and is made deep enough to more than accommodate a large can, placed on its side. The bottom of the hole is lined with a layer of stones to be heated (watch out for rocks that cannot be heated), and a base for the can is made of stones or firebrick. Shelves of wire screening should be placed in the can to hold the clay articles.

A fire may be necessary to dry out the ground before the real heating begins. The can is placed on the supports, and the ware stacked in. Cover is placed lightly on can—*not tightly*. The fire is kept going, and gradually increased until the can is red hot. It is kept at red-hot heat for several hours, then allowed to cool off gradually. When can is cool to the touch, it may be opened—but not before. The success of wood-burning kilns depends upon a good supply of hardwood and upon constant attention during the whole operation. The fire should come up gradually to its peak, and be kept that way for several hours. This process consumes the better part of a day, as well as plenty of wood, but it cannot be hurried. It is a good project for older campers to carry out; relays of fire tenders may be organized, and other craft or skill activities may be in process during the burning.

A sawdust fired kiln (Figure IV-19 *b*) is a very inexpensive but effective method of firing, as the sawdust is free from impurities.

Equipment needed: drill and bits for making 1/2-inch holes; a twenty-gallon metal trash can or grease drum.

Materials needed: mixture of medium and fine dry sawdust; wire mesh or screen slightly larger than diameter of drum; two common bricks.

Steps

1. Drill 1/2-inch holes 4 to 6 inches apart around drum, 6 inches from bottom. Fill with 6 inches of sawdust.
2. Place largest articles on the sawdust, 3 inches apart and 4 inches from sides of the drum.
3. Put a 6-inch layer of sawdust in and around articles.
4. On top of this 6-inch layer, put another group of articles, and repeat the layering.
5. If this fills the can, place 8 to 20 sheets of crumpled newspaper on top of the sawdust and ignite. Cover with mesh, chicken wire, to contain embers of burning paper.
6. After flame has burned out, sawdust is black, and wisps of smoke are seen, put lid on, resting on two bricks on edge of drum for ventilation.
7. After fire has completely burned out and no smoke is seen (which takes 24 hours), let the articles cool to touch before removing them.
8. Brush off sawdust and lightly sponge since the articles may be black from the firing.

Primitive kilns are not satisfactory for baking glazing articles, as there is no way of controlling the temperature of the fire.

Gas or electric kilns may be installed in craft centers, or green ware and bisque may be fired at commercial kilns in town. For the camp that has an extensive ceramics program, either of these methods of having objects fired will be satisfactory. For campers who are interested in a total craft experience in clay, the making and using of a primitive kiln will be a rewarding experience, in spite of the amount of wood consumed and the amount of work involved.

Placing ware for firing: All clay must be *absolutely* dry before being fired. Cracks that may appear in the ware while drying should be mended with slip, and the article dried again.

When stacking a kiln, put largest pieces on bottom shelves, and do not let pieces touch one another (Figure IV-19 *a*). Small pieces may be set inside large pieces without danger.

Finishing articles: Articles may be sanded with steel wool or fine sandpaper after bisque firing, to product a smooth surface. Some clays may be made nonporous by rubbing with wax. This is true of roughhewn articles that are not glazed.

PROJECTS

Modeling Figures, Dishes, Small Objects

Making figures, dishes, or small objects by manipulating the clay is known as *modeling.* Small figures, such as sitting (rather than standing) birds or animals, or small dishes in leaf shape, are good articles for beginners. Puppet heads and the making of camp pins or symbols may be a progressive step. Learning to handle the clay will involve free action in working with a small ball of clay, making all kinds of shapes at first, with no plan to fire or finish the article. The clay may be returned to the storage crock and used again and again. Modeling is especially delightful to young campers. When one has caught the feel of the craft, some creation will be so pleasing to the maker he will want to keep it, and then embark on a more advanced project.

Equipment needed: modeling tool; piece of oilcloth; knife.
Materials needed: ball of well-wedged clay; glaze as desired.

FIG. IV-20   FIG. IV-21

FIG. IV-22

FIG. IV-23   FIG. IV-24

Making an Animal Figure

Steps

1. Using the reverse side of the oilcloth piece as a working space, squeeze the clay roughly into the shape of the object (Figure IV-20 *a*).
2. Next define more clearly the head, neck, etc. Add legs by taking away clay with tool (Figure IV-20 *b*). Beginners should not attempt to make the standing animals, but should indicate legs that are folded into the body.
3. Keep adding more detail until the figure is satisfactory. Do not try to put in every little detail, but accentuate those that are prominent (Figure IV-20 *c*).
4. Protruding parts, such as ears, tails, and beaks, may be attached with slip.
5. Except for very small figures, hollow out part of the bottom and inside of the figure (Figure IV-21).
6. Dry and fire and glaze as desired.

Try a variety of animals and birds (see Figure IV-22).

Making a Puppet Head

Follow the same general steps as above, but plan a place to insert finger, and make neck long enough so that a costume may be attached. Puppet head features are usually exaggerated (Figure IV-23). Puppet heads can be made of self-hardening clay and painted with poster paints. (See also Chapter XIII).

Making a Leaf Dish

Steps

1. Find a leaf that has an interesting shape to serve as a design for a dish (avoid sharp points or deep cuts into leaf).
2. Pat out the clay in a square or oblong of desired thickness and size (Figure IV-24 *a*).
3. With a knife, cut out design.
4. With fingers, model the shape of the leaf as desired (Figure IV-24 *b*).

5. Put in veins, etc., with modeling tool.
6. Dry, fire, and glaze as desired.

Tile—Slab Method

Tiles may serve as table protectors for hot dishes, flower pots, or as plaques for wall decorations. The story of the nature lore of the camp may be recorded in tiles for a cabin, or many campers may make tiles for the facing of a new fireplace, especially if the clay comes from the campsite.

Equipment needed: guide sticks; piece of oilcloth; knife; water and brush; rolling pin or broom handle; small nails and hammer.

Materials needed: ball of well-wedged clay; glaze as desired.

Steps

1. Make a frame of guide sticks of desired size; 5 inches by 5 inches is good size for a tile (Figure IV-25). The height of the sticks will determine the thickness of the tile (1/2 inch is a good thickness).
2. Place ball of well-wedged clay on reverse side of piece of oilcloth on table. Roll out between two guide sticks until uniform in thickness (Figure IV-26).

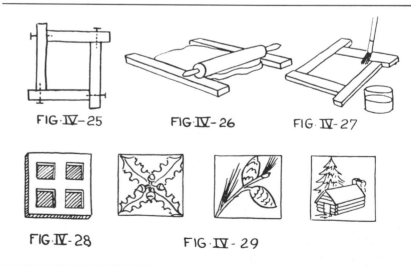

FIG·IV-25   FIG·IV-26   FIG·IV-27

FIG·IV-28   FIG·IV-29

3. Place frame on clay, and cut around inside of frame. Cut away excess clay, and press frame around clay piece. Leave for an hour. Free edges around frame with knife. Brush some water on edges next to frame, as these dry faster than center (Figure IV-27). Leave in frame overnight.
4. Remove frame next day, and brush edges of tile with water. Wet a strip of cloth that is long enough to go around all four edges, and wrap around the outside of tile. Keep this strip wet throughout a day.
5. Let tile dry for several days, turning it over occasionally so air will touch both top and bottom, to prevent warping.
6. When tile is leather-hard, turn bottom side up, and mark four square areas on bottom (Figure IV-28). With knife, cut out about 1/4 inch of clay in these squares, making the tile thinner except on edges and across center.
7. Decorate and fire as desired (Figure IV-29).

Note: Tiles to be used on tables should have pieces of felt glued on bottom; small patches may be used on the corners, or the whole base may be covered.

Flower Dish—Slab Method

The same method is used to make dishes, boxes with lids, etc., by the addition of sides. The project described might be for dish-gardens or flower holders for the camp dining room.

Equipment needed: paper and scissors for pattern; 1/2 inch guide sticks; rolling pin; modeling tool; water and sponge; oilcloth; plaster bat.

Materials needed: well-wedged piece of clay; slip; glaze as desired.

Steps

1. Cut a paper pattern for sides and bottom (Figure IV-30).
2. Place ball of clay on reverse side of oilcloth, and roll out between guide sticks to uniform thickness and to desired length (see Figure IV-26).
3. Using pattern as guide, cut out bottom, two sides, two ends. The *D* and *E* end should be 1 inch narrower than the bottom, to allow for thickness of sides, *B* and *C* (Figure IV-30).
4. Lay these cut-out sections on a plaster bat until they are leather-hard and do not bend when handled.
5. Run slip along one edge of base, and stand side *B* along edge (Figure

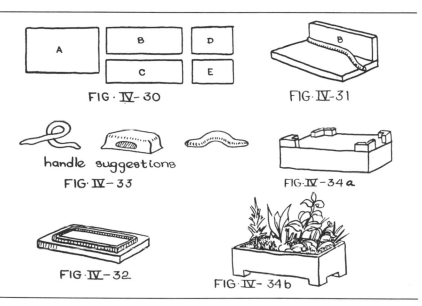

FIG · IV- 30   FIG · IV- 31

handle suggestions
FIG · IV- 33   FIG · IV- 34 a

FIG · IV- 32   FIG · IV- 34 b

IV-31). Roll a small coil of clay and place it in the seam, with a generous amount of slip. Smooth joint inside and out with modeling tool or fingers.
6. Erect the two ends and place coils in seams, as in step 5.
7. Place side *C* last, using coil in seam, as above.
8. Smooth inside and outside of box with modeling tool, sponge, or fingers.
9. Dry, decorate as desired, and fire.

Variations: Put handles or feet on the dish (Figures IV-33 and 34). See mug project for attaching handles (Figure IV-42).

Make a lid for a box by making a section like the bottom (*A*). Roll a small coil and attach with slip inside box, to keep lid from slipping (Figure IV-32). Allow to become bone-dry before firing.

Camp Pin Made by Casting

This project is one to use in making a number of identification symbols or pins. Two processes may be used in making the mold into which the clay is pressed.

Equipment needed: nail; hairpin; brushes for glaze; household cement; plaster bat; knife.

Materials needed: plaster of paris for mold; clay; glazes; pin-back; soft-soap grease.

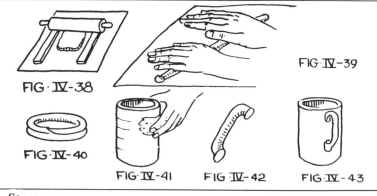

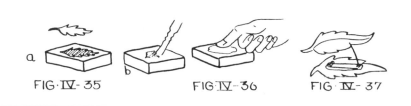

Steps

1. Model a pin from clay, let dry and then fire, then make a plaster of Paris mold from the pin. Grease the pin, then press into soft plaster, removing when the plaster is firm (Figure IV-35 *a*).

   Or, carve a mold from plaster. Plan the pin, and with hairpin and nailhead, carve the design in reverse into a block of hardened plaster (Figure IV-35 *b*).
2. Grease the mold with soft soap (made by cutting up soap, boiling, and cooling) using brush.
3. Press clay into mold, and level off with knife edge, even with mold (Figure IV-36).
4. Let stand about 10 minutes, and remove from mold with hairpin or sharpened twig.
5. Stand on plaster bat to dry.
6. When bone-dry, fire.
6. Glaze as desired, and fire again.
8. Attach pin-back with household cement (Figure IV-37).

Pottery Mug—Coil Method

This project employs a base and coils of clay laid on top of each other to make a cylindrical shape.

Equipment needed: piece of oilcloth; plaster bat; 2½-inch guide sticks; rolling pine; knife; brush and sponge; water; modeling tool.

Materials needed: ball of well-wedged clay; slip; glaze or slip as desired for decorating; fine sandpaper or medium steel wool.

Steps

1. Place ball of wedged clay in center of reverse side of oilcloth, between the guide sticks.
2. Roll out clay to uniform thickness (Figure IV-38).
3. Cut out shape of bottom, using paper pattern or a glass or other circle. Place this base on plaster bat.
4. Make a coil from a ball of clay the size of a walnut. Roll ball between the palms until it is elongated. Then place on oilcloth and roll with palms of both hands until it is a coil of desired thickness (Figure IV-39).
5. Brush a generous amount of slip on top edge of base. Lay coil carefully around base, on the edge, and press firmly in place. Cut ends of coil diagonally, and brush slip in cut surfaces as joint is made (Figure IV-40).
6. Lay successive coils in the same manner, but make joints of coils in different places, so none is directly over another. When cylinder is high enough, smooth out coils with fingers and wet sponge, inside and out. Shape as desired by pressure of fingers (Figure IV-41).
7. If a handle is desired, roll a coil and shape it on oilcloth. Be sure it is in good proportion to the size of the cup and is sturdy enough and long enough to allow for at least two fingers to grip it (Figure IV-42).
8. Using slip, wedge handle ends to mug (Figure IV-43).
9. Use modeling tool to smooth joints at handle.
10. Let dry gradually until bone-dry.
11. If smooth surface is desired, smooth with sandpaper or steel wool.
12. Decorate and fire as desired.

ADDITIONAL SUGGESTIONS

Leatherwork

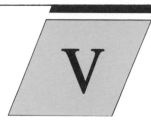

Man, from the earliest ages, has used hides for clothing and utensils. The Indians and pioneers used leather for many types of articles that are used in camping today—belts and ax sheaths, carrying cases and pouches, moccasins and jackets. For older campers, the experience of tanning a hide will be a satisfying project, although it requires time, effort, and patience. Most, however, will make use of leather that is already processed. Leather work calls for few tools, and scrap leather may be purchased to provide excellent material for beginners and for the making of small articles. These two factors contribute to the value of leatherwork in the camp program. Leather for large articles or for extensive projects is a relatively expensive material, so it is best for campers to begin by learning how to handle leather with scrap pieces. Progressive steps will lead to a great variety of activities that will warrant the use of the lovely textures and colors of larger pieces of leather.

Creativity in leatherwork comes in planning the article and in assembling and decorating it. After learning the simplest techniques in cutting, joining, and decorating leather, the camper will find many ways to develop skills. Nature provides appropriate designs for decorating leather, and many types of leather articles are useful in outdoor living. The commercial kits of leather articles have no place in a creative handcraft program, as they merely give the camper an experience in assembling an article, with none of the learnings, explorations, and satisfactions that come from creating his own article for use and for enjoyment. Such kits are more expensive than similar articles cut from whole or half hides.

Leather is a material processed from animal hide by tanning. The hides of various animals make different textures of leather; the various types are used for different purposes. Some leathers are soft and pliable; some are smooth textured, others are rough; some are soft enough to be used like cloth; some are natural color, and some are dyed in the skin. The hair is usually removed but is retained on a few leathers.

Tanning prepares hide for commercial use either by the vegetable process, using tannic acid, or by the mineral or chrome process, using chemicals. These processes produce different textures of leather: vegetable-tanned leathers are used for tooling, stamping, and carving; chrome-tanned leathers are tough and water-repellant and are used for shoes and garments, without decoration. Tanning a piece of hide is a good project for older campers; but, for most practical craft purposes in camp, the process is too long and too involved, and it is best to buy the leather ready to cut.

Leather is classified in three ways: by name of the animal (i.e., sheepskin); by the tanning process (i.e., chrome tanned); by the thickness and weight of the leather (i.e., medium-weight—three ounces per square foot).

TYPES OF LEATHER AND USES IN CAMP HANDCRAFT

Various types of leather may be used in camp handcraft:

—*Tooling calf* has a firm surface; it is durable; it is available in varying thicknesses and colors. It is used for all types of projects and is best for tooling and stamping. It is a relatively expensive type of leather for campers' use.

—*Tooling sheepskin* is a good material for beginners since it is less expensive than calf but used in the same general way. It may be tooled or stamped, but stretches a little in tooling. It should not be confused with the sheepskin used for parchment or diplomas, which is a thin, stretched, stiff skin. Sometimes sheepskin has the wool on one side and is used for caps, mittens, slippers, etc.

—*Tooling steerhide or cowhide* is similar to tooling calf but is heavier. It can be flat-tooled, stamped, or carved and is used for articles like belts and ax sheaths.

—*Suede* is usually lambskin which is tanned so that it has an undressed or rough surface not suitable for tooling. It is soft, easily sewed, and available in many lovely colors.

—*Pigskin* is a rough-surfaced leather, not suitable for ornamenting but with an attractive grained appearance.

—*Goatskin* is usually used for lacings which may be bought in varying widths and colors.

TOOLS USED IN LEATHERWORK

Tools for Cutting

sharp knife · skiving knife · metal or metal-edged ruler (household) · Try square · heavy sharp shears (household) · wooden cutting board · back

Tools for punching holes

punches · rawhide · wood · mallets · back · wooden cutting board · awl · spring · rotary · drive

Tools for decorating

modeling · tracing · stamping · orange stick · sponge · metal hammer · front · cutting board

Tools for setting fasteners

snaps · eyelets

Other tools

needles · lacing · sewing · or for clamping

Materials

lacing · thong · snaps · eyelet · buckles · paste wax or shoe polish · leather cement · household cement for stiffening

PLATE V

—*Deerskin, elkskin, and horsehide* are usually chrome-tanned, as shown by the blue-green edge on the skin. These are good leathers for moccasins and garments, but they cannot be tooled, stamped, or carved.

—*Skivers* are very thin leathers, generally used for linings.

—*Rawhide* is hide from which the hair has been removed but which has not been through a tanning process. Instead of tanning, the hide is dried on a frame and becomes stiff. To be used, it must be rubbed with neat's foot oil and tallow which makes it waterproof, soft, and oily. It is often used for thongs and shoelaces which are useful for many projects.

—*Scrap leather* may be bought in bundles, by the pound. It is suitable for practice of techniques, and for many beginners' articles. Bundles are inexpensive; but, before purchasing, it is important to be sure that the pieces are large enough for practical purposes.

Lacings may be cut from the same material as the article (see Figure V-4) or purchased in contrasting colors and leathers. Plastic lacing, under many commercial names, may also be purchased; it is used for braided articles, such as lanyards, and for lacing. It is less expensive than leather but does not have the wearing qualities. Some plastic is flammable, and this type should not be purchased for campers' use.

There are many craft supply houses that carry all types of leather and leatherwork supplies and tools. These companies have good advice on types of leather needed for various purposes. For names and addresses of such suppliers, write to the American Camping Association for a copy of the Buyer's Guide, published annually.

TECHNIQUES

Working in leather calls for special skills and techniques. It is good for the novice to practice these techniques on scrap leather before attempting a finished article. Since much of the value in leatherwork comes from planning the article, creating the pattern and the design for decorating, and utilizing the various techniques, it is assumed here that the camper will have a hand in these steps. (Ready-to assemble kits are available from craft supply houses, but these are not included here.)

Techniques in leatherwork include cutting leather, punching holes, lacing and stitching, decorating, making folds, corners, and gussets, and attaching fastenings such as buttons and snaps. These techniques form the basis for the steps in the projects which are presented later in the chapter.

Cutting Leather

Equipment needed: A hardwood cutting board—use the top side for cutting with knife, the underside for punching with drive punch; sharp knife and sharp shears; metal ruler or metal-edge ruler; pencil.

Steps

1. Make patterns of objects from thin cardboard (old file folders are good).
2. Lay leather on cutting board, smooth side down, rough side up. Place patterns on leather, and mark with pencil (Figure V-1). Place patterns carefully to make best use of leather without waste.
3. Use a metal ruler to guide straight edges; cut along edges of pattern with sharp knife, holding almost perpendicular (Figure V-2).
4. Cut slowly, drawing knife toward you; go over cutting if necessary, but do not *pull* apart; be sure to cut completely through leather. Hold ruler and leather at side to avoid cutting yourself if knife slips.

When cutting from whole skins, use back sections for choicest large pieces, as these are freer from blemishes, scars, and scratches. Use outside pieces for small sections, such as belt loops, gussets, fringe.

Cut suede or thin leather with sharp shears.

Cutting a Thong for Lacing

Most lacing is purchased ready-cut, but it may be cut from a circle or disc of leather to match the leather used in the article. Lacings are thin and narrow and are difficult for the novice to cut. Thongs are thicker and wide; they are made of heavier leather (generally rawhide) and so are more easily cut.

Steps

1. Make a disc of leather (Figure V-3); length of thong will depend on width of thong as it is cut:

From a 4-inch disc, 16.7 feet of 1/16-inch thong; 8.3 feet of 1/8-inch thong.

From a 3-inch disc, 9.4 feet of 1/16-inch thong; 4.7 feet of 1/8-inch thong.

2. Mark off the disc in right angles (Figure V-3 at *A* and *B*).
3. Make a cutting board by fastening a side piece to any board (Figure V-4).

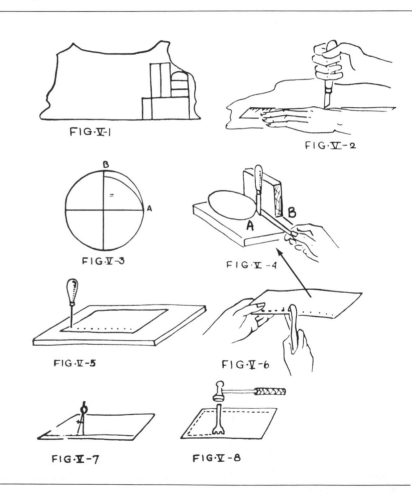

FIG·Ⅴ-1 FIG·Ⅴ-2 FIG·Ⅴ-3 FIG·Ⅴ-4 FIG·Ⅴ-5 FIG·Ⅴ-6 FIG·Ⅴ-7 FIG·Ⅴ-8

4. Stick the point of a *sharp* knife into the board at a distance from the side piece to give the desired width, blad cutting *away* from you. This distance determines the width of the thong.
5. Place leather disc at knife edge, close to side piece. Start with tapered cut from *A* to *B*, reaching desired width at *B*. Pull cut thong toward you, with even tension, cutting disc in a spiral to center.

Punching Holes

Holes are punched in leather prior to lacing or stitching to ensure even spacing, to reduce strain on the lacing and the leather, and for ease in pulling thread or lacing through the leather. Holes are pierced with an awl or punched with a leather punch.

Equipment needed: Leather punch, with spacer, or drive punch and mallet; awl; cutting board; ruler and pencil and divider.

Steps in using an awl: Awls are used to make small holes for stitching.

1. Place leather, right side up, on underside of cutting board.
2. Mark light line about 1/8 inch to 1/4 inch from edge with ruler.
3. Mark dots for holes, spacing evenly about 1/8 inch to 1/4 inch apart.
4. Push awl through, from right side to back, on dots; make holes the desired size by controlling the distance the awl is pushed through the leather (Figure V-5).

Punches are used to make larger holes, for use with lacing or thong. There are drive punches and spring punches. Some spring punches have several different sized punches, in a rotary device, and some have a device on the side that simplifies spacing.

Steps in using punch without spacer

1. Mark light line about 1/8 inch to 1/4 inch from edge, and mark dots for holes as for awl, above, or use divider (Figure V-7).
2. Place punch on spot, and squeeze firmly.

Steps in using punch with spacer

1. Mark light line about 1/8 inch to 1/4 inch from edge to guide punch.

2. Make first punch.
3. Adjust spacer to desired distance between holes; hook spacer in first hole, and punch second hole on line; continue to end, working from left to right (Figure V-6).

Steps in using drive punch

Drive punches are cheaper than spring punches; they make a variety of sizes and shapes of round holes and slits; some of them make multiple impressions. They are used to make holes far from an edge.

1. Mark line with dots with awl, as above; place leather on underside of cutting board.
2. Place punch upright over a dot; strike sharply on end with a metal hammer (Figure V-8). Continue to end.

For folds and seams, be sure holes in both sides of seams or folds match (Figures V-9 *a* and *b*); mark carefully before punching. An awl may be used to mark through one set of holes for the second set. Strings tied in first and last holes keep the leather pieces from slipping while being punched (Figure V-10). Skive all edges before punching (see below).

For corners, make a single hole at corner (Figure V-11) and space adjacent holes from this corner hole. Round corner of leather.

For gussets or side pieces: A gusset is an inserted piece of leather, used to make a side piece, either straight or tapered.

Steps

1. Make pattern for gusset, with pattern for main piece. Cut both pieces.
2. Punch holes in main piece, then mark and punch holes to correspond in gusset piece, as far as beginning of curved bottom (Figure V-12).
3. Put gusset in place, and tie to main piece at top and at last holes before curve (Figure V-13).
4. Locate middle hole (*M*) in main pieces; push awl through it, marking place for *M* on gusset; punch holes in gusset; tie *M*s together.
5. Locate other holes on gusset in similar manner; punch; ease leather into place to make accurate fit (Figure V-14).
6. Lace with any desired stitch.

Making Folds

Steps

1. Have leather piece cut to size.
2. Dampen on both sides.
3. Measure and mark places for fold.
4. Lay ruler or straightedge firmly in place where fold is to be made (Figure V-15); fold leather over ruler; press down with heel of hand along length of fold.
5. Remove ruler; pound fold with rawhide mallet (Figure V-16).

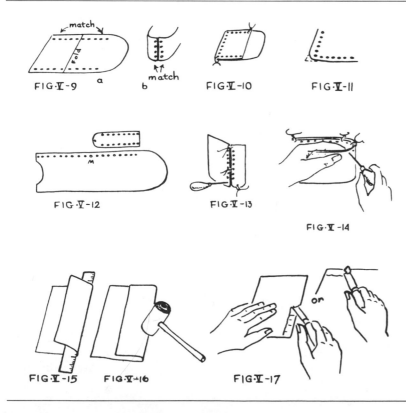

FIG·V-9   FIG·V-10   FIG·V-11

FIG·V-12   FIG·V-13

FIG·V-14

FIG·V-15   FIG·V-16   FIG·V-17

Skiving

This is a process of thinning edges of leather when two or more thicknesses join, preventing a bulky edge or seam. A skiving knife is used (Figure V-17) to shave off small pieces of leather along the edge of the underside of leather, making a long bevel. Avoid taking off big pieces or cutting too deeply. All edges to be joined should be skived for about ½ inch from edge.

Lacings are skived when two pieces are joined; the top of one piece and the underside of the other are skived for about 1 inch, making the joint about the thickness of the rest of the lacing.

Lacing

One method of joining pieces of leather together is by lacing or thonging with a leather strip, called a *lacing* or *thong*. Single edges are trimmed with similar lacing stitches.

Seams are made, or edges trimmed, by threading a narrow strip of leather through a series of small holes, spaced evenly, near the edge of the article. The size of the holes, the distance between them, and the distance from the edge of leather varies with the size of the object and the size of the lacing; 1/8 inch to 1/4 inch will be the usual distance, the same distance being used between holes, and from holes to edge (see Figures V-5—14);

Lacing is generally a narrow strip of goatskin; it may be a wider strip, about ½ inch, called *Florentine*. Thongs are heavier strips, generally rawhide; thongs are used with heavy leather. Lacing is usually bought ready-cut though it may be cut of the leather from which the article is made. Thongs may be purchased ready to use or may be cut from discs (see Figure V-4). Rawhide shoelaces, available in hardware stores, are often used in camp articles.

Equipment needed: Punch; ruler and pencil; awl; lacing.

Steps

1. Punch holes as needed.
2. Point threading end of lacing, and stiffen with household cement.

3. To start a piece of lacing, insert end between layers of leather, and down through bottom part of first hole. Fasten end with rubber cement and hold until cement sets. Bring lacing up over edges, and down in top of next hole, according to desired stitch (Figure V-18). Stitches are described in following section.
4. Work from left to right, threading from top to bottom.
5. Turn lacing as it is pulled through so that the smooth side is always in place on the top of work. Pull stitches evenly as lacing progresses.
6. Run finished edge between fingers as a small part of lacing is completed to get stitches lined up evenly. Pull lacing through holes with same tension, pulling firmly, but not tightly, into place (Figure V-19).
7. When turning a corner, lace twice in corner hole (Figure V-20).

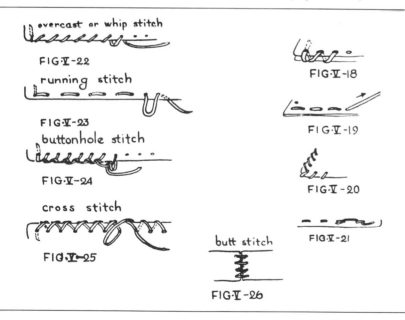

overcast or whip stitch

FIG·V-22

running stitch

FIG·V-23

buttonhole stitch

FIG·V-24

cross stitch

FIG·V-25

butt stitch

FIG·V-26

FIG·V-18

FIG·V-19

FIG·V-20

FIG·V-21

8. End lacing in similar manner to starting, tucking last inch between layers and fastening with rubber cement.
9. To start or end lacing on single piece of leather (without layers), run lacing under first few and last few stitches on underside, fastening with rubber cement (Figure V-21).

10. To join pieces of lacing, skive top of one piece of lacing and underside of the other for ½ inch, so together they are about the thickness of the lacing. Spread ends with rubber cement, and hold in place until dry. Place this joint where it is flat and where it will not receive much wear.

Some Common Types of Lacing Stitches

—*Overcast or whip stitch* (Figure V-22): measure lacing 2½ times distance to be laced. Insert through bottom hole, from between layers. Bring lacing up in front, down into first hole through both thicknesses, up over edge to second hole, into second hole, then to third, etc., to end. Finish by going into last hole twice and end as above.
—*Running stitch* (Figure V-23): measure lacing 1¾ times distance to be laced. Bring lacing up through first hole, down into second, up into first again, down into second, up into third, down into fourth, etc. Finish by going back on last stitch, fastening as above.
—*Buttonhole stitch* (Figure V-24): measure lacing five times distance to be laced. Start as in overcasting; after pulling lacing through second hole pass end over loop and down. Pull to left. Put lacing through third hole, loop and pull to right. Continue to end, and finish in overcasting.
—*Cross stitch* (Figure V-25): measure lacing five to six times distance to be laced. Overcast from one end to the other; turn and come back in same holes, crossing on edge of leather. Start in middle of lacing, using both ends to lace, as in lacing a shoe. Be sure to lace so that the top stitch goes in the same direction each time.
—*Butt stitch* (Figure V-26): measure five to six times distance to be laced. Start at top of seam, holding edges to meet, not overlap. Lace like a shoe, with horizontal stitches on outside of seam.

Stitching

Seams may be joined by stitching with needle(s) and waxed thread, twine, fine cord, or similar material. Stitching is usually used on soft and thin leather.

Equipment needed: Heavy, large-eyed needles or four-sided leather needles; waxed thread (carpet thread is good) or string or cord; awl; cutting board; ruler and pencil.

To wax thread: cut off desired length, and pull between thumb and piece of beeswax or paraffin.

Two types of stitches are described:

One-Needle or Imitation Cobbler's Stitch

Steps

1. Punch hole with awl, using underside of cutting board.
2. Measure thread three and one-half times length of seam; thread in one needle.
3. Put needle up last hole on right, leaving a length of thread hanging, about one-half the length of seam. This is a take-up thread.
4. Carry thread across the top of article and down into first hole on left, leaving a loose thread (*a-b*) across top (Figure V-27).
5. Put needle up through second hole onleft, in front of *a-b* thread; go over the *a-b* thread, and back down in the same hole. (Figure V-28). Pull thread down so that the *a-b* thread is pulled into the space between the layers of leather (Figure V-29), concealing the interlocking of the threads. This dip takes up a little of the take-up thread at each stitch.
6. Bring needle up through third hole, in front of thread, over and back down, in back of thread as above (*up* in front, *over,* and *down* in back).
7. Continue to end of seam. Finish by working back one or two stitches, bring thread out between layers of material.
8. To turn corners: measure the *a-b* thread for full length of stitching. Start in last hole at one corner, as above; carry thread along the top of the article for the full length of the seam, catching *a-b* thread at corners with paper clips (Figure V-30). Remove clips as *a-b* is caught at corners in stitching.

Cobbler's Stitch or Saddle Stitch (with two needles)

Steps

1. Punch holes with awl, using underside of cutting board.
2. Measure thread three times length of seam.
3. Thread one needle, and put through first hole on left; pull half way through. Thread other end of thread in other needle.

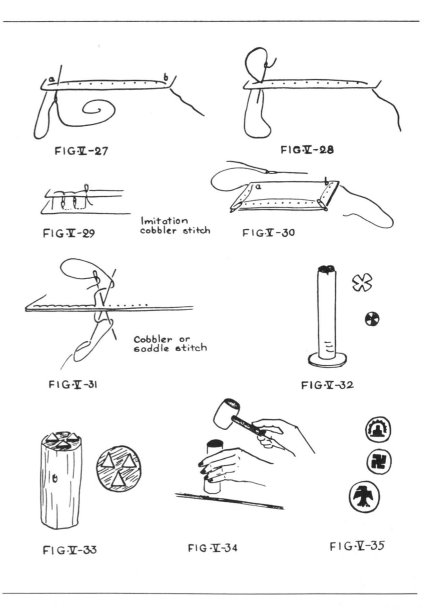

FIG·V-27   FIG·V-28

FIG·V-29   Imitation cobbler stitch   FIG·V-30

Cobbler or saddle stitch

FIG·V-31   FIG·V-32

FIG·V-33   FIG·V-34   FIG·V-35

4. Put top needle *down* through second hole and bottom needle *up* through same hole (Figure V-31).
5. Take top thread in left hand and bottom thread in right, and pull until interlocking loop formed by the threads is between layers of leather (Figure V-31).
6. Continue to end.
7. End by working back two stitches, drawing threads out between layers, cutting off all but an inch. Tuck ends between layers and fasten with rubber cement.

Decorating Leather

There are a number of ways of decorating leather; smooth leather like calfskin or steerhide may be decorated in designs by stamping, tooling or modeling, carving, beading, or pyrography. Each method of decorating calls for special tools and techniques: these are described in the following sections.

Stamping

This method of ornamenting uses wood or metal stamps with designs carved or filed in the end. It is one of the simplest ways to decorate leather.

Equipment and materials needed: Staming tools—these may be purchased in Indian symbols or other designs, or handmade by: (1) cutting off the point of a heavy nail, or using the head, and filing a design (Figure V-32), or (2) cutting a design with a knife in the end grain of a hardwood stick (Figure V-33); cutting board; rawhide or wooden mallet; tracing tool; water and sponge; tooling calf, sheepskin, or cowhide.

To make a design for stamping: a design for stamping is usually an all-over design, or repeated pattern, as for a border. The design should be fitted to the place, i.e., a design with curves for a round area, a long repeat pattern for a belt, and one with straight lines for a rectangular space. Stamping designs should be clear and compact. The stamp may be used over and over so repetition of the design is possible.

Steps

1. Dampen leather on both sides with sponge (not too wet). Place leather right sige up on cutting board.
2. Mark with tracing tool where each unit of design will go.
3. Place stamping tool in place; hold vertical and hit top of stamp sharply with mallet to make impression in leather (Figure V-34). Repeat as desired. Try to make first impression hard enough with first blow of hammer to avoid "fuzziness" by repeated blows.
4. Practice on scrap leather to get even impressions and to see how design works out before using on article to be finished.

Commercial stamps, with Indian designs, are very useful in telling a story, Indian style (Figure V-35).

Tooling

This method of decorating utilizes metal tools, known as modeling tools, to depress lines and areas in leather.

Equipment and materials needed: Hard tooling surface of marble, masonite, glass, etc.; tracing tool or orange stick; modeling tools; rubber cement or masking tape; water and sponge; wax to polish; tooling calf, tooling sheepskin, or tooling cowhide.

To make a design for tooling: make it suitable in size and shape to the article. Tooling is a process of impressing lines and wider areas in the surface of the leather. Usually large areas are left high, and lines and small areas are depressed. Initials, leaves, acorns, campfires, etc. make simple first steps in tooling. (See designs for bookmark, Figures V-37 and 40).

Steps

1. Draw design on paper, and transfer as follows: lay leather piece face down on hard surface and dampen back. Turn over and dampen front. *Do not soak leather* so that water oozes out when pressed (Figure V-36).

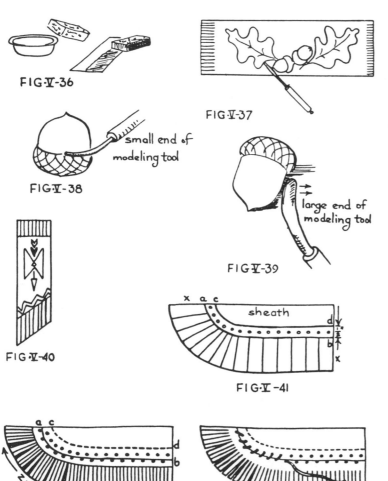

FIG·V-36

FIG·V-37

FIG·V-38

small end of modeling tool

FIG·V-39

large end of modeling tool

FIG·V-40

FIG·V-41

sheath

FIG·V-42

FIG·V-43

2. Fasten paper design on front of leather with rubber cement or masking tape.
3. Go over design with tracing tool (Figure V-37).
4. Go over design with small end of modeling tool (Figure V-38).
5. Using large end of tool, press down the background around the edges of design (Figure V-39). Press harder near design, and lift tool gradually as you leave the design area. For greater detail in the design, use the small end of the tool.
6. If the leather dries, dampen whole piece, or water will leave a stain.
7. When tooling is finished, let leather dry, then polish with paste wax and rub with soft cloth or your hand.

Making Fringe

This type of decoration is used on ends of straight strips, such as a bookmark, and on seams of such articles as sheaths, jackets, and Indian costumes.

Equipment and materials needed: Sharp knife or heavy sharp shears such as kitchen shears; awl; cutting board; ruler and pencil; material—part of the main piece, or extra piece of same material.

Steps for fringing a straight piece (as a bookmark)

1. Mark line at each end for depth of fringe (Figure V-40).
2. Mark dots for desired width of fringe at each edge and at each line. Connect with light pencil mark and ruler.
3. Cut with shears, following marks.

Steps for fringing a knife sheath

1. Use shape of sheath, punched ready to lace, as pattern, and draw around edge on leather (line *a-b*) Figure V-41.
2. Extend line at point of sheath and at top (Figure V-41 *x*).
3. One-half inch or 3/8 inch above this line draw another line (*c-d*) to correspond.
4. Measure depth of fringe from line *a-b*, along *x*, and mark same depth for entire length by putting dots about every inch, the same distance from line *a-b*. Connect dots for outside edge of fringe (Figure V-42).

5. Cut out shape of fringe.
6. With awl, mark through holes punched in sheath piece, for holes in fringe to correspond.
7. Mark off line for second row of holes below line *a-b*, putting dots for holes between the holes above this line (Figure V-43).
8. On under side of leather of fringe piece, mark off with pencil width of fringe strands, keeping lines at right angles to edge of sheath or line *a-b*. When planning for strands at curve (Figure V-42) cut out narrow slivers, wedge shaped, to make strands uniform width (Figure V-43).
9. Cut with sharp knife and cutting board or with shears.
10. Insert fringe between layers of sheath, and lace with overcast stitch (Figure V-43).

Other Ways of Decorating Leather

Of the several other ways of decorating leather, some are used extensively in certain parts of the country, as the carved leather of the West; some, as carving or beading, are more advanced than the steps already described. For campers who are ready to advance into new techniques, these additional methods will be of interest; any complete book on leathercraft will give details.

Carving is a method of decorating thick leather, such as cowhide, by cutting the design in low relief with a special swivel blade knife. A combination of carving and stamping is currently very popular in Western type belts and purses.

Beading is a method of decorating by sewing beads on leather; it is often carried out in Indian designs and symbols. Several beads may be strung on a thread, and sewed in place; or in places receiving hard wear, beads may be sewed singly or in pairs. Beads for borders are first sewed on a strip, and the strip laced in place on the leather, as on a belt.

Pyrography is a method of decorating by burning with a heated point, generally an electrically heated wood-burning set. Primitive tools may be fashioned from nails, heated in the fire. Cowhide, steerhide, and pigskin in natural colors are often used as the base for pyrography.

Finishing Leather

Smooth leathers may be finished with an application of either liquid or paste wax or leather shoe polish; the leather is hand-rubbed or polished with a soft cloth for the final finish.

Attaching Fastenings

Leather may be fastened with thread, lacing, thongs, snaps, eyelets, or rivets. The metal accessories are called 'findings'; some of them require special setting tools. Buckles and straps are usually stitched on, though rivets may be used; speedy rivets are often used for straps or to attach rings, such as D-rings. Split rivets reinforce leather at points of strain as on an ax sheath.

Attaching Buckles

Buckles used for belts and straps are usually of two types; metal with tongues or carved wood without tongues (Figure V-44). These are attached in similar fashion.

Buckles with tongues require a hole punched near the end of the belt or strap or in a separate piece of leather for the tongue to pass through.

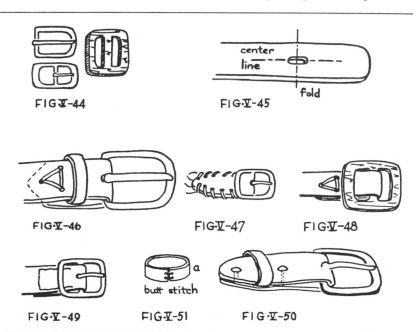

FIG·V-44

FIG·V-45

FIG·V-46

FIG·V-47

FIG·V-48

FIG·V-49

FIG·V-51

FIG·V-50

—Method No. 1 (to attach in end of belt): punch a slot of two or three holes along a center line; even off sides of slot with knife, if necessary; fold over at this point, and insert tongue (Figure V-45). Mark off three holes for lacing, and punch with small punch. Spread inside with rubber cement, and clamp together while lacing. Lace in triangle and finish off by cementing ends under stitches on back (Figure V-46).

—Method No. 2 (separate piece, as with braided belt [see Figures II-50 and 51): punch holes on edges of extra piece (Figure V-47); make hole for tongue; cement, lace, and finish as above.

Buckles without tongues need no hole in the strip; slip strap over crosspiece of buckle, narrowing as necessary to fit; fold and punch, and finish as above (Figure V-48).

Small buckles on straps and buckles for camera case straps or other equipment are attached by Method No. 1 above or by sewing with one-needle cobbler's stitch (Figure V-49).

Rivets are often used to fasten buckle straps instead of lacing (Figure V-50).

Belt loops or 'keepers' are metal or leather loops inserted between stitches or between rivets. Leather loops are stitched with butt stitch (Figure V-51) before being inserted (Figure V-50).

Making Buttons for Leather Articles

Buttons for leather may be made of wood, leather, bone, coconut shell, or similar materials. They are attached by leather lacing or thong or by needle with waxed thread. Heavy cowhide may be cut in desired shapes, then tooled or stamped. Holes are bored, or slits cut (Figure V-52). See Chapter Ten for making wooden buttons.

To attach buttons, two methods may be used.

—Method No. 1: pierce two small holes in proper place on main piece of leather. Insert lacing and tie underneath with square knot (see Figure II-16). Cement ends under knot.

—Method No. 2: lacings may be fastened with three holes (Figure V-53); pierce holes in proper place. Put end *x* down *a*, up *b*, down *c*; put end *y* down *c*, up *b*, down *a*. Cross ends underneath, and cement.

To attach toggles: use a lark's head (see Figure II-22) or a clove hitch (see Figure II-19) around toggle, and fasten ends as above.

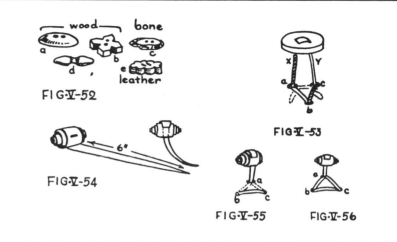

FIG·V-52

FIG·V-53

FIG·V-54

FIG·V-55   FIG·V-56

Steps for pioneer button

1. Use a 10-inch by ¾-inch strip of soft thin leather, such as calf, or a shorter piece of thicker leather, such as cowhide.
2. Taper both sides of one end to a 1/8-inch tail about 4 inches from the wide end.
3. Make a crosswise slit through roll (Figure V-54).
4. Start rolling at wider end; roll just past slits; tuck tail in slit and out at bottom, using an awl to hold the roll.
5. To attach: punch three holes in a triangle not more than 1/2 inch apart (Figure V-55).
6. Insert tail piece down hole *a*, up through *b*, down into *c*, and back into *a* again. Tuck under stitches, and cement end. Leave as much of the shank protruding as necessary, according to the thickness of the leather to be buttoned (Figure V-56).

Buttonholes are usually slits cut in leather with a sharp knife; the slit runs parallel to edge of material. For a thick button, or a double-headed rivet, the buttonhole should have two smaller slits at end, like a capital *I;* for a heavy strap or heavy leather, a small hole may be punched at each end of the slit (see knife sheath, Figure V-83).

Setting Eyelets

Small metal eyelets are used for reinforcing punched holes for lacing where there will be wear and pull on the opening. Large metal rings are called *grommets;* these are seldom used in leather work, except in large heavy bags. Directions for setting grommets may be found in Chapter Sixteen.

Equipment needed: Eyelet; hammer; punch; setting tools—these may be bought commercially, including anvil and setting tool, or made from a 16-penny nail, filed flat, then filed to have a shank (Figure V-57).

Steps

1. Punch hole in leather.
2. Push eyelet through from right to wrong side.
3. Place leather on anvil or pad of newspaper with eyelet flange up; insert setting tool in center of eyelet flange.
4. Hit tool on end sharply with hammer (Figure V-58) to spread flange.

Eyelets that come in two sections are set in similar fashion, except that second part is placed over the flange before hammering.

Setting Metal Rivets

Speedy rivets (obtainable at a notions counter) are used to fasten straps, to finish belts, for Western style decorating, to fasten D-rings on straps. No setting tools are required; a hole is punched, and the rivet inserted, top and bottom in the hole; a sharp blow with a hammer closes the rivet (Figure V-59).

Setting Snaps

Snap fasteners are utilized on pocketbooks, ax sheaths, and so forth. A special snap setting kit, including tools to use and the snaps, may be purchased from any craft supply house.

Equipment needed: Snap setting tools; hammer; punch; snaps—two parts to each.

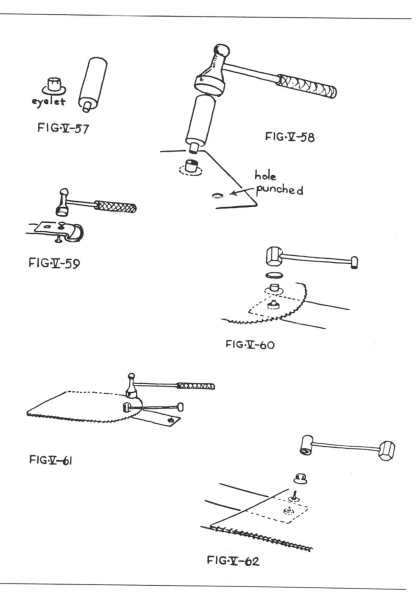

eyelet

FIG·V-57

FIG·V-58

hole punched

FIG·V-59

FIG·V-60

FIG·V-61

FIG·V-62

Steps

1. Punch hole in desired spot, as on a flap.
2. Fold flap over; mark with tracing tool or pencil the corresponding spot on main piece.
3. Place large lower section of snap on large end of anvil and from underneath in hole in flap (Figure V-60).
4. Lay top of snap on assembled parts, and place large end of hammer on it. Hold hammer steady with one hand, and strike a sharp blow on hammerhead with another hammer (Figure V-61).
5. Put layers of newspaper or cardboard under other piece of leather where other part will be set to prevent marring underpiece (Figure V-62). Put pointed end of snap through hole from back, and lay it on small end of anvil which is tucked underneath (Figure V-62).
6. Place top section of second part over point; put small end of hammer over this. Hold steady, and strike with a sharp blow with other hammer.
7. The tension of the snap may be adjusted by squeezing bottom part with pliers or by giving a light tap with hammer.

Slits for Straps and Belts

Slits for belts, straps, and tongues are cut before the article is assembled.

For *slits in sheath or belt purse,* if lightweight leather is used, mark lines with awl, and cut carefully with sharp knife on cutting board (Figures V-63 and 64).

If heavyweight leather is used, mark lines with awl, and indicate spots for holes at top or at top and bottom of slit. Using knife, straightedge, and cutting board, cut on line, keeping knife blade against straightedge. With punch make one hole at end of line for rivet-head slit or a hole at each end for sheath slit *(Figures V-63 a, b, c).*

For *straps on cases,* such as camera cases, which often have shoulder straps that go under the bottom of case for added strength, slits to hold the strap in place are cut in side pieces and bottom before assembling. Tongues on flaps may be secured in the same fashion. Mark lines to be cut, use straightedge and cutting board, and cut carefully with sharp knife (Figure V-64).

PROJECTS

Bookmark—a Simple Project in Tooling

This project utilizes all the steps necessary in tooling; it is a good beginner's project in planning and in carrying out a design from nature.

Equipment needed: Hard tooling surface; tracing tool; modeling tool; water and sponge; rubber cement; wax.

Materials needed: Small piece of tooling calf or sheepskin—scrap leather may be used.

Steps

See preceding pages in this chapter for techniques used in this project.

1. Make a design on paper (Figure V-65).
2. Cut leather desired shape and size.
3. Transfer design to leather (Figure V-65).
4. Tool design (Figure V-66).
5. Cut fringe (Figure V-67).
6. Finish by waxing and rubbing.

Belt Purse—a Simple Project in Lacing

This project includes first steps in planning, in lacing, and in setting snaps. It may include simple tooling or stamping.

Equipment needed: leather punch; knife, snap setting tools; tooling or stamping tools; rawhide mallet; water and sponge; rubber cement; wax.

Materials needed: any light-weight leather, tooling or nontooling—scrap leather may be used; lacing; snap set.

Steps

See preceding pages in this chapter for techniques used in this project.

1. Cut piece of leather (5 inches or 6 inches by 9 inches is a good average size).

2. Punch holes along edges for lacing; do not punch across end *A-B* (Figure V-68).
3. Cut slits for belt (Figure V-69).
4. Tool or stamp if desired.
5. Lace with desired stitch.

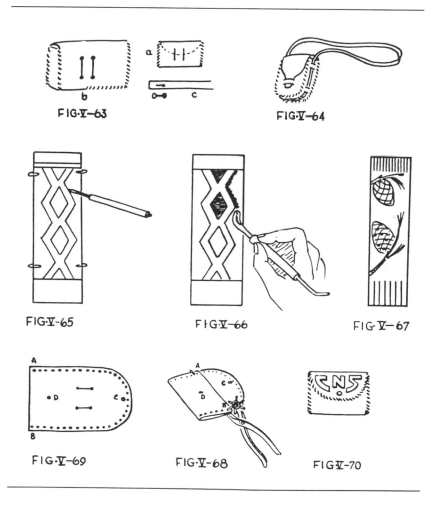

FIG·V–63

FIG·V–64

FIG·V–65

FIG·V–66

FIG·V–67

FIG·V–69

FIG·V–68

FIG·V–70

6. Punch hole (*C*) in center of flap, about 1 inch from edge (Figure V-69); fold over; mark through this hole for hole (*D*); punch (Figure V-68).
7. Set snaps (Figure V-70).
8. Finish by running laced edges between fingers; place between layers of paper and pound with mallet.
9. Wax and polish.

Miser's Pouch

This is another type of purse to be worn on the belt. Tradition says that the forty-niners used similar pouches to hold their gold nuggets. Scrap leather that is soft and easily crushed is good for this project.

Equipment needed: Knife or scissors; awl; needle and waxed thread; ruler; shears.
Materials needed: Piece of soft leather, size desired—one large piece folded, or two pieces stitched together; two small rings, plastic or metal.

Steps

See preceding pages in this chapter for techniques used in this project.

1. Cut leather as desired; 9½ inches by 8 inches is a good size.
2. Lay ruler 1/8 inch from edge and mark for holes; punch with awl (Figure V-71). Make holes on sides 1 and 2; on side 3 leave a 3-inch opening (*A-B*) at center, without holes.
3. Stitch with cobbler's stitch all but opening (*a-b*).
4. Slip rings over ends, to center.
5. *To use:* slip rings down one end; put article or coins in other end; slip rings to this end, locking in the coins; put something in other end, slip one ring toward that end (Figure V-72). Hang over belt (Figure V-73).

Variation: In a *jug purse* (Figures V-74 and 75), opening is at top, and the purse looks like a jug when ring is held in place by handle.

Belts

Making belts presents a variety of possibilities for campers; these are especially good projects for boys. The simplest belts will be those without

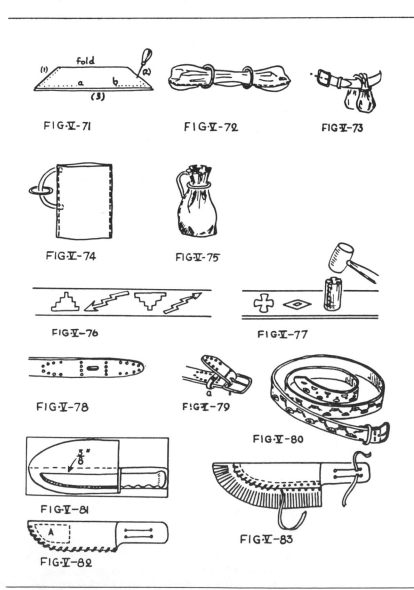

FIG·V-71

FIG·V-72

FIG·V-73

FIG·V-74

FIG·V-75

FIG·V-76

FIG·V-77

FIG·V-78

FIG·V-79

FIG·V-80

FIG·V-81

FIG·V-82

FIG·V-83

decoration, employing the techniques of fastening buckles and loops. Belts may also be braided, as shown in Chapter II on Braiding and Knotting. Advanced projects will include belts that are tooled or stamped or carved. Except for the braiding or decorating, the process is similar to that given below.

Stamped Steerhide Belt

Equipment needed: Stamping tools; punch; awl; rawhide mallet; knife; rubber cement.

Materials needed: Strip of tooling steerhide, desired width and length; lacing; small strip for loop; buckle. A kit of materials for a belt may be purchased from craft supply house.

Steps

See preceding pages in this chapter for techniques used in this project.

1. Make a plan for the design (Figure V-76).
2. Transfer design to belt.
3. Stamp design (Figure V-77).
4. Attach buckle and loop *a* (Figures V-78 and 79).
5. Cut other end into rounded point; try on belt and mark place for hole where belt fits. Add two holes evenly spaced on either side of the first hole (Figure V-80).

Knife Sheath

This is a more advanced project, entailing cutting a pattern to fit a specific knife. It is a good plan to make a paper pattern first to be sure of all steps. The sheath may be stamped or tooled; a fringe (see Figure V-41) may be added.

Equipment needed: Knife; punch; awl, rubber cement; stamping or tooling tools.

Materials needed: Cowhide or similar stiff, tough leather; lacing; short thong; lighter leather for fringe, if desired.

Steps

See preceding pages in this chapter for techniques used in this project.

1. Making pattern: lay knife on back of leather; draw around it, allowing 3/8 inch margin around blade (Figure V-81).
2. Cut out with sharp knife.
3. Dampen leather; fold over, right side out (Figure V-82).
4. Punch holes for lacing 1/8 inch from edge, 1/4 inch apart; cut slits for belt (Figure V-82).
5. If fringe is desired, measure, cut, and make fringe.
6. Lace with running stitch or whip the edges; fringe is laced in place with the rest of the lacing (Figure V-83).
7. Thong is placed at slits to tie around knife handle (Figure V-83).

Ax Sheaths

Making sheaths for personal axes is a good project for older campers. Three types of sheaths are given here; the steps, in general, are the same for each type. The value of this project is the planning for the specific ax and for the desired type of sheath.

Equipment needed: Knife and cutting board; awl; rawhide mallet; needle and waxed thread; snap setting set; pencil.
Materials needed: Heavy cowhide; goatskin lacing or thong; snap and/or buckles.

Steps

See preceding pages in this chapter for techniques used in this project.

1. Make paper pattern, leaving about 1/2 inch margin on edges (Figure V-84).
2. Lay pattern on leather; draw around it. Use piece doubled, with fold at back, or use two single pieces joined with butt stitch at back (Figure V-85).
3. Cut and punch an extra piece (x) 3/8 inch wide, the length of the sheath edge at cutting edge of ax; this is to lace into sheath to prevent ax edge from cutting lacing (Figure V-84).

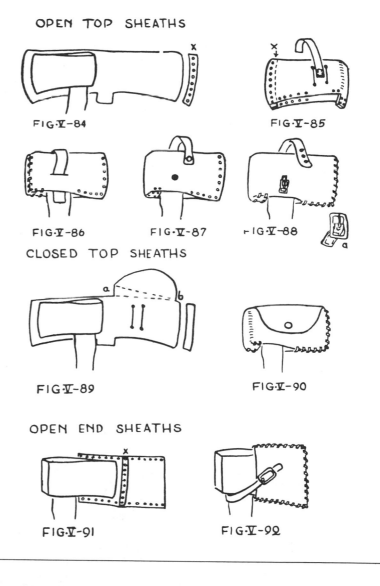

OPEN TOP SHEATHS

FIG·V-84   FIG·V-85

FIG·V-86   FIG·V-87   FIG·V-88

CLOSED TOP SHEATHS

FIG·V-89   FIG·V-90

OPEN END SHEATHS

FIG·V-91   FIG·V-92

4. Punch holes, punching one side first, then marking through holes for other side, before punching second side.
5. Punch holes and cut slits in back of sheath for belt slot (Figure V-85).
6. For a strap fastener (Figures V 85-88); cut a strap needed length (about 6 inches) and desired width for buckle, or about 1 inch for a snap. Attach the strap to back of sheath with waxed thread, using running stitch. Set snap, or if buckle is used, cut a leather tongue (Figure V-88 *a)* and sew with waxed thread, using running stitch. If no snap or buckle is desired (Figure V-86), cut slot for strap in sheath, and make the strap long enough to fit into slot and down through opening.
7. Lace edges with whip stitch or cobbler's stitch, with goatskin lacing or a thong cut from same leather as sheath (Figure V-88). Lace in strip *x*.
8. Flatten lacing with rawhide mallet.

Steps for open-top sheath (Figures V-84-88)

1. Follow directions above.
2. Dampen cut-out leather; fold over, making two folds at back so edges are even.
3. Attach strap and buckle or snap fasteners.
4. Lace as above.

Steps for closed-top sheath (Figures V-89-90)

1. Follow general directions above, adding piece at top (*a-b*) to fold over top of ax head.

Steps for open-end sheath (Figures V-91 and 92)

This type of sheath is particularly suitable for large axes and for those not carried on belt.

1. Follow general directions above, leaving 1/2 inch margin on end and 3/4-inch margins on top and bottom. Cut reinforcing piece (*x*) 1/2 inch wide (Figure V-91). One piece of leather may be used, but the fold needs reinforcing, as the ax edge cuts a fold easily.
2. Cut strap for buckle long enough to fit around handle under head of ax (Figure V-92).
3. Sew strap and lace as above.

Tooled Bookcover

A bookcover of tooling leather can be made any size to fit a particular volume. This is a project that entails planning, cutting, making pockets, and tooling of some outdoor design.

Equipment needed: Knife; modeling tools; punch; awl; ruler and pencil; rawhide mallet.

Materials needed: Tooling calfskin; lacing.

Steps

See preceding pages in this chapter for techniques used in this project.

1. Make a paper pattern to be sure of actual size. Make the cover 1 inch wider and 1 inch longer than actual size of book; allow for the back of the book (Figure V-93).
2. Cut leather from pattern.
3. If pockets are desired, add leather strips to fit at *A* and *B* (Figure V-93). Strips are usually about 2 inches or 3 inches wide for an average size book.
4. Make design, transfer to leather, and tool before punching holes.
5. Mark off line 1/4 inch from edges, all around; punch holes 1/4 inch apart. Punch holes in three sides of pocket strips at same time so holes coincide with cover holes (Figure V-94).
6. Lace with whip stitch or buttonhole stitch.
7. Tie in piece of lacing in top center hole for bookmark (Figure V-95).
8. Place cover under layers of paper; pound edges with rawhide mallet.
9. Finish with wax and polish.

Variation: Make of suede, with no tooling; this is a simpler project.

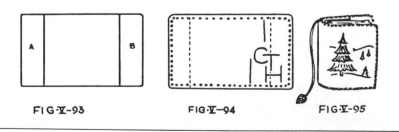

FIG·V-93   FIG·V-94   FIG·V-95

Autograph, Photograph, Memory, and Log Books

Two types of leather covers for books are shown here. Covers may be decorated by any appropriate method, or plain leather or suede may be used. The making of a log book cover or a photo album cover is a good group project for the camp library.

Equipment needed: Knife; tooling, stamping, or carving tools; shears; ruler and pencil; punch; awl; rubber cement.
Materials needed: Leather as desired; lacing, if desired; cardboard and lining papers; thong; pages.

Steps for cover #1—using heavy leather, such as cowhide

See preceding pages in this chapter for techniques used in this project.

1. Cut leather 1/2 inch larger on all four sides than the size of paper to be used (Figure V-96).
2. If the cover is to be decorated, make design, transfer, and tool, stamp, or carve as desired. Include in the design the placing of the two holes for the lacing (Figure V-97).
3. Punch holes for lacing (Figure V-96).
4. Polish leather.
5. Assemble with punched paper, and insert thong from back to front through the pages. Tie with square knot (see Figure II-16) on top (Figure V-98).

Steps for cover #2—using thinner leathers cemented to cardboard

See preceding pages in this chapter for techniques used in this project.

1. Cut cardboards for back and front covers; make a hinge on front cover by cutting off 1 inch on left side (Figure V-99).
2. Cut leather pieces 1/2 inch larger on all sides than cardboard pieces (Figure V-100).
3. If the cover is to be decorated, make design, transfer, and tool or stamp as desired. Plan for hinge and holes for lacing in the design (Figure V-100).

4. Spread rubber cement on back of leather, and on one side of each cardboard; wait 5 minutes and lay cardboards in place on leather. Mark places for cardboards before spreading cement. Place cardboard piece for hinge with 1/16 inch space (Figure V-100).
5. Press from center to all sides to eliminate air bubbles.

Steps for corners

1. Draw line 1/2 inch in from edges on cardboards; cover this 1/2 inch margin with rubber cement, and let dry five minutes.
2. Fold over edges of leather, one side at a time.

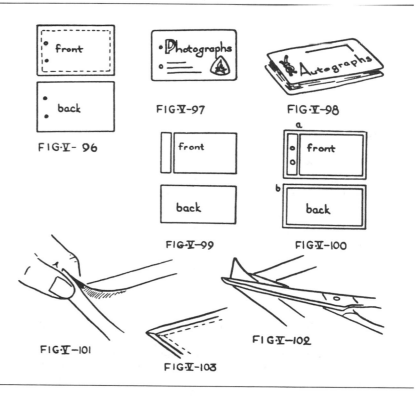

FIG·V-96
FIG·V-97
FIG·V-98
FIG·V-99
FIG·V-100
FIG·V-101
FIG·V-102
FIG·V-103

3. At corners, pinch edges of leather between thumb and forefinger close to cardboard (Figure V-101). With shears, cut off surplus leather about 1/16 inch from flat surface to make a flat corner or mitre (Figure V-102).
4. Flatten leather down with one edge of mitre on top, making a flat corner.

Steps for lining

1. Cut lining papers of construction or craft paper, 1/4 inch smaller than completed covers, including hinge section.
2. Cover one side of paper, cardboard, and half of leather fold with rubber cement; let dry 5 minutes, until both sides are "tacky."
3. Press together, pressing air bubbles out toward edges.
4. Put both covers side by side on newspapers; cover with paper, and press under weights for 24 hours.
5. Polish leather (except suede).
6. Insert thong and pages (Figure V-98) and tie with square knot (see Figure II-16).

Moccasins

There are many types of moccasins, Indian and Eskimo being the most usual. Some are for indoor wear, some for outdoor wear. They may be beaded, fringed, or painted. A simple indoor type is described here.

Equipment needed: Knife; two needles and waxed thread; paper, pencil, and stapler; awl.
Materials needed: Horsehide, elk, or deerskin; thong.

Steps

See preceding pages in this chapter for techniques used in this project.

1. Make a paper pattern first: stand on paper; draw around one foot, being sure to keep pencil vertical (Figure V-104). Make another pattern for other foot.

2. Make another line 1 inch away from foot outline, following shape around toes, from just below large toe joint, and to a place on opposite side (points *A* and *B*, Figure V-105).
3. At points *A* and *B* add an extra inch for flap, and carry past heel approximately 1 inch (Figure V-105). If a fringe (Figure V-113) is desired, add an extra 1/2 inch on the flap sections.
4. Make two small cuts, starting 1/4 inch from base of heel to edge, slightly on diagonal (Figure V-105).
5. Cut tongue roughly the shape of top of foot (Figure V-106).
6. Staple paper pattern together at tongue and at heel, making edges meet (Figure V-107). Try on and adjust for satisfactory fit. Make and fit pattern for *each* foot.
7. Trace pattern on under side of leather.
8. Cut out leather pieces.
9. Cut pairs of slits through which to thread thong for tighter fit. Use knife or slit punch on sides and tongue (Figures V-105 and 106).

Steps for sewing heel

1. Bring upper sides of heel together and sew this seam with two-needle cobbler's stitch, first skiving edge to make them flatter (Figure V-108). Make holes with awl; use waxed thread and needles.
2. Pinch edges together when sewing, to get firm seam (Figure 109). Grasp threads with both hands and pull, keeping even tension.
3. Flap may be cut off and sewed to bottom edge of heel (Figure V-110), or it may be turned up and sewed with running or cobbler's stitch (Figure V-111).

Steps for sewing tongue

1. Pin tongue in place at several places on sides (Figure V-112), "easing" the extra leather on side pieces evenly between pins.
2. Use an awl to make holes for stitching.
   Note: Sewing of tongue will be easier if moccasin is tacked to a wooden form. This form may be made from piece of pine 1 inch thick, cut to shape of foot and inserted in the moccasin (Figure V-112).
3. Start sewing on left side and sew toward toe, using two-needle cobbler's stitch. Reinforce starting and ending stitches with two overcast stitches.
4. If fringe is desired, cut fringe on flap (Figure V-113).

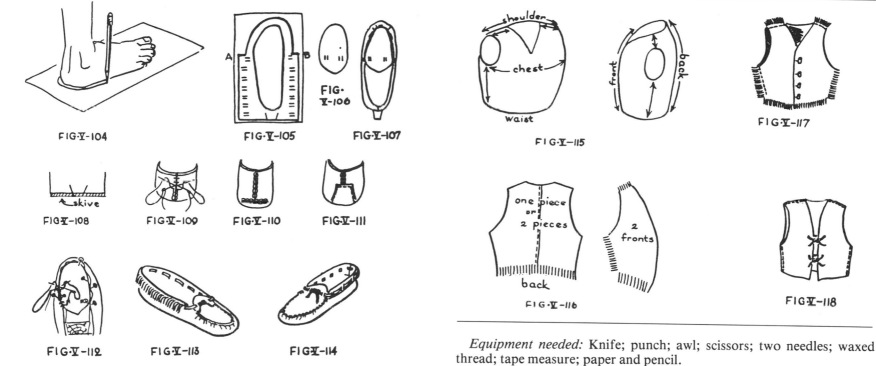

FIG·Ⅴ-104   FIG·Ⅴ-105   FIG·Ⅴ-106   FIG·Ⅴ-107

FIG·Ⅴ-108   FIG·Ⅴ-109   FIG·Ⅴ-110   FIG·Ⅴ-111

FIG·Ⅴ-112   FIG·Ⅴ-113   FIG·Ⅴ-114

FIG·Ⅴ-115   FIG·Ⅴ-116   FIG·Ⅴ-117   FIG·Ⅴ-118

5. Run thong through slits from tongue to heel and back to tongue. Tie over tongue with square knot (see Figure II-16) or bowknot.
6. If no fringe is included, thong may go through double thickness of leather (Figure V-114).

Variations: Tongue may be decorated with beads or with an oil-painted design. This is done before the tongue is stitched into place.

Vest

This is an advanced project; it is especially good for older campers. The materials are more expensive than most projects, but a vest justifies the cost if the project is carefully developed.

Equipment needed: Knife; punch; awl; scissors; two needles; waxed thread; tape measure; paper and pencil.

Materials needed: Quarter skin or more of soft, pliable leather such as suede or tooling sheepskin; lacing; leather for fringe, if desired; thong for buttons or ties.

Steps

See preceding pages in this chapter for techniques used in this project.

1. First—and most important—make a paper pattern. Use an old vest for a pattern, or make a paper one to fit (Figure V-115). Add extra on front, for lap-over, if desired; or plan to tie with thong (Figure V-118). Add fringe on shoulders, sides, and bottoms of front pieces, and on bottom of back piece, if desired (Figure V-117).
   Try pattern on, and have someone pin to fit.

2. Cut leather by pattern. Back may be in two pieces; allow for seam and join with cobbler's stitch on wrong side (Figure V-116).
3. Seams may be stitched with cobbler's stitch with two needles, or with thongs or lacing and punched holes, using running stitch (Figure V-117).
4. Buttons may be monkey's fists (see Figures II-54-57), pioneer buttons (see Figures V-54), or of elkhorn or similar materials.
5. Put vest on to mark places for buttons and buttonholes. Cut buttonholes with knife.
6. Fringe is stitched into seams.

Camera Cases

This is a good advanced project for older campers. The main problem comes in the planning and making of a pattern to fit the individual camera. The same steps are used in making cases for other equipment, such as field glasses.

Equipment needed: Knife; punch; awl; mallet; snap setting tools; ruler; pencil; rubber cement; modeling or stamping tools; shears.
Materials needed: Cowhide, horsehide, steerhide, or upholstery leather; lacing, buckles; leather for straps; snaps, rivets, and D-rings; thin cardboard for pattern.
See preceding pages in this chapter for techniques used in these projects.
In making the pattern, one main piece to cover top, front, bottom, and back, with two pieces for sides, may be planned; or each side, front, back, etc., piece may be cut separately, and laced together (this makes use of smaller or scrap pieces).

Case for Films, Lenses, Gadgets

Steps

1. Wrap thin cardboard strip around camera: do not make snug, as leather is thicker than cardboard (Figure V-119 **A**). Cut this to fit, with lap-over for snap. Allow just enough for seams (**A**). Lay camera on side, draw shape, allowing just enough extra for seams. Round corners slightly. Cut pieces for sides (Figure V-119 *B*). Pin or staple cardboard pattern together, and "try on" (Figure V-120); adjust as needed.

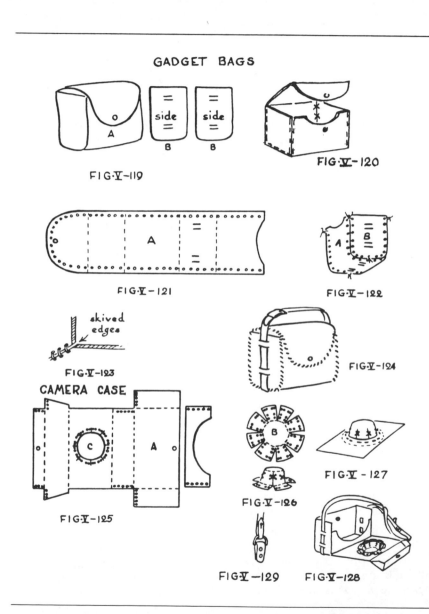

GADGET BAGS

FIG·V-119

FIG·V-120

FIG·V-121

FIG·V-122

skived edges

FIG·V-123

FIG·V-124

CAMERA CASE

FIG·V-125

FIG·V-126

FIG·V-127

FIG·V-129

FIG·V-128

2. Place pattern on underside of leather; trace around and cut out.
3. Mark slits for strap, if desired; cut with knife.
4. Mark line 1/4 inch from edge to guide punching; punch holes (Figure V-121). Punch A-piece first; make sure holes on B-pieces correspond. (See Figure V-122 for inserting side pieces.)
5. Tool or stamp initials or design before lacing.
6. Set snaps before lacing.
7. Start lacing with whip stitch in center of flap, and lace both ways, three or four stitches on one side, then three or four on the other, until B-pieces are reached. Join B-pieces to A-piece (Figure V-122). Skive edges for better fit (Figure V-123).
8. Attach strap and buckle, making strap either hand grip or shoulder length (Figure V-124).

Case for 35mm. Camera

Steps

1. Pattern: make cardboard pattern, as in Figure V-125, measuring each side or face of camera carefully.

   For lens housing (B), make pattern as in Figure V-126; do not make this snug. Staple pattern into place, and "try on" for fit; adjust as needed.
2. Trace around pattern A on underside of leather; cut out; cut slits for strap as indicated; punch (Figure V-125).
3. Cut circle for lens housing (B); dampen leather, and shape over a cup or glass about size of lens; cut flange cuts; punch two holes on sides of cuts (Figure V-126).
4. Set snaps in flap and case.
5. Tool, stamp, or carve initials or design, if desired.
6. Cut openings in A-piece for lens cover to fit through from back to front (Figure V-125 c).
7. Spread flanges of lens housing; score on underside and fold. Punch holes in A and B to correspond. Lace in place with running stitch or sew with cobbler's stitch (Figure V-127).

8. Dampen leather, and make folds before lacing.
9. Skive edges.
10. Lace as shown (Figure V-128).
11. Make a strap and insert. Attach with rivets and D-rings if desired (Figure V-129).
12. Hammer edges with mallet, under paper, to flatten lacing.

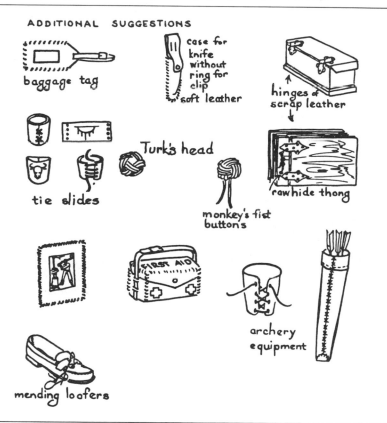

ADDITIONAL SUGGESTIONS

baggage tag

case for knife without ring for clip soft leather

hinges of scrap leather

Turk's head

tie slides

monkey's fist buttons

rawhide thong

archery equipment

mending loofers

Metalwork

VI

Creating articles from metal may well be included in a camp handcraft program. Tin craft is a native craft carried on in the Southwest by Indians and Spanish Americans. Many types of projects are developed, including the use of tin for animals, birds, masks, ornaments, and utensils. Tin cans provide materials for many camp projects. Other metals, such as copper, brass, aluminum, pewter, and nickel silver must be procured in sheets for craft use. Metal is a medium that cannot be used in the natural form. It must be secured in processed form.

This chapter will deal with projects that teach how to handle metal and metal tools with dexterity and with safety and will include making camping equipment, camp furnishings, and camp symbols, and making articles that combine the use of metal with other materials, such as wood. There are many possibilities in metal crafts, including jewelry and utensil making which are not included here because the projects require extensive equipment or do not seem to fit into a program of outdoor living as do the simpler activities suggested in the chapter.

MATERIALS USED

Materials used in metalwork may include:

—*Tin:* a bluish-white metal, malleable at ordinary temperature; also tin plate (as in cans) which is a thin sheet of steel covered on both sides with tin.
—*Copper:* a reddish metal; very malleable.

—*Brass:* an alloy of copper and zinc, reddish yellow in color; malleable.
—*Aluminum:* a bluish-silver-white metal noted for lightness and resistance to oxidization; malleable.
—*Pewter:* an alloy with tin as its chief constituent; very malleable.
—*Silver:* a white metal capable of a high polish; very malleable.
—*Nickel silver:* a silver-white alloy of copper, zinc, and nickel, sometimes called German silver; malleable and relatively inexpensive.
—*Foil (30 gauge):* a very thin sheet of metal; suitable for tooling, like leather.

TERMS USED

Some terms used in metalwork are defined:

—*Malleable:* capable of being shaped or stretched by beating with a hammer or by the pressure of rollers.
—*Anneal:* to heat and let cool, to make metal softer, and less brittle —necessary when raising bowls, etc., as hammering hardens metal.
—*Chasing, embossing, spotting, or tapping:* ways of decorating metal with small hammers.
—*Raising:* a method of making a depression in a piece of metal to form a bowl, dish.
—*Piercing:* a method of making a design of holes in metal, usually with a nail-like tool.
—*Saw-piercing:* the process of cutting out a design of holes in metal with a jeweler's saw.
—*Beveling:* filing or sanding an edge of metal to eliminate a right angle.
—*Concave surface:* surface hollowed out like a depression.
—*Convex surface:* having a rounded-up surface, like a hill or mound.
—*Bench pin:* a wedge-shaped piece of hardwood with a *V*-shape cut sawed into narrow end; used as a working surface.
—*Ball-peen hammer:* a metal hammer with a ball on one end and a flat surface on other; used for shaping metal.

TECHNIQUES

General Safety

It is important to learn to handle tools and metal with safety as well as with dexterity. This is especially true with tin for the edges of this metal are very sharp. Cotton work gloves should be worn when handling tin or other thin sheet metals, and edges of the metal should be turned and flattened.

A good working space, such as a table or stump with vise and bench pins and logs that can be slipped into cans, will help in the handling of metals.

Flattening Metals

Wooden or rawhide mallets are used to hammer metal; these do not leave marks as metal hammers do. The *down* stroke of the mallet is firm, and the mallet should *slide along* the metal as it strikes, rather than bouncing up and down (Figure VI-1).

Making Fold or Bending Edges

A fold or angle is made by flattening the edge of the metal against a wood or metal strip held in a vise (Figure VI-2 *a*). The fold will be made more easily if the front edge is beveled slightly (Figure VI-2 *b*).

Place metal strip in vise between two pieces of wood; tap with mallet to bend for angle or fold. For flat edge, take metal out of vise, and continue bending edge on wood surface until it is flattened against main strip (Figure VI-3). To turn four sides of a strip, cut corners diagonally, then turn, pounding corners together (Figure VI-4).

To bend edges on a curve, snip the edge with 1/4-inch cut every 1 inch to 1½ inch. Bend back with pliers, then hammer flat with mallet (Figure VI-5).

Rounding

Use a pipe or smooth hardwood stick to round a piece of metal, using mallet to form in desired shape (Figure VI-6).

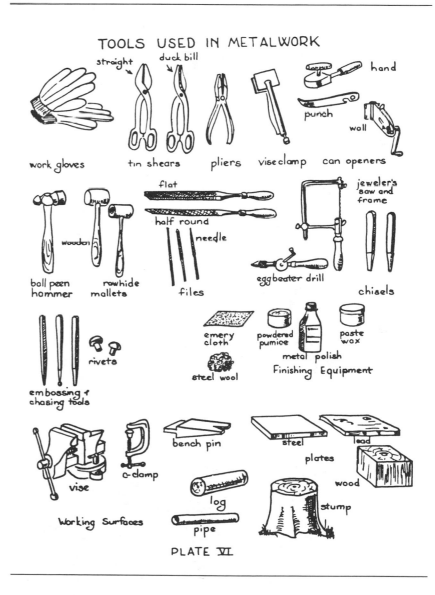

TOOLS USED IN METALWORK

work gloves — straight, duck bill — tin shears — pliers — viseclamp — can openers — hand — punch — wall

ball peen hammer — wooden — rawhide mallets — flat — half round — needle — files — eggbeater drill — jeweler's saw and frame — chisels

embossing & chasing tools — rivets — steel wool — emery cloth — powdered pumice — metal polish — paste wax — Finishing Equipment

vise — c-clamp — bench pin — steel — lead — plates — wood — stump — log — pipe — Working Surfaces

PLATE VI

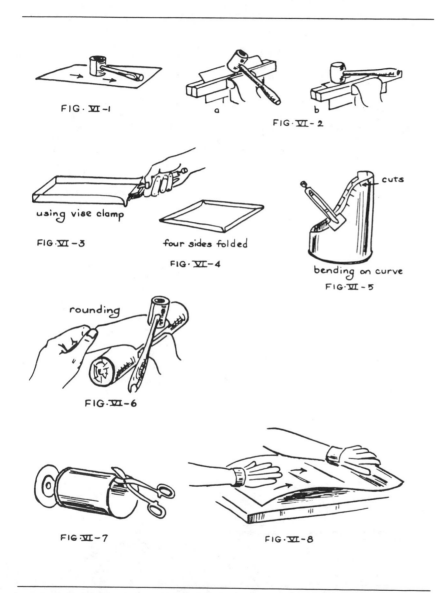

FIG · VI – 1

FIG · VI – 2

using vise clamp

FIG · VI – 3

four sides folded

FIG · VI – 4

cuts

bending on curve

FIG · VI – 5

rounding

FIG · VI – 6

FIG · VI – 7

FIG · VI – 8

Making a Sheet from Tin Can

A flat piece of tin may be made from a tin can. This is a good practice step in handling tools and in establishing good safety practices. A #10 (gallon) can makes a piece 6½ inches by 18 inches.

Equipment and materials needed: Tin shears; pliers or vise clamp; smooth cutting can opener; work gloves; mallet; vise; wooden work surface; cans to make strips of the desired size—must be clean and free from rust.

Wear work gloves when working with metal.

Steps

1. Cut off top and bottom of can with can opener.
2. Cut off both rims with shears or can opener.
3. Cut off seams with shears, cutting 1/2 inch from center of seam on both sides (Figure VI-7).
4. Flatten strip by putting concave surface down on workbench, picking up back edge with left hand while rubbing toward back with heel of hand (Figure VI-8). This process prevents the dents and marks that hammering may make.
5. Fold edges as in techniques (above).

Cutting Edges

Edges of metal are cut with tin shears or snips of which there are two general types, the straight and the duckbill (Figure VI-9). The straight shears (*a*) are used for cutting straight lines and the duckbilled (*b*) for curved lines. Draw the outline to be cut with pencil, using a ruler for straight lines. Follow the lines, cutting at the center of the blades. The job is simplified by using a firm working surface and by resting the bottom blade of the shears on the surface as the cut is made. Separate the two edges as the work progresses for ease in the cutting (Figure VI-9 *a*).

For *fine cutouts,* a jeweler's saw is used (Figure VI-10 *a*). This is similar to a very fine-toothed blade. The saw blade is placed in the frame with the teeth pointing *down* so that the cut in the metal is made as the saw is *pulled* down through the metal (Figure VI-10 *c*). The blade is inserted in the top clamp first, then the top of the frame is pushed against edge of

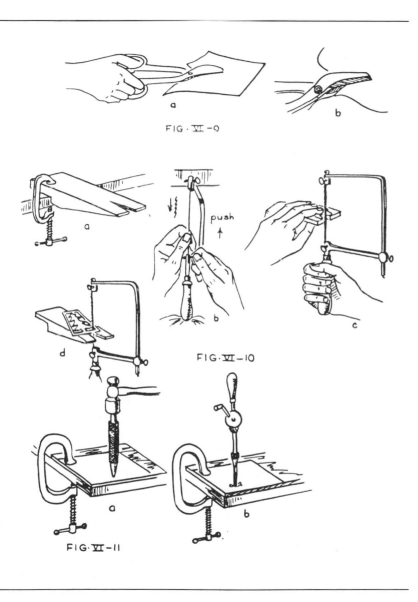

FIG·VI-9

FIG·VI-10

push

d

FIG·VI-11

bench, springing the frame slightly, and the other end inserted in the bottom clamp (Figure VI-10 b). To saw, keep blade vertical, pulling saw down with eveny strongs, then push up with lighter pressure, drawing back slightly.

To cut out a design: when a design calls for cutout parts, drill a small hole in the metal with an egg-beater drill (Figure VI-11 a, b). Insert one end of the saw in the hole, clamp blade in the frame, and saw section as above (Figure VI-10 d).

To turn inside corners: saw with a steady motion until the corner is reached. Continue sawing, almost in the same spot, pulling back on saw blade slightly while slowly turning blade in proper direction, then proceed forward. This makes an enlarged hole in which to turn the blade, preventing snapping the blade which occurs when blade is turned too quickly.

Drilling Holes

An egg beater drill is used to make holes in metal. Place metal on piece of scrap wood, and clamp both to workbench, so that when the drill has perforated the metal, it will sink into the scrap wood instead of into the workbench surface. A small indentation should be made with a punch or a nail, so the end of the drill will settle in the depression and will not slip around (Figure VI-11 a). Place drill in the depression, holding upright with left hand, exerting a little pressure to keep in place. Turn handle clockwise to make the hole. Remove drill by pulling with left hand, continuing the turn of the drill (Figure VI-11 b).

Cutting with Chisel

Heavy metal, such as a heavy can, may require the use of a chisel and hammer to make a cut. The chisel is placed on the spot, and a sharp blow of the hammer on end of chisel forces it through the metal. The chisel is then moved along the line, and the action repeated. Sometimes it is possible to cut with the chisel at an angle, continuing the cut smoothly without removing and replacing chisel (Figure VI-12 a). Use of a log the size of the inside of can simplifies the cutting as the log holds the shape of the can and prevents it from buckling (Figure VI-12 b).

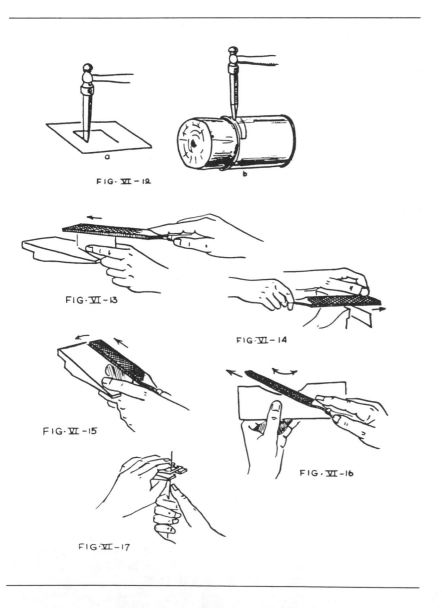

FIG. VI-12

FIG. VI-13

FIG. VI-14

FIG. VI-15

FIG. VI-16

FIG. VI-17

Filing Edges

When edges of metal are not turned under to make a fold, they must be smoothed with a file. Large metal files used for outside edges are either flat or half round. Needle files used for small edges, as in the center of pierced designs, may be triangular, round, oval, flat, or half round, making it possible to smooth edges in very small places.

To file an edge: hold metal piece against bench pin, in vise, or on edge of workbench with left hand, and file with forward strokes of the file in right hand, lifting at end of stroke (Figure VI-13). If metal is clamped in vise, left hand may be used to guide and to lift the file (Figure VI-14). File teeth do not cut on backward pull.

To file outside of curve: hold as above, and make the forward stroke incline or conform to the direction of the curve, rocking the file up and over the curve (Figure VI-15).

To file inside of curve: hold metal on edge (Figure VI-16) and file with the rounded side of half-round file, filing at right angles to metal.

To use needle files: hold file in vertical position, and use in same manner as saw and frame, above (Figure VI-17).

Fastening Metal to Metal or Wood

Metal parts are fastened to other metal parts by soldering, by riveting, by nailing or screwing, or by the slit and tab method. The simpler types of projects described in this chapter do not call for soldering in the usual method using blow torch and solder since most camps will not have equipment for this. Fine jewelry work or projects with pewter, copper, and silver will require the blow torch method.

Liquid solder, which may be purchased in tubes at any hardware store, may be used for simple projects. The surfaces to be joined are cleaned with steel wool, a small amount of solder is spread on, and the pieces are clamped together and left for several hours (Figure VI-18). Follow directions on the specific tube.

Riveting is a method of joining metals by a small metal rivet. Drill a hole through both pieces of metal; place rivet in hole so head of rivet is on top or where it will be most readily seen (Figure VI-19 *a*). Turn piece over, and hammer edges of rivet on underside, spreading to create a flange which will hold rivet in place (Figure VI-19 *b*). Handles or seams may be fastened in this way, and the rivet may become part of the design of the

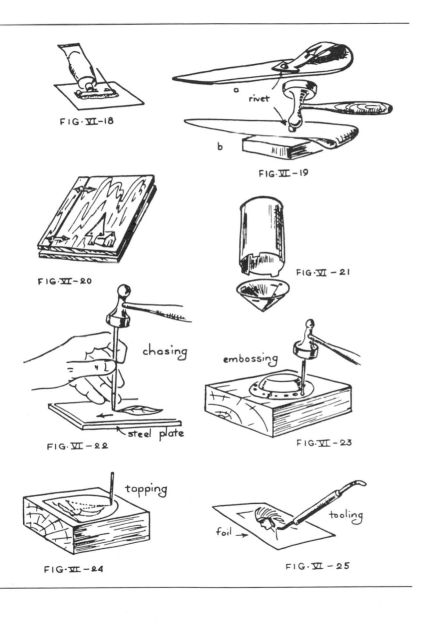

FIG·VI-18

FIG·VI-19

rivet

a

b

FIG·VI-20

FIG·VI-21

chasing

FIG·VI-22

steel plate

embossing

FIG·VI-23

tapping

FIG·VI-24

tooling

foil

FIG·VI-25

article. These are not *split* rivets such as are used to fasten leather.

Screwing and nailing are used to fasten metal to wood, as in securing metal hinges to a book cover or applying a metal design to a wooden surface. Drill small holes in desired places with egg-beater drill, and use tiny brass screws or escutcheon pins to go through metal into wood (Figure VI-20). Escutcheon pins are small nails with convex head and with short (about 1/4-inch) shanks, usually of copper or brass.

Slit and tab method is used in putting together parts of such metal objects as a lantern or box (Figure VI-21). See Figures VI-46-49.

Decorating Metals

Design may be applied to metal by a number of methods, some of which have to do with marking the surface with metal tools, some with cutting out designs, and some with etching with chemicals.

Chasing, Embossing, Spotting, Tapping, and Tooling

These are methods that are similar to each other and also similar to techniques used in decorating leather. The process includes hitting a metal tool with a hammer, creating an impression on the metal:

—*Chasing* makes a shallow groove or line in the face of the metal (Figure VI-22). Chasing tools have chisel, rounded, or curved ends with which impressions are made. A chasing tool is held vertical, guided by the last two fingers, as the other end is hit sharply with a hammer.

—*Embossing* raises a design from the back of the metal (Figure VI-23). A round-end tool is used to make depressions on the back of the metal, causing the design to be raised on the front.

—*Spotting* covers the surface of the metal with closely spaced spots made by hitting the metal with a ball-peen or chasing hammer. The metal is placed on a smooth metal plate. The hammer bounces on the surface.

—*Tapping* makes a series of closely spaced dots, usually in outlining a design (Figure VI-24). Nails may be used as tapping tools. This method is often used with a thin metal applied to wood. Tin, copper, or brass are good media for tapping.

—*Tooling* is a method that is similar to the method of tooling leather. The same type of design and the same tools are used (Figure VI-25). The material to be tooled must be 30-gauge aluminimum, copper, or brass foil. This may be purchased in sheets and is easily cut with shears. The working surface may be a pad of newspaper. Modeling with the bowl of a spoon on the reverse side of the foil is sometimes used to produce large raised areas.

Cutout Designs

These are obtained by piercing or by cutting with a saw:

—*Piercing* is a method of making a design of holes in metal. It is done with nails filed in desired shapes (Figure VI-26). It may be done from the outside of the object, leaving a smooth surface (Figure VI-27 *a*), or from the inside, making a rough surface on the outside (Figure VI-27 *b*). This method is used in making lanterns to give an interesting lighting effect (see Figures VI-45 and 46).

—*Cutout designs* are made by cutting away the edges of metal (Figure VI-28) or making a design cut out within a frame of the metal by saw piercing (Figure VI-29). Chasing and embossing are sometimes used to complete the work on such designs (see Figures VI-22 and 23).

Applied Design

This is done by applying a design of metal to wood, metal, or other base. The design is created by any of the methods described above and applied by one of the fastening techniques (Figures VI-30; see also Figures VI-18 and 21).

Etching

This process of decorating metal uses nitric acid to eat away a portion of the metal in making the design. Nitric acid should be handled carefully. It should be stored in a tightly corked bottle and kept away from other metals as the fumes will rust iron or steel.

Steps

1. Make design and transfer to metal with pencil or carbon. Go over lines with scriber, such as phonograph needle inserted in a handle.
2. Use asphaltum varnish to paint smoothly those parts of design to be left high on the metal. Cover back and edges of article, too. Let dry. This protects parts of the design not to be etched in the bath (Figure VI-31 *a*).
3. Using a three to one proportion of nitric acid and water; place water in glass dish (pyrex pie plate or custard cup) and slowly add acid.
4. Place article in acid bath *carefully* to avoid splashing.
5. Leave until exposed metal is covered with small bubbles.
6. Remove from bath with wooden tongs or spring clothespin (Figure VI-31 *b*).
7. Rinse well in clear water.
8. Remove varnish with rags and kerosene. Surface which came in contact with the bath will be pitted; surface coated with varnish will be smooth and shiny (Figure VI-31 *c*).
9. Oxidize if desired (see below).
10. Polish as desired (see below).

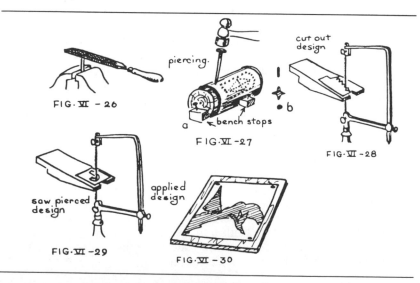

FIG·VI – 26

piercing.

cut out design

FIG·VI –27

a   bench stops   b

FIG·VI – 28

saw pierced design

applied design

FIG·VI –29

FIG·VI – 30

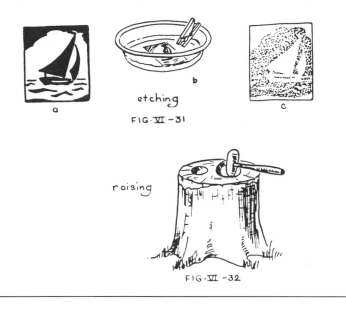

etching

FIG. VI-31

raising

FIG. VI-32

rubbed with ammonium sulphide or liver of sulphur which oxidizes the surface (turns it dark). It is then rubbed with powdered pumice or powder cleanser, leaving the low spots dark and the high spots brightly polished. This is used on cooper, brass, nickel silver, and on metal foil designs. This method is sometimes called antiquing.

Tin is polished by rubbing with steel wool; this should be sufficient to give a satin finish. If the article is to be used out-of-doors, it should be lacquered. A thin coating of wax will keep tin from rusting.

Copper and brass are polished with a powder cleanser or powdered pumice.

Nickel silver is polished with powdered pumice or a good grade of silver polish. Jeweler's rouge is also used.

Pewter is polished with kerosene and lamp black.

All need to be rubbed briskly with soft flannel or felt for a high polish at the end.

PROJECTS

Candle Sconce from Tin Can

This project may be made from any size can: #10 cans make good footlights for dramatic presentations, and #5 cans are a good size for sconces by fireplaces.

Equipment needed: Rawhide mallet; vise; file; pliers; tin snips; decorating tools.

Materials needed: Clean cans of desired size; paper, scissors, etc., for pattern; small nail to hold candle.

Steps

1. Make a paper pattern by wrapping paper around can to get size. Fold in half, and draw shape of sides as desired. Cut both sides out at same time (Figure V-33 *a*). Draw shape on can.
2. Cut can to pattern (Figure VI-33 *b*), leaving 1/4-inch edge to turn under (see Techniques for turning edge, Figure VI-5). Flatten with hammer (Figure VI-34).
3. Hammer nail through bottom, from outside, so point of nail will hold candle in place; or make a collar as in Figure VI-37.
4. Decorate as desired (see Techniques).

Raising

This is a method of making a large depression in a piece of metal, to make a bowl, plate, or tray (Figure VI-32). A rawhide mallet and a ball-peen hammer are used with a mold hollowed out of a block or a stump or with a "jig" to make the desired shape or on stakes (see Figures VI-42 and 43).

Finishing Metal

Metals must be cleaned and polished to get a good finish. When this has been obtained, the object can be sprayed or painted with lacquer to retain that finish. This is essential for objects used outdoors, such as lanterns and signs. Many prefer to keep a hand-rubbed finish on copper and brass objects, however.

Oxidizing is a method of darkening part of the metal and of polishing the high lights to give a contrast in polish. The object is dipped in or

Candle Sconce with Cutout Design

This is a good project to use in cabin or dining hall where candles are used; the background protects the wall or post from the smoke of the candle. A strip of tin from a #10 can (see Techniques, Figures VI-7 and 8) will be good material for this sconce.

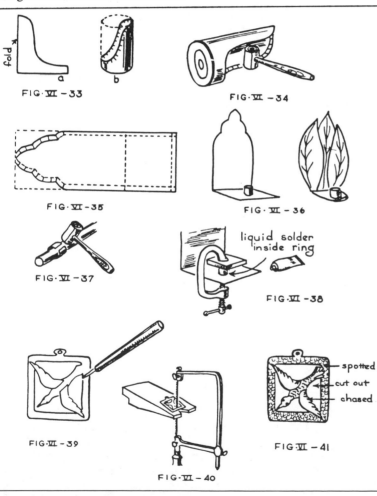

FIG·VI–33

FIG·VI–34

FIG·VI–35

FIG·VI–36

FIG·VI–37

liquid solder inside ring

FIG·VI–38

FIG·VI–39

FIG·VI–40

FIG·VI–41

spotted
cut out
chased

Equipment needed: Tin snips; work gloves, stick or pipe for bending; rawhide mallet; egg-beater drill; liquid solder; fine steel wool.

Materials needed: #10 tin can—clean and rust free; paper, etc., for pattern.

Steps

1. Make paper pattern, deciding on shape, size, etc. Make design and trace on the metal (Figure VI-35).
2. Cut metal 1/2 inch wider than design on each side. Turn this 1/2-inch edge under (see Techniques, Figures VI-2, 3, 5), and hammer flat.
3. Cut design (see Techniques, Figure VI-9 *b*) as desired (Figure VI-36).
4. To make holder for candle, make a strip about 1¼ inch by ¾ inch. Turn back ¼ inch on long edges. Roll strip around stick or pipe the thickness of a candle, overlapping ends for seam (Figure VI-37).
5. Bend bottom of sconce as desired (Figure VI-36).
6. Fasten seam and attach candle holder with liquid solder (Figures VI-18 and 38).
7. Drill hole at top for hanging on wall or post.
8. Rub with steel wool.

Simple Saw Piercing—a Tent or Cabin Symbol

This is a good beginning project in metal crafts. Each member of the group may make his own design, or there may be a symbol already in use which can be modified by each camper. Copper and German silver are less expensive metals than silver, and they make good first project materials. The following project may be a pin or small, flat symbol to wear on a thong or chain.

Equipment needed: Jeweler's saw and frame; egg-beater drill; bench pin; rawhide mallet; files; polishing equipment.

Materials needed: Pieces of copper or other metal of desired size; paper, etc., for design.

Steps

1. Make a design the exact size of finished project. Transfer it to the

metal by tracing over carbon paper with hard pencil, then scratching with a sharp point, such as a needle placed in a stick for a handle VI-39).

2. Drill holes in which to place saw blade. Cut out (see Techniques, Figure VI-29) parts of design (Figure VI-40).
3. File edges (see Techniques, Figures VI-13-17), outside and inside (Figure VI-41).
4. Polish and add pin, if desired (see Techniques, Figure VI-18).

Variations: Use ball-peen hammer for spotting or tapping frame of design, or any part. Use chisel or filed nails to add to design (Figure VI-41).

Etch design (see Techniques).

Raising a Shallow Bowl or Dish

This project is included here because the making of the mold in a stump is a good correlation with woodworking. A shallow dish or bowl may be used in camp dining hall for a dish garden or in tent or cabin groups for a table utensil. The project may be as simple as the shaping of the dish or may be extended to include some type of design that is saw pierced, chased, embossed, or spotted on the edges.

Equipment needed: Wood gouges and sandpaper; rawhide mallet; ball-peen hammer; pencil and dividers; decorating tools, as desired; polishing equipment.

Materials needed: Stump or wooden block; circular disc of metal—copper, aluminum, etc.—6 inches to 8 inches in diameter is a good starting size.

Steps

1. Make a mold (Figure VI-42) the desired size and depth by scooping out the stump or block (see Techniques in Chapter X). Sand smooth.
2. With pencil and divider, mark rim of dish.
3. With the ball end of the hammer, begin to pound the center of the disc into depression, rotating disc while hammering in same area, avoiding the rim (Figure VI-43).

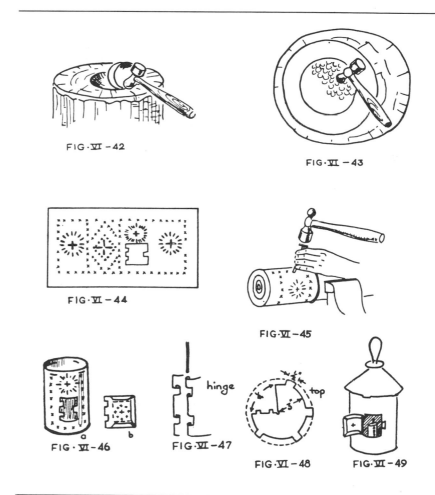

FIG·VI—42

FIG·VI—43

FIG·VI—44

FIG·VI—45

FIG·VI—46

FIG·VI—47

FIG·VI—48

FIG·VI—49

4. If the metal becomes hard and difficult to work, it must be annealed or softened. Heat the metal in a hot wood fire, and plunge into a pail of water. This may need to be repeated several times.
5. When the dish is the desired shape, file edges, and polish as in Techniques, above.

A Colonial Lantern (nail pierced)

This is a more advanced project, included to show decorating with nail piercing and also slit and tab construction. Materials may be tin cans or sheet tin.

Equipment needed: Vise; 10-penny nails; file; hammer; pliers; tape; cold chisel; log (size of can); tin shears; work gloves; long finishing nail.

Materials needed: #5 juice can and strip end from #10 can or sheet tin; coat hanger or wire; thin cardboard for pattern.

Steps

1. Make a cardboard pattern of all parts; fit together, adjusting as needed. Draw design for piercing on pattern (Figure VI-44).
2. Place log in vise horizontally, and slip can over end (Figure VI-45).
3. Fasten paper on can with tape.
4. File nails to shapes desired, and follow design, pounding nail through pattern and through can. Log keeps can in shape through piercing (Figure VI-45).
5. Cut out hole for door, using chisel and tin shears. Leave two 1/2-inch tabs on left for hinges (Figure VI-46 *a*).
6. Make four slits for top along top edge—1/2-inch slits just below rim (Figure VI-46 *a*).
7. From another piece of tin, cut a door 1 inch higher and wider than hole with tabs to correspond to hinges (Figure VI-46 *b*). Bend edges of three other sides 1/4 inch, and hammer flat.
8. Bend tabs on hinges of door and lantern around heavy finishing nail, so they fit together as hinges (Figure VI-47).
9. Make a circular top from disc 7 inches in diameter. Draw 6-inch circle with allowance for 1/2-inch tabs to correspond with slits in lantern. Cut out one quarter of the disc (Figure VI-48).
10. Bend top around, and insert tabs in slots. Bend tabs inside lantern to fasten top (Figure VI-49).
11. Make handle from wire or coat hanger. Cut a 3-inch disc to put at top of lantern to keep heat from hand (Figure VI-49).
12. Put small nail in bottom to hold candle.

SUGGESTIONS FOR ADDITIONAL PROJECTS

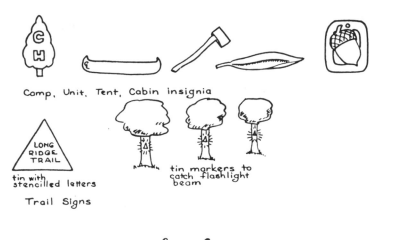

Comp. Unit, Tent, Cabin insignia

tin with stencilled letters

Trail Signs

Signs using metal on wood

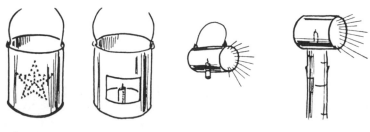

Lanterns

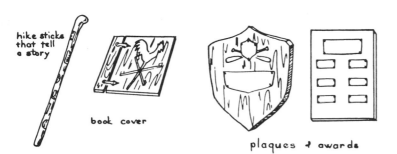

hike sticks
that tell
a story

book cover

plaques & awards

Metal foil applied designs

Corners & markers on
trip boxes, program chests, etc.

copper — 2" or 3" x 6"
or nickel silver

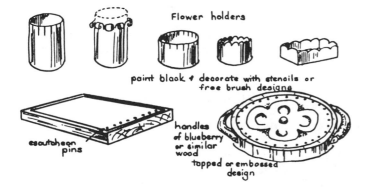

Flower holders

paint black & decorate with stencils or
free brush designs

escutcheon
pins

handles
of blueberry
or similar
wood

tapped or embossed
design

Printing and Stenciling

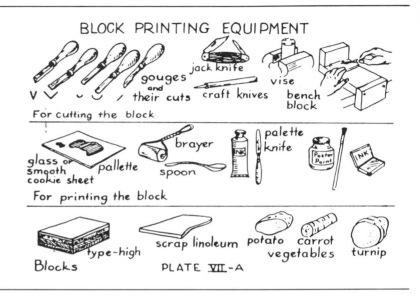

VII

BLOCK PRINTING EQUIPMENT

gouges and their cuts · jack knife · vise · craft knives · bench block

For cutting the block

glass or smooth cookie sheet · pallette · brayer · spoon · palette knife · Poster Paint · INK

For printing the block

type-high · scrap linoleum · potato carrot vegetables · turnip

Blocks   PLATE VII-A

Printing and stenciling are good crafts for campers to use in creating arrangements for logbook covers, end papers, and invitations; in making nature recordings; and in developing insignia for camp equipment and gear. Natural materials form an excellent base for many of the arrangements that can be made or for designs for block print or stencil. Experimentations with all kinds of materials found on the campsite will stimulate creative, imaginative activities as campers look for shells, acorns, grasses, or leaves to be used for printing.

Block printing is one of the oldest arts; wood blocks were used by the Egyptians and the Chinese as early as the fourth century. The variety of methods that can be used and the simplicity of beginning steps make it an interesting present-day camp craft.

The materials and equipment used are simple and inexpensive, and much of the equipment can be adapted from tools and materials found in all camps.

Block printing with vegetable, eraser, stick, or linoleum blocks and stenciling with various types of stencils are described in this chapter.

DESIGNS FOR BLOCK PRINTING

The design is cut into the block so that what is left of the original surface will print on the paper or cloth. Everything else is cut away and will not print; the background part will be the color of the material on which the block is printed (Figure VII-2). The block is inked and turned over on the material to make the print.

When making a design (Figure VII-2), consider the place in which it will be used, and make it fit the border, corner, or over-all plan of the printing on the particular material. Unless the design is symmetrical, it must be planned in reverse. Experimentation with the cutting tools and bits of linoleum or other block materials will show the variety of textures and lines that may be obtained. Straight lines are good for beginners.

Light lines or spots on the material will guide the placing of the block during printing.

TECHNIQUES IN PRINTING

Potato or Eraser Prints

A design cut on a firm vegetable is the simplest type of block to make; it may be made on any vegetable that has a firm surface, such as a potato, carrot, turnip. The design is cut on a piece of raw vegetable; this cut surface will change as the piece of vegetable dries, so it must be used for printing immediately after it has been cut. For a more permanent block, a piece of artgum or a square eraser may be used.

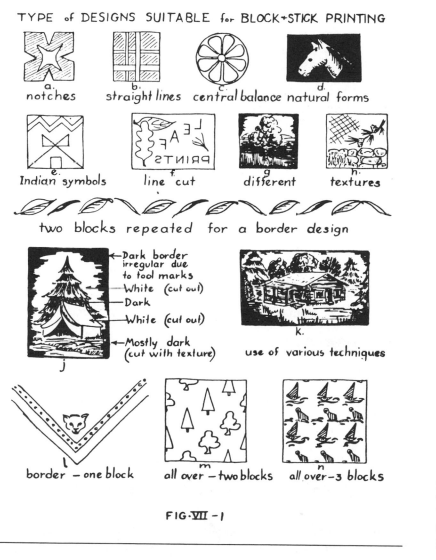

TYPE of DESIGNS SUITABLE for BLOCK+STICK PRINTING

a. notches
b. straight lines
c. central balance
d. natural forms

e. Indian symbols
f. line cut
g. different
h. textures

two blocks repeated for a border design

j.
- Dark border irregular due to tool marks
- White (cut out)
- Dark
- White (cut out)
- Mostly dark (cut with texture)

k. use of various techniques

l. border — one block
m. all over — two blocks
n. all over — 3 blocks

FIG·VII–1

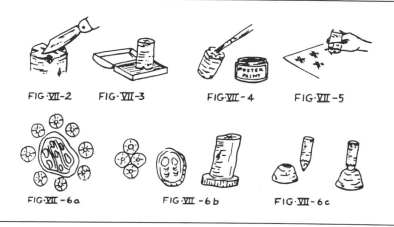

FIG·VII–2   FIG·VII–3   FIG·VII–4   FIG·VII–5

FIG·VII–6a   FIG·VII–6b   FIG·VII–6c

Equipment needed: Jackknife; stamp pad or poster paint and brush; bench block; working surface for printing.

Materials needed: Material for block—vegetable, eraser, etc.; material for printing—paper or cloth.

Steps

1. Cut vegetable into cube-shaped pieces, with end the desired size for the block.
2. Cut design in end with jackknife (Figure VII-2).
3. Use stick like a rubber stamp; press design end into stamp box (Figure VII-3); or apply poster paint to design with brush (Figure VII-4).
4. Press design end of stick into place on paper or cloth (Figure VII-5). Hold stick straight, press firmly, do not wiggle it, and try to make the impression the first time. Repeat step 3, then 4, in a new spot.

Make and use blocks made of erasers in same way.

Variation: Interesting patterns can be made with cross sections of things found on the campsite—acorns, nuts, weed stems, etc. Experimentation will bring delightful results. Combine prints and colors for variety (Figure VII-6 *a*). For easy handling of the cross-section pieces, mount on small sticks with glue or household cement or with a point on end of stick (Figure VII-6 *b* and *c*).

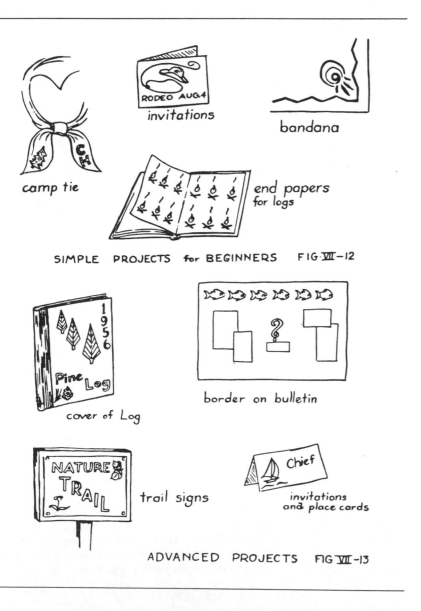

SIMPLE PROJECTS for BEGINNERS   FIG VII-12

ADVANCED PROJECTS   FIG VII-13

Stick Printing

This method uses a design carved on the end of a stick; it is a step in progression from potato printing as the block is more difficult to cut. Since the block is more durable and lasts indefinitely, it is better than vegetables and erasers for repeated use.

Equipment needed: Very sharp knife or wood-carving tools; sandpaper; vise to hold stick while carving; inking equipment (see above).
Materials needed: Piece of branch, kindling, or any wood; paper or cloth to be printed; printing materials (see above).

Steps to make block

1. Sand end of stick very smooth to prevent the grain of wood from printing too.
2. Plan the design on paper, and either transfer it to stick with carbon paper or draw it free hand (Figure VII-2).
3. Put stick in vise to hold while carving; cut design. Cut or sketch same design on other end of stick to guide the placing of the stick while printing.

Print in same manner as for potato print (Figure VII-3-5).

Linoleum Block Printing

For this method, linoleum is the material for the block. Linoleum blocks are long lasting, and may be used over and over in printing. This is a good method to use in group projects, since once the block is cut, any number of people can use it for printing. Cabin or tent ties, camp kerchiefs or bandanas, invitations or programs, camp stationery, and insignia on equipment may all be printed with blocks.

Linoleum blocks are usually made on battleship linoleum or similar material; remnants are usually available at floor covering stores. Commercial blocks of linoleum mounted on wood are available from craft supply houses.

Equipment: For cutting—linoleum cutting gouges, bench block; for making design—pencil, paper, carbon paper; for printing—brayer or roller, piece of glass, big spoon or rolling pin, hard surface for working, newspapers or magazines, palette knife, kerosene and rag for cleaning.

Materials needed: Linoleum blocks; material to be printed—paper, cloth, etc.; printer's ink in desired colors.

Steps

1. Practice cutting first. Use cutting tools and bits of linoleum to discover what you can do with the various tools. Make some straight cuts, some curved, some snakelike, some cross-hatched. Try picking with the point of a tool to give interesting texture. Cut deep, then ease off at the end of the stroke. Draw a leaf or petal, and cut out the inside with the large curved gouge, leaving the veins raised. Remember that letters must be in reverse. (Check general instructions on designs at beginning of section—Figure VII-1).
2. To make design: draw on paper the size of block. Plan the design for the place where it will be used. Make it simple for first projects. Plan some contrast of light and dark (Figure VII-1).
3. Transfer design to block with carbon paper and pencil.
4. To cut design in block: place block on bench block against back edge. Hold the block with one hand and the cutting tool in the other (right-handers hold cutting tool in right hand, etc.). Be sure fingers of the hand holding the block are *always* behind the tool, in case it slips. Hold tool with ball of handle in palm of hand. Cut carefully, removing small bits at first, not too close to design lines; then smooth off as you finish.
5. To print the block: plan printing steps first. Have block ready to use. Make a smooth working space with newspapers or magazines spread out, and paper, cloth, wood or other material to be decorated pinned in place on the papers. Mark spots for printing, or draw lines to guide the placing of block on the material.

   Squeeze out 1 inch of printer's ink on piece of glass and spread it evenly over 4-inch area with palette knife. Ink the brayer by rolling it over the inked area until it is evenly inked (Figure VII-7). It should be "tacky," i.e., make a noise when rolled over the ink. If it isn't tacky, add more ink.

   Place block on newspaper and roll brayer over block, so ink is spread evenly over all raised parts (Figure VII-8).

   Pick up block and place it *ink side down* on paper, in exact place

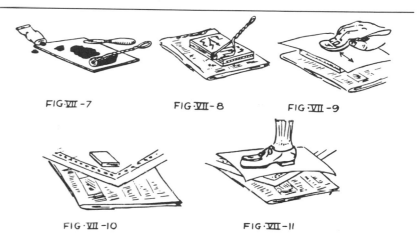

FIG·VII-7   FIG·VII-8   FIG·VII-9

FIG·VII-10   FIG·VII-11

for printing. Turn paper and block over carefully. Rub paper with bowl of big spoon (Figure VII-9) or rolling pin. Pull paper off carefully, and place paper to dry. Or, place block on designated place on cloth (Figure VII-10). Cover with paper and stand on block (Figure VII-11). Rotate weight so that entire block has even distribution on the cloth. Remove paper and block.

6. Clean equipment by scraping extra ink from glass with palette knife, and wipe glass, knife, and brayer with newspaper. Saturate rag in kerosene, and wipe all equipment clean. Dispose of rag with newspapers.

Wood blocks are also used for block printing. The designing and cutting of such blocks are good progressive steps for campers who develop a real interest in this craft. The gouges, however, need to be stronger than those made for linoleum.

STENCILING

This is a method of decorating which employs a stencil—a sheet with holes or cutout areas in it. Ink, paint, crayons, or similar materials are brushed into the holes, so that the design of holes is transferred to the paper, cloth, wood, or other material to be decorated.

Stencils are used to mark equipment, such as canoe paddles, packs, or food containers, or they may be used to make a to-be-repeated design for invitations, book covers, bandanas, ties, signs, and so forth. The uses are very similar to those for block printing, but the processes of making and using the stencil are different.

Equipment needed: Sharp knife or single-edged razor blade in holder, or X-acto knife; sharp, pointed scissors; palette of glass or waxed paper; stencil brushes; pins; pencil and paper for design; newspaper or magazines; compo board; working surface; cleaner for brushes.

Materials needed: Stencil paper or back of mimeograph stencils; watercolor, oil, textile, or poster paint or wax crayons; paper, cloth, wood, etc., or pieces of equipment to be decorated.

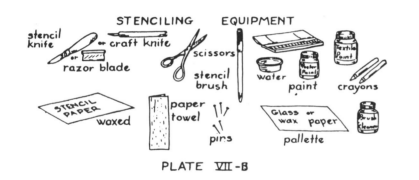

STENCILING EQUIPMENT

stencil knife — or craft knife — or razor blade — scissors — stencil brush — water — paint — crayons — STENCIL PAPER waxed — paper towel — pins — Glass or wax paper — pallette — Brush cleaner

PLATE VII-B

TECHNIQUES IN STENCILING

Stencil—Simplest Type

A stencil is a design of holes or cutout areas; the edges of the holes must be very definite, and each hole must be separate from every other hole.

Steps

1. The simplest stencil is one variegated "hole," as a tree. Cut the design from paper first; fold a 2-inch by 2-inch square in half with fold on the left. Make an evergreen tree sketch with pencil or paint on one half

(Figure VII-14). Be sure the top and the bottom cuts are on the fold so that there will be a complete piece of paper surrounding the cutout (*x* in Figure VII-14).

2. Cut out the tree, being careful to leave the paper at the Xs intact. Unfold the paper, and the design will be the same on both sides of the fold. Transfer to a piece of stencil paper, and cut out.

3. To print: place paper or other material on which the design will be printed on a smooth working space of newspapers and compo board on table. Fasten stencil in place with pins (Figure VII-15), especially at loose points.

Make a work space for the paint. Use poster or watercolor paint for the first try. Have a piece of paper towel for wiping brush (Figure VII-16). Dampen brush and dip in paint. Wipe off excess paint on towel.

Starting 1/2 inch from edge of cutout design, brush over edge of stencil toward center of cutout space (Figure VII-17). This gives a crisp edge and keeps the center light, creating more "form" to the design. Hold the brush at a slight angle (Figure VII-17). The paint *should not be thick,* and there should be no piling up of paint along the edge of the stencil. Repeat stroking, if necessary, to make color darker in some spots.

Take out pins; take stencil off carefully. It is best to let the paint "set" a few minutes before removing stencil.

Variation: Move the stencil back a little, and make a second tree behind the first (Figure VII-18). The second tree will be partly hidden; make it lighter in color to give effect of distance. Experiment for interesting effects.

Stencil—With a Series of Open Areas

Steps

1. Make a design on paper, giving consideration to the space in which it will be used. Make the design of a series of "holes," being sure that no areas or holes are joined to other areas (Figure VII-19). On the paper, pencil in the "holes" of the design which will be cut out; hold the design up against the light to get the effect of the stencil.

FIG·VII-14　　FIG·VII-15　　FIG·VII-16

Brush strokes

FIG·VII-17　　FIG·VII-18

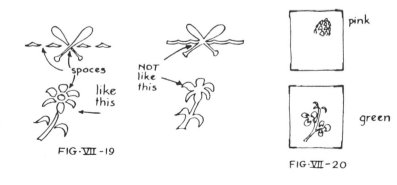

spaces

like this

NOT like this

FIG·VII-19

pink

green

FIG·VII-20

2. Trace the design on the stencil paper with carbon. Using a very sharp knife or razor blade, cut out each section of the design. Keep knife straight so the edges are cut square and not slanting.

Making a Design with More Than One Color

Steps

1. A single sheet of stencil paper may be used if there is space between the different colors (Figure VII-19).
2. If colors are to be joined together (Figure VII-20) a stencil for *each* color must be made. Mark the four corners of the stencil, and mark corresponding spots on the paper or cloth to be sure the stencils register so that each part of the stencil falls in the right spot to make the total design.

Using Textile Paint on Cloth

Textile paint is a special paint that can be applied to cloth. The cloth may be washed, once the paint has dried. Textile paint, in sets of colors, is available at craft supply houses; directions for use are included in the set.

Steps

1. Pin cloth on newspapers or magazine, and pin stencil in place. Use same technique as with water color (above), being sure to use small amounts of paint and to clean excess off brush on paper towel before applying to cloth. If the brush has too much paint, the paint will pile up under stencil edges and will also make the cloth too stiff. Do the painting gradually.
2. Lift stencil off carefully; clean after each use.
3. Let paint dry, and press as directions in set of paints indicate.
4. Clean stencil and brush with cleaner that comes in set or with carbona or similar cleaning fluid.

To stencil on wooden articles, follow same directions for making stencil. Use oil or enamel paint.

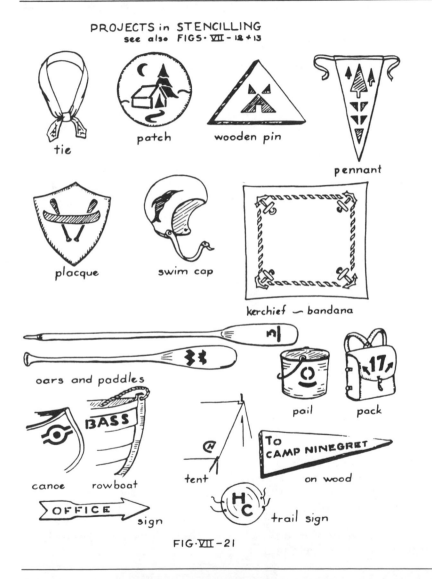

PROJECTS in STENCILLING
see also FIGS· VII - 12 + 13

tie

patch

wooden pin

pennant

placque

swim cap

kerchief — bandana

oars and paddles

pail

pack

BASS

canoe   rowboat

tent

To CAMP NINEGRET
on wood

OFFICE
sign

H C
trail sign

FIG·VII-21

PROJECTS

Spatter Printing

This is a simple type of stenciling in which the paint or ink is sprayed over a shape or natural object which keeps the ink from touching the material. Stencils may be cut out, as in the simplest step in stenciling, or letters, natural grasses, leaves, and branches may be used to make the design.

This method is commonly used in making leaf prints for nature records. From this simple first step, very creative and interesting designs may be made for attractive invitations, decorations, end papers, and the like.

Equipment needed: Spattering tools—brush and knife or screening, spray gun or atomizer; straight pins; flat working surface; newspapers or magazines; shallow pan or dish for paints.

Materials needed: Ink, poster paint, dye, liquid shoe polish, etc.; construction or other paper, or cloth, as desired.

Steps

1. Select leaf or other design. Leaves, grasses, etc. are best for spatter printing after being pressed flat. Choose paper and contrasting ink or paint; sharp contrast is best.
2. Place paper on work surface on top of several thicknesses of newspaper or magazines.
3. Pin leaf or stencil in place, putting pins at points and depressions, so that the leaf or stencil lies very flat against paper. Slant pins toward center of leaf or away from edge of stencil cuts so pins will not retard spraying (Figure VII-27).
4. Spatter print by one of these methods:

   With brush and knife: dip brush in ink or paint in shallow dish; shake off excess. Hold near paper and leaf. Draw knife blade across the brush, holding brush with bristles at slight angle (Figure VII-22), drawing knife *toward* you, making a spray of ink. Move the brush and knife around so the ink sprays in desired places, at desired intensity. (Practice will be needed to get spattering even, without blots.) Avoid getting too much ink or paint on brush.

   With brush and screen: dip brush in ink or paint; shake off excess.

Hold piece of fine wire screening in place, and "scrub" or brush with the brush, moving around, as above (Figure VII-23). Practice again! A good method for screening is to make a frame of a cigar box; remove one long side; tack screening across top of box; cut box top down slightly, so it will slip into the box; pin paper and leaf on the box top; slip into the box, under screen; brush across the screening (Figure VII-24). This is a good method to use when a number of objects will be printed, as invitations or programs.

With sprayer or similar tool: proceed as above, using sprayer instead of screen and brush. Or, place paper and leaf on an easel or a board fastened to a tree (Figure VII-25).

On textiles: spatter printing on cloth may be done with dyes, waterproof ink, or textile paints. The cloth should be stretched *tightly* on working surface before the stencil or leaf is pinned in place.

Variations: over-all design will be obtained by placing many leaves or stencils over the entire surface as for end papers (Figure VII-26).

A *positive* stencil will be obtained by drawing a leaf on stencil paper, cutting out the shape of the leaf and spatter printing the shape of the leaf (Figure VII-27).

Lettering is done by cutting letters out of paper and pinning them in place (Figure VII-28). Cutouts of animals, fishes, etc. may be used in the same way.

For *an advanced project,* use a spray of leaves, grasses, flowers, etc. Place as desired; spatter all over, then remove a few pieces of grass, leaves, etc. Spatter again. Repeat the removing of a few pieces. Repeat these two steps until desired effect of shading is obtained. This is especially good for wall hangings, special illustrations, etc.

The real craftsmanship of this project comes in creating good arrangements, in making interesting color contrasts, and in carrying out the project in a craftsmanlike manner.

Blueprinting

This process uses leaves, grasses, etc., to make a design on architect's blueprint or ozalid print paper. Exposure of the paper to the sun turns it

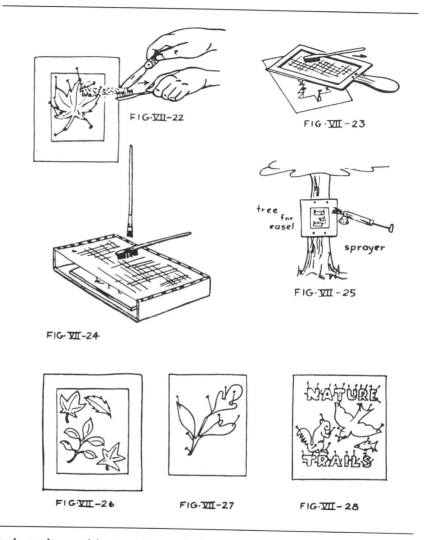

FIG·VII–22

FIG·VII–23

tree for easel

sprayer

FIG·VII–25

FIG·VII–24

FIG·VII–26

FIG·VII–27

FIG·VII–28

dark, and any object, such as a leaf, placed upon the paper keeps that part of the paper from changing color. Good arrangements of the design makes blueprinting a good craft for campers.

Equipment needed: Printing frame; pan of water to hold paper; sunlight.

Materials: Blueprint paper.

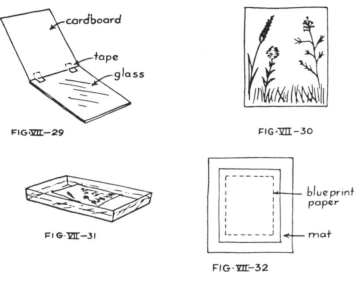

FIG·VII–29

FIG·VII–30

FIG·VII–31

FIG·VII–32

blueprint paper

mat

FIG·VII–33

Printing frame may be a commercial one, as used in photography, or one made from a piece of glass and a piece of cardboard, each about 6 inches by 9 inches or 9 inches by 12 inches, with hinges of adhesive tape (Figure VII-29). Blueprint or ozalid paper can be purchased from an architect's supply house. Have the sheets cut to required size at the supply house. Sheets must be kept in dark wrapper and must be handled carefully, as exposure to light will spoil them.

Steps

1. Arrange design of grasses, leaves, maple keys, twigs, pressed flowers, etc., on the piece of glass (Figure VII-30).
2. Place blueprint paper over the design on the glass, sensitive side *down.*
3. Close frame carefully so the cardboard flattens the leaves, etc. between the blueprint paper and the glass.
4. Hold frame, glass side up, in the sun for several minutes or until the paper is greenish gray.
5. Take into shade; open frame; remove paper and immerse it in pan of water, exposed side *down* (Figure VII-31).
6. Be sure it is thoroughly wet. Leave it in the water from 15 to 60 seconds. (Experiment with bits of paper, washing them for varying lengths of time, to get the best color for your purpose.)
7. Take paper out, and press on blotter pad of newsprint paper to absorb water.
8. Dry in shade, weighing down at corners to keep flat.

Variations: If a *dark margin* is desired, cut another cardboard frame a trifle smaller than the blueprint paper, and lay it on the glass before making arrangement of leaves, grasses, etc. (Figure VII-32).

Silhouettes may be cut from paper and arranged as desired.

Lettering on menus, invitations, etc. may be done with India ink on tracing paper and incorporated into the design (Figure VII-33).

Ozalid prints are similar to blueprints, but can be made in red, blue, or black. The developing process is different.

Steps

1. Follow steps 1, 2, 3, for blueprints.
2. Expose frame to sun for 15 to 25 seconds for red, for 20 to 35 seconds for blue, and 40 to 50 seconds for black.
3. Working in the shade, remove print from the frame, roll into a cylinder, print-face inside, and place in a #10 can inverted over a dish of concentrated ammonia covered with screening. (Concentrated ammonia may be purchased at a drug store.) The ammonia fumes develop the print by bringing out and setting the color. Use new ammonia as old ammonia loses its strength.
4. Remove after 3 or 4 minutes. Under-fuming makes the print colors pale; over-fuming makes them harsh. Experimentation will give the desired color.
5. Spread in shade to dry, as in step 8, above.

Other types of prints: crayon prints, ink-pad prints, carbon prints, and smoke prints are other types of prints used in making nature records. See Chapter XV pages 143-144.

Sketching and Painting

VIII

Sketching and painting are good means of individual expression for campers. A new appreciation of the out-of-doors is gained by the camper who looks for beauty and translates that beauty to paper with pencil, crayon, or brush. The making of a picture can be a very satisfying experience, even for the camper who tries it for the first time. The picture is a personal expression, a description of some scene which has impressed him and a means of describing his impression by line and color rather than by spoken or written words. For many campers, the first stimulation to draw something comes from an enthusiastic counselor or from the activity group, and when they learn that the fun of making lines and forms or of blending colors is the important result, not the making of a finished portrait, they relax and begin to sketch with ease and with pleasure. This positive approach, this willingness to try, is the first step in helping campers know the joy of sketching and painting. Enthusiasm is contagious, and once started, the activity will soon be enjoyed by many who may have thought they couldn't draw at all. Since the equipment is relatively simple and inexpensive, it can be provided easily for a group, and several campers can enjoy the activity at the same time.

In sketching and painting, the artist makes his own interpretation; he may leave out what he does not like, and emphasize what he wants to emphasize. This point of view helps the beginner realize that he does not need to make his picture like any other picture, but rather that he has great freedom to record what he wishes to record.

Sketching is an art which is recorded with pencil, charcoal, or crayon. *Painting* is an art which employs brush and transparent water color, poster paint, or oil paint.

Beginners in sketching and painting should be encouraged to try scenes in the out-of-doors first. The challenge of groups and of individuals in action may be met as the artist gains confidence. Sketching is a good beginning activity, and it is an especially good group activity, with each camper making his own sketch but also having the fun of seeing what other campers develop. In a group it is easy to catch the enthusiasm of the counselor who finds good in each expression and who encourages freedom of execution. In a group, too, one quickly finds that no two sketches are alike, but that each artist has an individual approach which makes each sketch or painting his own.

As campers progress beyond the first steps in groups, they have a new-found pocket craft, and a small sketch book and pencil slipped into a pack or pocket will provide additional enjoyment for hikes, quiet times, or special occasions.

TERMS USED

These are some of the terms used in sketching and painting:

—*Composition:* the arrangement of the picture, an organization of line, shape, mass, and color to make a whole. (The important part, the *center of interest,* should be near the center of the picture; some part should lead the viewer's eye into the center of interest.)

—*Design:* Organization of line, mass, shape, texture, color, and motion growing out of personal or group explorations of materials; may be in two or three dimensions.

—*Line:* A means of indicating form, motion, and emotion in two dimensions.

—*Form:* Mass or shape to make or construct, conceive, arrange, or compose.

—*Color:* Hue.

—*Balance:* A distribution of line, shape, mass, or color which results in an equalization of weight, either symmetrical or asymmetrical.

—*Symmetrical:* Balanced; having corresponding parts equal in size, shape, and relative proportions from a longitudinal line.

—*Asymmetrical:* Lacking in symmetry; having unequal balance of parts.

—*Emphasis:* An effect that is brought out clearly or distinctly by position, color, or size.

—*Perspective:* The art or science of representing on a flat surface three-dimensional objects as they appear to the eye.

—*Rhythm:* A finely spaced or measured sequence of the elements of design.

—*Value:* A quality of color which distinguishes light from dark colors.

—*Shade:* A representation of a surface in shadow by a dark color.

—*Block in:* To sketch or indicate objects in the picture very roughly, with no detail.

EQUIPMENT NEEDED

Be sure to have a sketching or painting surface and tool for *each* member of the group.

For Sketching

Large sheets of paper—12 inches by 18 inches a good size; newsprint or drawing paper, or any clean surface.

Drawing boards—boards slightly larger than the paper to be used; these may be heavy cardboard, masonite, plywood, or similar material. Corrugated cardboard is not recommended, as the surface is not firm enough, and ridges will show on the sketch.

Improvised easels—see Figure VIII-1.

Sketching materials—soft pencils (#2B are best) with broad edges rather than points, or wax or pastel crayons. Colored chalk may be used instead of pastel crayons; it is less expensive and is a good beginning medium. Charcoal bits may be picked from the campfire, or artist's charcoal sticks may be purchased. Making charcoal will be a good project for older campers. Felt-tipped markers are also useful for sketching.

Soft erasers—kneaded rubber, soft rubber, or artgum.

Fixative—a thinned shellac used for preserving pastel, charcoal, and chalk pictures; may be purchased in aerosol cans or in spray bottles.

For Painting

Large sheets or paper—18 inches by 24 inches a good size; manila, bogus, or antique paper for poster paint; antique, charcoal, or water-color paper for water color; canvas board, canvas panels, or canvas-like paper for oil.

Drawing boards of flat surface. See Sketching section for materials.

Improvised easels—see Figure VIII-1.

Brushes—flat 1/4-inch, 1/2-inch, 3/4-inch, or 1-inch artist's bristle brushes for poster paint or oil; #9 and 1-inch wash brushes of oxhair, camel hair, or sable for water color.

Painting materials—poster, oil, or water-color paints.

Turpentine and linseed oil for oil paints, *water* for poster and water-color paints.

Palettes—white plate for water colors, muffin tins for poster paints, masonite or plywood for oil paints.

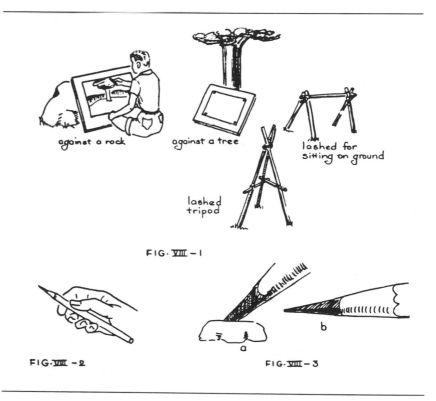

against a rock   against a tree   lashed for sitting on ground

lashed tripod

FIG. VIII – 1

FIG. VIII – 2

FIG. VIII – 3

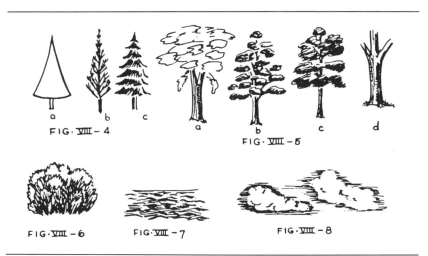

FIG·VIII-4

FIG·VIII-5

FIG·VIII-6   FIG·VIII-7   FIG·VIII-8

TECHNIQUES IN SKETCHING

Using a Pencil

Hold the pencil across the hand (Figure VIII-2), *not* between the fingers as in writing. Use a broad edge on the pencil rather than a fine point, or flatten lead on a small stone for a wedge-shaped point (Figure VIII-3).

Helps on Indicating Outdoor Subjects

Practice making strokes to get the feel of what can be done. Do not try to reproduce *each* part, as each tree or each leaf, but rather give an impression of leaves, clouds, branches, trees, etc. Here are some suggestions:

—For *evergreens:* use a tall, narrow triangular shape (Figure VIII-4).
—For *elms, oaks, maples:* show general shape, and trunk, noting how branches grow out of the trunk (Figure VIII-5).
—For *bushes:* show general shape (Figure VIII-6).
—For *water:* indicate with horizontal strokes, with light between (Figure VIII-7).

—For *clouds:* use light areas against darker sky (Figure VIII-8).
—For *grass:* use vertical strokes for high grass, horizontal strokes for close clipped grass (Figure VIII-9).
—For *stones:* show general shape, with dark sections to indicate three dimensions (Figure VIII-9).
—For *bark:* follow contour of tree, noticing general characteristics of the bark (Figure VIII-10).
—For *fur:* make lines follow contours of animal's shape; make pencil stroke go the way the fur grows (Figure VIII-11).

Practice sketching unrelated objects, such as trees, bushes, clouds, and then put some of them together in your own imaginative picture before trying to sketch some specific scene.

Helps on Sketching People

Do not try to make a portrait. Just indicate shape, height, and some characteristics that identify each person. Start by making figures that do not need features at first, then begin to add details as you gain confidence.

People may be made by a formula. Look at other campers and notice how their legs and arms are hung on their bodies. Notice that elbows come opposite the waist; hands reach almost to knees; side view, sitting, distances from shoulder to waist, from center of hip to knee, from knee to ground, are almost equal; children have larger heads than young adults or adults in proportion to rest of bodies, their legs are straighter; adults are roughly 7½ to 8 heads high. (Figure VIII-12)

Selecting a Subject for a Sketch

Make a *finder* or window through which to look; curl fist (Figure VIII-13 **A**) or make a square or rectangle of thumbs and forefingers (Figure VIII-13 **B**). This will limit your outlook and help you select a view that you like. Turn your head a little one way and another to help choose the picture that pleases you and that you want to sketch. What is selected should have something of interest in the center, something to keep the eye from running out of the picture and some background. Try to avoid having something that cuts the picture in half, either vertically or horizontally—the horizon or a single tree or post.

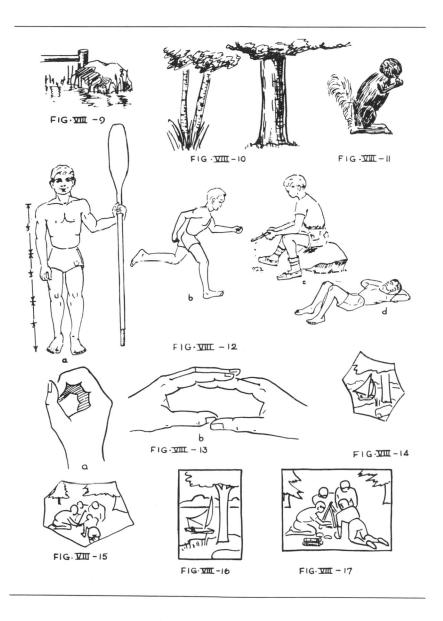

FIG·VIII–9

FIG·VIII–10

FIG·VIII–11

FIG·VIII–12

FIG·VIII–13

FIG·VIII–14

FIG·VIII–15

FIG·VIII–16

FIG·VIII–17

For example, in Figure 14, the boat is to be the center of interest, the tree stops the eye from running out of the picture, the background is the other side of the picture, and the tree is off center one way, the edge of the pond is higher than the center the other way. The rock in the foreground may or may not be included in the final sketch, depending on the size and shape of the sketch and the desire of the artist.

For *group action,* catch what you want to portray as the *center of interest.* In Figure 15, the group is laying a fire; all faces are turned toward the fire so the viewer finds himself looking toward the fire, too. In making the sketch, one person may be made to stand out or each member of the group may have equal value.

Making a Sketch

Translate *what you want* of what you saw in the finder; keep it simple, and do not try to put in each little detail. Decide whether the picture will be better if placed horizontally or vertically. Then *quickly* sketch in a few light lines, locating the various parts of the picture. This is called *blocking-in* (time limit—two minutes). Starting with just a few lines makes it possible to revamp the sketch as you progress, eliminating or adding as you like (Figures VIII-16 and 17).

Adding value to the sketch: when the sketch has been blocked in, look at the scene and decide which parts are light, which are dark. Indicate this on the sketch by adding some dark strokes to give contrast as well as to heighten interest. Use varying degrees of shading to produce the variation of lights you wish (Figures VIII-18, 19, 20).

FIG·VIII–18

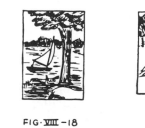

FIG·VIII–19

FIG·VIII–20

Using Crayons—Wax Crayons, Pastel Crayons, or Colored Chalk

Using color requires more thought than using black and white. Colors like those in the objects being sketched should be used. Shadows are made with blue, purple, or green (known as cool colors). Black should be used sparingly when making an outdoor sketch. Shadows should be made on the sides of people or objects that are away from the sun; a shadow on the ground, known as a cast-shadow, needs to be dark also (Figure VIII-20).

Use crayons lightly at first, covering part of the color with more of the same to deepen color; to give the sketch depth, do not completely cover first color. From a distance the eye will see both colors side by side and mix them visually.

In using pastel crayons or colored chalk; choose colors nearest like the subject matter, applying one on top of the other or side by side. Color may be blended by rubbing with finger. Lighten colors by adding white. Colors seem truer on gray paper. Colored charcoal paper is good for a picture which is "vignetted" or blurred on edges, leaving paper color around edges.

Using Charcoal

Charcoal, being black, reduces a picture to black, white, and grays. After sketch is blocked in, put in lightest spot and darkest black (usually these are close together). Then limit rest of picture to three values of gray, making five values in the picture. This simplifies the picture and eliminates unimportant details.

How to Fix Charcoal and Pastel Sketches

To preserve the picture, charcoal fixative is used for charcoal, pastel fixative for pastel or colored chalk. The fixative is applied from an aerosol can or spray bottle; the spray is held two feet from the picture and applied in even sweeps across the picture and back.

TECHNIQUES IN PAINTING

Painting is the art of making a picture with a brush and some type of paint. For beginners, poster paint or opaque water-color paint, with large paper, is a good medium. More advanced media are water-color paints, acrylics, and oil.

Using Poster Paint

Fasten piece of newsprint, antique, manila, or bogus paper on drawing board and prop against a wall, tree, rock, or easel.

With a small brush and a color like light brown, brush in, in no more than two minutes, the location of each part of the picture. Starting with center of interest, paint that area, and the areas around it that are approximately the same color. Do this simply, with no detail. When the whole picture has been painted, go back and put in details like windows, clothing, shadows, etc. Make a *quick* painting rather than one that is tediously and meticulously done.

When using poster paint, it is possible to place two wet colors beside each other with no danger of the colors running together.

Paint large areas with wide brushes, detail with small brushes. Add white poster paint to other poster paint colors to lighten the color; do *not* add water to lighten colors. Add water to poster paint to keep it the consistency of heavy cream.

Wash brushes with water.

Using Watercolor Paints

Watercolor is the most difficult medium to control. It is a very wet medium when used correctly. A direct approach of *put it down and leave it* is the best policy; otherwise, any changes will show when the paint is dry.

Mix paints on plate or other white surface, mixing enough color for each area to be painted. Add water to color to lighten it. Two adjoining areas should be painted with a narrow strip of unpainted paper between them, or one area should be painted and let dry before applying the adjacent color. If this is not done, the two colors will run together.

Experiment with the paint to see what can be done with various colors, using long sweeps of the brush. Try a gray sky, looking like rain, a dead tree or a living one, or perhaps a splash of red sunset. This may be called a "mood" picture.

Paint on a horizontal surface, if possible, so the colors will not run down in long drips and spoil the picture.

Wash brushes and palette with water.

Here are some suggestions to help in working with watercolor paints:

—*Sky* is sometimes indicated first as a wash or light blue area, flowed on smoothly by overlapping one row with the next, carrying color continuously across the paper with one stroke of a loaded wash brush or a 1-inch bristle brush. Let dry, and then paint over it, putting in trees, buildings, or other objects that come in front of the sky.

—*Clouds* are white spaces left on white paper—not painted. Pale purple used as a shadow on the lower parts will indicate fluffy clouds.

—*People* are painted rather than drawn. Do not outline arms, legs, or body. The head may be shown simply with hair or hat, without features.

—*Foliage* may be suggested by touching brush repeatedly to paper, not drawing any shape, just brush blots, probably yellow-green. Use green and blue-green for the differences in light and shadow.

Using Oil Paints

This is similar to painting with poster paint, except that the paint is used with turpentine and linseed oil rather than water. Oil paint is usually thicker in consistency than poster paint.

Colors may be painted over, changed, scraped off—and the picture may be started again.

Canvas is the surface on which oils are usually used. Canvas panels are cheaper than canvas used on a stretcher. There are also some tablets of paper simulating canvas that may be used with oil paints. This type of paper is good for beginners' projects.

To begin to paint, squeeze paint from tubes around edge of palette, then mix in center of palette with turpentine and linseed oil to make a consistency easy to apply. Do not make too thin, or the paint will be like a stain rather than a paint.

Colors may be laid on top of each other. High lights, such as the whitest spot on a shiny surface, may be added on top of other paint with a brush *loaded* with thick paint.

Painting should be left to dry at least 24 hours before being touched again.

Clean brushes with kerosene and rag, then wash with soap, rubbing brush on cake, then in palm of hand, and repeating until no more color comes from brush.

Scrape unused paint from center of palette with palette knife, and throw away. Colors around the edges may be saved from day to day, as a skin forms on outside, leaving paint in a plastic condition underneath.

USE OF SKETCHING AND PAINTING IN CAMP ACTIVITIES

Sketching and painting are activities in themselves; as such, they are included in camp program for the purpose of appreciation and expression. These two arts may also be used to good advantage in other forms of program, and these are briefly suggested here:

—For *log books, memory books, favors, special events,* see Chapter Seventeen on Favors and Decorations for suggestions of many ways in which these techniques may be used.

—For *dramatics,* see Chapter Thirteen on Correlation with Dramatics for suggestions on making scenery, masks, puppets.

—In *games:* a number of games employ the skill of sketching. These are often played to help the camper catch the feel of quick sketching and to sharpen his power of observation. One player from a team may view some specific object—a leaf, a piece of camp equipment, a picture of a camp building; he then returns to his group and makes a quick sketch, adding to the sketch until someone recognizes the object. The sketching and the quick identification by the group are the purpose of the game, but there can be other good results in the fun of the game and the merriment of the group.

Another game is good for quiet hours or campfires. Each player in turn sketches someone in the group, using major characteristics in his sketch, such as a plaid shirt, curly hair, glasses, etc. He "exhibits" his sketch, and the rest of the group guesses which one has been the subject.

Games such as these help everyone to make quick observations of key characteristics and promote skill in the quiet sketching of the "block in" stage. They also help to break down campers' inhibitions and resistances toward sketching.

EXHIBITS

Since exhibits will often be an outgrowth of this activity, some suggestions on planning and carrying out exhibits are given here.

Black and white sketches may be mounted on colored paper, or colored paper may be interspersed among the pictures. When several pictures are put on a large board, try to keep some edges of pictures even to create top, side, and bottom margins of a block outline (Figures VIII-21 and 22).

Hang pictures at or near eye level.

Create a neutral background for a better appreciation of the pictures. Cover display space with gray bogus paper or manila paper, or if tackboard is used, paint it gray or cream. The colors of pictures show to best advantage against a neutral background. Charcoal or pencil sketches may be mounted or matted with three borders even and larger space at bottom.

Group small pictures together, formally or informally.

Captions lettered on black or white strips explain and add interest to the exhibit.

Photography is a related art since it has to do with picture-making. It has been included in Chapter XXI.

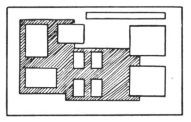

FIG. VIII - 21

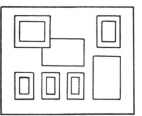

FIG. VIII - 22

Weaving

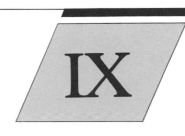

IX

Weaving is a craft that has come down through the ages. It was an essential home craft of the pioneers and early settlers; Indian tribes still create rugs and materials on handmade looms. Weaving is a craft of people who lived by the skill of their hands; they used the materials to be found around them, sometimes natural materials such as reeds and rushes, sometimes materials such as flax or wool which they raised and processed. Some weaving calls for extensive equipment, such as table or floor looms, but there are simple looms that may be made by campers; some of these are portable and may be used for pocket crafts. Woven belts with hand-carved buckles, camp symbols, mats for sitting on the floor or ground, decorative hangings for cabin walls—any of these may introduce campers to the fascinating world of weaving with natural materials. Basic campcraft skills of lashing, knot tying, and toolcraft are put to good use in making and setting up the simple looms which are presented in this chapter.

TERMS USED

The following are some of the terms used in weaving:

—*Weaving* consists of interlacing one set of thread, yarn, or strips with another set.
—A *loom* is the apparatus on which the weaving is done.
—*Warp* and *weft:* a loom contains a set of stationary strips, threads, or yarns that are known as the *warp.* Horizontal, interlacing strips or threads are called the *weft,* or sometimes, the *woof.*

TOOLS USED IN WEAVING

shuttle
wood weaving needle
heddle stick
heddle rod
comb
wood → beaters

Looms used in weaving

frame   tube   T-D   small Navaho   large Navaho

Materials used in weaving

string for warp
yarn, wool or cotton
grasses

PLATE IX

—A *shuttle* is used for this interlacing; it may be a large-eyed wooden needle or a forked wooden strip around which the yarn or thread for the weft is wound (Figures IX-1 *a* and 1 *b*).
—A *beater* is used to press the weft into place as the weaving progresses; usually a comb is used as a beater with a small loom (Figure IX-2); sometimes wooden beaters with teeth are used.
—Simplest weaving is the *darning stitch weaving* in which the weft is woven under and over the warp (Figures IX-7 and 8).

—More advanced weaving employs the use of a *shed* or space through which the shuttle may pass without being interlaced over and under the warp threads. One method (see Navajo loom, Figures IX-26-32) uses a heddle stick and a heddle rod. The *heddle stick* is a strip of wood which is woven under one set of warp threads; when turned on edge, a shed is created for the shuttle. The other set of warp threads is attached by loops to a *heddle rod;* when this rod is pulled forward, a second shed is created for the return of the shuttle to the starting side (Figure IX-3 *a* and 3 *b*).

—Another method is to make a *harness* of several wooden or metal heddles, each with an eye through which a warp thread is strung (Figure IX-4); these heddles, in the harness, are moved up and down to create shed (see T-D Looms, Figures IX-24 and 25). Table and floor looms (not included here) use a number of similar harnesses.

TECHNIQUES

To Make a Frame Loom

A frame loom is the simplest type of loom; others are described in specific projects in the following pages. This project makes use of rough, dried sticks, or wooden dowels, and the skill of lashing.

Equipment needed: Knife with reamer; sandpaper; hammer; ruler and pencil; glue or household cement.

Materials needed: Four sticks, size to be determined by size of loom; wood matchsticks for pegs or brads; cord for lashing; string for warp.

Steps

1. Trim ends of dried sticks or dowels, making them desired sizes.
2. Notch corners, or shave off ends, top sides of the *A* sticks, under sides of *B* sticks. Whittle off whole length of tops of *B* sticks to make flat for brads or pegs (Figure IX-5). Sand ends and top.
3. Lash at corners with square lashings (Figue IX-5).[1]
4. With ruler, mark a pencil line across middle of top of *B* sticks; mark 1/2-inch spaces between spots for lashing.

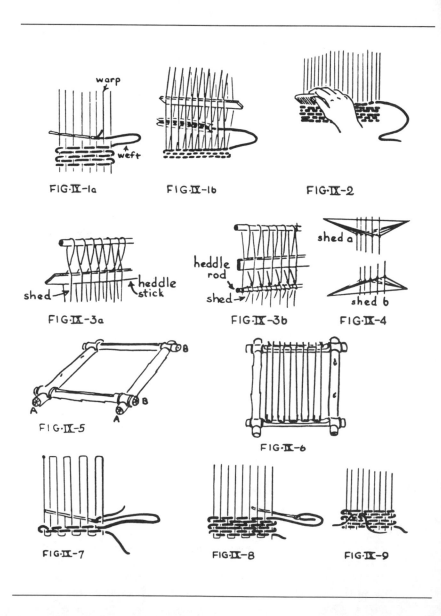

FIG·IX-1a   FIG·IX-1b   FIG·IX-2

FIG·IX-3a   FIG·IX-3b   FIG·IX-4

FIG·IX-5   FIG·IX-6

FIG·IX-7   FIG·IX-8   FIG·IX-9

5. If wooden pegs are to be used, whittle to desired length, point one end and round the other; make holes at spaces with reamer of knife. Insert pegs with a drop of glue or cement. If brads are used, hammer in at marked spaces. If loom is to be used extensively, fasten small screw in each corner, under lashing, to make more secure.

To string a frame loom, start warp thread at upper left-hand peg or brad; carry warp to first peg at bottom; carry along to second peg on bottom; carry up to second peg at top (making threads parallel); carry across top to third peg, down to third peg at bottom; continue to end of frame (Figure IX-6). Start and end thread with clove hitch (see chapter on Braiding and Knotting, Figure II-19).

Darning Stitch Weaving

This, the simplest form of weaving, is a good practice step. Use frame loom, as for mat (see Figures IX-16 and 17), or weave strands or strips without a loom, as for mat (see Figures IX-18-19).

Equipment needed: Frame loom; flat whittled needle or upholstery needle; comb for beater.
Materials needed: Thread, string, yarn, etc., for warp; same for weft, as desired.

Steps

1. To weave: thread needle with piece of yarn or other material about 24 inches long. Have loom ready with warp wound in place. Starting at either side, weave needle under warp thread 1, over 2, under 3, over 4, etc., across to other side (Figure IX-7). Pull needle through, then pull yarn through loosely, leaving small end at starting side. Press into place with comb.
   Return, threading needle over the odd-numbered warp threads and under the even-numbered warp threads to other side. Press into place.
   Repeat these two rows to end of weaving. Do not pull weft threads tight at turns between rows, but leave a slight loop at ends (Figure IX-8).
2. To add pieces to weft: when the end of piece of yarn or thread is reached, lay end of a new piece beside old end two to three warp threads

back (Figure IX-9); any loose ends may be snipped off even with material at end of weaving.
3. To begin or end weft: weave weft thread or yarn back between first or last two rows of weaving. Cut off any extra.

Preparing Natural Materials

Grasses, palmetto strips, reeds, and similar materials are used in the natural state for weaving many projects. Preparation of such materials is the same as for basketry and is described in Chapter Three on Basketry.

Natural dyes are good to use in camp weaving projects. Suggestions for making and using such dyes will be found in Chapter Fifteen on Correlation with Nature.

Designs for Weaving

Designs for simple weaving projects are usually made with straight, rather than curved, lines. The design should be worked out full-size on paper; this pattern may be slipped under the frame to follow in the weaving. Combinations of interesting colors and shapes serve to individualize projects of campers; crayons or paint are used on pattern to indicate colors. A symetrical design is made by folding full-size paper in half vertically and then in half horizontally. The design is worked on one quarter and transferred to the other three sections, being sure corresponding lines match or register (Figure IX-13).

Steps to Weave a Design

1. Make a paper pattern of design, full-size.
2. Wind several small shuttles with background color; wind separate shuttles with colors for design, or thread needles with colors.
3. Start at bottom of loom and weave 1/2-inch selvage with warp thread (Figure IX-14 z).
4. Proceed with design in color A (Figure IX-14).
5. With a needle threaded with background color B, fill in two lower corners, joining B weft with color A. Be sure to loop color B around the last warp thread used for color A, to avoid a slit in the material.
6. Use shuttle wound with b when the background color goes across the entire width of material.

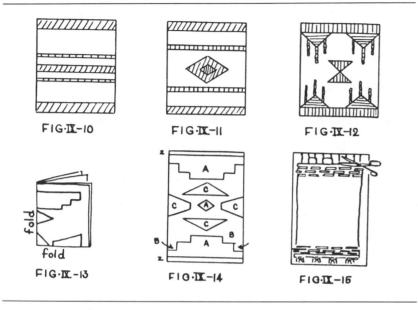

FIG·IX-10   FIG·IX-11   FIG·IX-12

FIG·IX-13   FIG·IX-14   FIG·IX-15

7. Use needle for small design areas; count warp threads on both sides of design, to ensure evenness of design. Count rows of background color *B* between colors *A* and *C*, and repeat on upper half of material (Figure IX-14).
8. Finish design with 1/2 inch selvage of the warp material.

To take material from loom: cut warp threads at top and bottom of loom (Figure IX-15); tie together in pairs with square knots (see chapter on Braiding and Knotting, Figure II-16).

PROJECTS

A Mat of Natural Materials (with loom)

This is a beginner's project in making a loom and using it for the simplest type of weaving. Materials used will depend upon the material available in abundance in the camp. Suggestions for preparing the material are to be found in Chapter Fifteen on Correlation with Nature.

Equipment needed: Knife; ruler; pencil; sandpaper; scissors.
Materials: Sticks for loom, lashing twine, pegs or brads; string or twine for warp; for weft—rushes, palmetto, lauhala, grasses—gather with good conservation practices—strips should be approximately the same width and long enough to go across the loom.

1. Make frame, and string it (see preceding pages).
2. Weave one piece of material as in darning sticth (Figures IX-7-9). Let material protrude about 1 inch beyond warp at each edge.
3. Weave second row, as above, repeating untill all of the warp is covered (Figures IX-16 and 17).
4. Trim ends at sides evenly.
5. On side edges, weave an extra piece of warp thread for strength. It may be a different color, for variety.
6. Finish as in Figure IX-15.

This may be a place mat, table runner, sit-upon mat, or door mat, depending on size and material used.
Strips of rags may be used for weft, in the same manner.

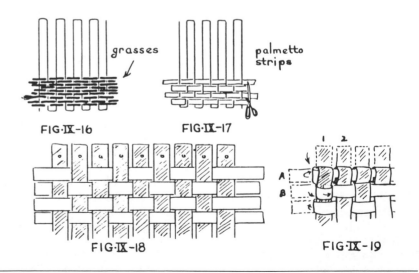

grasses   palmetto strips

FIG·IX-16   FIG·IX-17

FIG·IX-18   FIG·IX-19

A Mat of Strips (without loom)

This is a simple weaving project that calls for no loom; the mat, some-times known as a situpon is useful for camp floors, campfire seats, etc. Natural materials such as palmetto may be used, or heavy wrapping paper, oilcloth, newsprint, cut into strips. Salvaged pieces of canvas or paper are also suitable. The mats may be painted and shellacked or varnished to waterproof for outside use; plain paper and cloth may be decorated by stenciling or block printing. These mats make a good group project for camp equipment.

Equipment needed: Scissors; working space, as a table or board; thumbtacks.

Materials needed: Twelve or sixteen strips of material about 24 inches long and three inches wide; paper should be double width, folded in half, lengthwise, for strength.

Steps

1. Lay half the strips side by side close together, vertically, to form the warp. Thumbtack the top of each strip to hold in place on table.
2. Weave a strip as in darning stitch (see Figures IX-7-9) over and under the vertical strips, and push up toward the tops that are tacked down.
3. Weave the next strip in alternate fashion, under and over, and continue until all the cross strips are in place. Remove tacks and even off the ends, leaving about 6 inches on ends for folded edges.
4. To finish; fold each strip over end strip; tuck end under same strip (Figure IX-19). No. 1 strip is folded back, over and under *A* strip; No. 2 strip is folded forward, over and under *A* strip; continue alter-nately folding back and forward across top and bottom. At sides, *A* strip is folded in back of No. 1 strip, and under right side of No. 1; *B* strip is folded in front of No. 1 strip, and under right side of No. 1; continue alternately to bottom of side.

Variations: The shape of this mat can be varied by the number and size of the strips. For a rectangular placemat, make strips 1 inch to 2 inches wide, vertical strips 14 inches long, horizontal strips 20 inches long.

Belt of Tube Weaving

Tube weaving, also known as cylinder and Swedish tube weaving, is a beginner's weaving method. Small-bore tubes are used to hold the warp threads; the weft is woven around the tubes, and the woven material slipped off as the work progresses. This is a good pocket craft. When hollow reeds or bamboo shoots are found on the campsite, they make very satisfactory tubes; metal tubes are usually used; macaroni may also be used, but as it is easily broken, is not too satisfactory; also plastic drinking straws.

Equipment needed: Six or more tubes of hollow reeds or bamboo shoots or similar material about 9 inches long, 1/16-inch in diameter.

Materials needed: Six strands wool, cord, string, etc., each length of waist plus 12 inches; six small bits of wood for stoppers to keep ends from slipping through reeds; toggle button (see Chapter X on Woodworking).

Steps

1. Thread strands through reeds, knotting 6-inch ends together with an overhand knot (see chapter on Braiding and Knotting, Figure II-21); tie stopper bits of wood on each strand (Figure IX-20). Tie other ends of strands loosely at other end.
2. Tubes are kept at top of strands. Start weaving at bottom of tubes (Figure 20 *x*) with long, single strand of weft (yarn, cord, etc.), over and under, from left to right, then back from right to left. Start, join, and end weft strands in middle of tubes, not on edges of material.
3. When weaving covers about half the length of tubes, slide it off tubes, in direction of arrows in Figure IX-20, pulling up for new weaving. As the weaving progresses, it will cover the remaining parts of the six strands and be at the loose knot at opposite end from the tubes.
4. When desired length is reached, untie top knot, slide tubes and stoppers off, and finish as desired.

Steps to make belt

1. Weaving should cover strands, except for about 6 inches on either end. Make a loop at one end of one or several strands of the warp. Sew

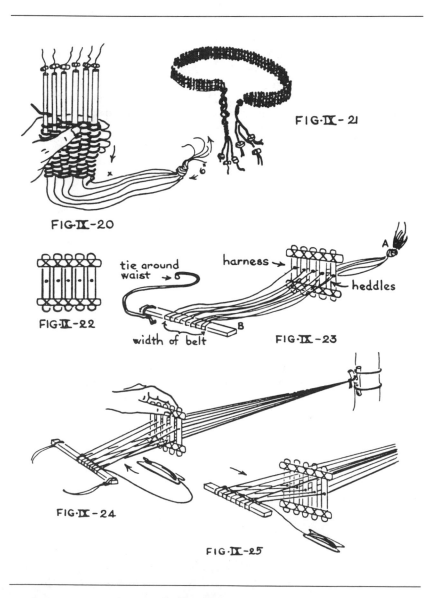

FIG·IX-21

FIG·IX-20

FIG·IX-22

tie around waist →

harness →

heddles

width of belt

FIG·IX-23

A
B

FIG·IX-24

FIG·IX-25

ends together, trim off extra, and cover with whipping (see chapter on Braiding and Knotting, Figures II-10-14).

2. See Chapter X on Woodworking for suggestions for buckles, buttons, or toggles; attach toggle or buckle as shown in Braiding and Knotting chapter, Figures II-8 and 9. Or, tie whittled bits of wood or shells, acorns, or similar objects to ends that are made by braiding three double strands on each end of belt (Figure IX-21); knot with square knot (see chapter on Braiding and Knotting, Figure II-16).

Belt Made with a T-D Loom

This type of loom is used to make a narrow fabric, as for a belt or a headband. This is a beginning step in using a loom with a "harness"; the weaving is tighter and firmer than that done by tube weaving. The making of the loom is an interesting project.

Equipment needed: Knife; sandpaper; egg-beater drill and small drill; peg; comb for beater; shuttle to hold weft.

Materials needed for loom and belt: Seven small strips of thin wood, whittled and sanded, as tongue depressors; string to lash; one stick 10 inches to 12 inches long, with cord tied to each end, to go around waist; yarn or string for warp and nine lengths yarn or string for weft; toggle or buckle.

Steps to make loom

1. Bore holes with drill in center of five of the small strips of wood, the heddles.
2. Lay these five heddle strips side by side, 1/4-inch apart and lash (see any campcraft book) them to cross pieces, top and bottom (Figure IX-22). This is the *harness*.
3. Thread nine strands of warp thread through the holes in the heddles and between the sticks (Figure IX-23) to make warp. Tie all strands at top with an overhand knot (Figure IX-23 *A*). For overhand knot, see chapter on Braiding and Knotting, Figure II-21.
4. Tie other end of strands evenly to the long stick (Figure IX-23 *B*), spaced as desired for width of weaving.
5. Hook overhand knot on peg and tie stick around waist, so strands are taut, and the harness is in place.

6. Wind shuttle with weft.

Steps to weave

1. With loom in place, start at the *B*-stick end; with left hand raise harness with right hand push shuttle through the shed from right to left (Figure IX-24). Catch with left hand and pull through, pulling yarn in place firmly, but not tight.
2. Use comb as a beater.
3. Lower harness so a new shed is formed (Figure IX-25); push shuttle from left to right, pull yarn into place, use comb as beater.
4. Continue length of belt, allowing for buckle and loop.
5. Finish ends as in chapter on Braiding and Knotting (Figures II-6 and 7).

Weaving with Navajo Looms

This type of loom is used by women of the Navajo Indian tribes to make rugs and materials. It is a particularly good camp project as the making of the loom utilizes trees and toolcraft and lashing. The first project given here is a good group project; the second, an individual project.

Grass Mat Made with Navajo Loom

Equipment needed: Tree; saw; hand ax; knife.
Materials needed for loom and weaving: Two poles or saplings, about 4 feet long; four stakes, about 20 inches long, pointed at one end, cut straight at other; binder twine or string; grasses, rushes, cattail leaves, sedges, or similar natural material—be conservation-wise in gathering!

Steps to make loom

1. Lash (see any campcraft book) one 4-foot pole to tree (Figure IX-26 *A*).
2. Tie nine pieces of binder twine to pole, five of them 5 feet long, four of them 6 feet long, so they alternate, one 5 feet then one 6 feet, etc. (Figure IX-26). Use clove hitches (see chapter on Braiding and Knotting, Figure II-19).
3. Drive stakes in ground, in front of tree, so the 5-foot pieces of twine can be tied to them with clove hitches (Figure IX-26). Tie these strings—1, 3, 5, 7, 9—to the stakes.

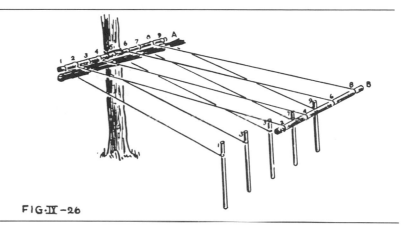

FIG. IX-26

4. Tie other strings—2, 4, 6, 8—to the other long pole (*B*), so the pole will drop *outside* the stakes (Figue IX-26).

This pole will serve as a heddle to make sheds for the weaving.

Steps to weave

1. Lift up pole *B*. Put long bunches of grass (size of fist) or other materials at top of warp strings, close to pole *A* (Figure IX-26).
2. Drop pole *B* down to ground, outside stakes; place bundles of grass next to first bundles.
3. Raise pole *B*, and continue steps 1 and 2 to end of weaving.
4. Cut strings at poles and stakes; tie ends of 1 and 2, 3 and 4, etc., together with square knots (see chapter on Braiding and Knotting, Figure II-16) at both ends of mat.
5. Trim ends at sides.

Weaving with Small Portable Navajo Loom

This type of loom (Figure IX-27) may be used to make a mat, or cloth, or similar material; the material is closely woven, and more "finished" in appearance than with other Navajo loom. This project calls for progression in weaving, in construction, and in making the design of interesting colors and shapes. An added step in progression would be to dye the weaving material with natural dyes (see Chapter XV on Correlation with Nature).

Equipment: Knife; saw; sandpaper; beater or comb; shuttle, 6 inches to 8 inches long; paper, etc., for design.

Materials needed for loom and weaving: Two forked sticks, 34 inches long, thicker than thumb, for uprights *A*; two straight sticks, 24 inches long, thicker than thumb, for stretchers *B*; two straight sticks, 20 inches long, thick as little finger, for yarn beams *C* and *D*; one straight stick, 24 inches long, thick as thumb, for hanger *E*; one straight stick, 20 inches long, thick as little finger, for heddle rod; one strip of thin wood ¼-inch thick, 1½-inch wide, 20 inches long, for heddle; lashing twine; warp thread; weft of yarn of desired colors.

Steps to make loom

1. Round ends of all sticks, and sand smooth. Notch ends of heddle rod *H* (see Figure IX-30).
2. Square lash the forked sticks *A* and cross sticks *B* to make frame (Figure IX-27). Notch before lashing for extra strength.
3. Lash, temporarily, yarn beams *C* and *D* at desired places, depending on length of cloth to be woven (Figure IX-27).

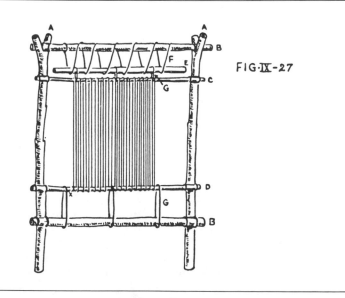

FIG·IX-27

4. String warp for desired width, as follows: with loom in horizontal position, tie end of warp thread at *x* (Figure IX-28); bring thread down over *front* of beam *D*, up and over *front* of beam *C*, down and in front of beam *D*, always bringing thread over beams from front to back. This makes thread cross at *M* (Figure IX-28). Space threads evenly, and keep tension uniform through stringing.
5. Fasten hanger stick *E* to top stretcher *B* by a piece of twine (Figure IX-27 *F*). Attach yarn beam *C* to *E* in three or four places with twine (*G*); attach yarn beam *D* to lower stretcher *B* in similar fashion. Remove temporary lashing of yarn beams *C* and *D* to uprights *A*, so yarn beams hang loose. Control tension of warp by *F*.

Steps to make sheds

1. Insert heddle stick so that it passes *under* odd-numbered warp threads and *over* even-numbered warp threads (Figure IX-28). Turn the heddle stick so that top edge is toward you, to create shed No. 1 (Figure IX-29).
2. Tie on heddle rod, to make shed No. 2, as follows:

   With heddle stick flat, pass a ruler or odd stick *under* even-numbered threads, below heddle stick; turn edge of ruler toward you, making temporary shed No. 2.

   Run a piece of twine (about three times width of warp) through this second shed from left to right, and remove temporary stick.

   Hold heddle rod *H* to right of warp (Figure IX-30); fasten right end of twine to left end of heddle rod, loosely, with two half hitches (see chapter on Braiding and Knotting, Figure II-20); push end of heddle rod to left across warp, catching twine with left forefinger, between first two even-numbered threads; throw two half hitches over end of rod, and push end through to next two even-numbered threads. Proceed from right to left, picking up twine between even-numbered threads. The twine lies *over* odd-numbered threads, and *under* even-numbered threads; the heddle rod is on top of all threads.

   Tie end of twine at left end of rod, with clove hitch (see chapter on Braiding and Knotting, Figure II-19). Notches on heddle rod will help hold the loops in place.

   Heddle rod now lies across warp; when lifted, it pulls even-numbered threads forward, creating shed No. 2 (Figure IX-31).

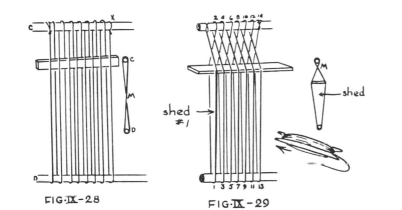

FIG·IX-28   FIG·IX-29

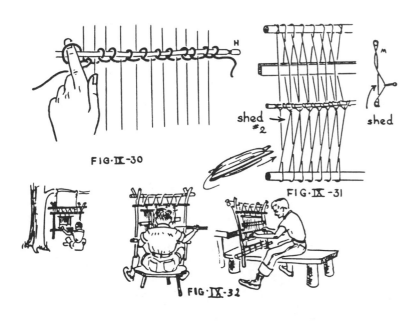

FIG·IX-30

FIG·IX-31

FIG·IX-32

Steps to weave

1. Check general suggestions for making and weaving design (Figures IX-10-15).
2. Make design and wind shuttles and thread needles.
3. Start with ½-inch selvage of warp thread, holding loom as in Figure IX-32.
4. Starting with shuttle of first color, make shed with heddle stick, and pass shuttle from right to left (Figure IX-29).
5. Pull heddle rod forward, making second shed, and pass shuttle from left to right (Figure IX-31).
6. Work in pattern to end, finishing with ½-inch selvage of warp thread.
7. Remove from loom by cutting warp threads and tying in pairs.

1. Hammett, Catherine T. *The Campcraft Book*. Martinsville, IN: American Camping Association, 1987.

Whittling, Woodworking and Woodcarving

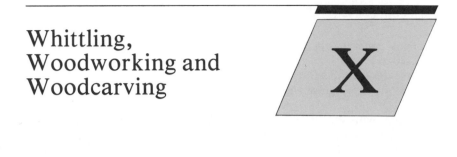

If there is one craft that is a natural for campers, it is this one which has to do with wood and a jackknife or other tools. Nearly every camper has a knife (or wishes he had one), and learning to use it safely and well is one of the basic skills in campcraft. So it is a natural step to using a knife for whittling. Coupled with this is the fact that wood is the one material that is found almost universally; good conservation practices dictate wise use of wood found on the campsite, but it is generally found in sufficient supply to make this the most practical craft material found in the out-of-doors. A beginning appreciation of the twigs and sticks one can pick up in the woods and the careful cutting and use of green sticks for cooking or construction will grow into real appreciation of wood carving and a feeling for wood. When a camper grows to the point of smoothing a piece of well-finished wood because it looks and feels so good, he will have progressed far along this particular craft trail.

Any knife will do some kind of job in getting the first marshmallow stick, but soon the camper realizes that he needs to know how to get his knife in good condition, how to keep it that way, and how to handle it with skill. These first steps will include the counselor's teaching of safety for himself and his fellow campers and consideration for the forest's trees and bushes. Any book on campcraft or woods lore will give these steps. This chapter is designed to help the counselor lead his campers beyond the steps of campcraft to the satisfaction of the pocket craft of whittling or to the more advanced steps of woodcarving and carpentry. Woodworking is one more of the oldest arts, and the same articles and expressions that were used by primitive men and by pioneers make this another good handcraft for the camp program.

MATERIALS TO USE

Materials for wood projects will vary from pieces of wood picked up in the open to bits of scrap lumber, from slabs cut from logs to selected pieces of fine-grained wood for woodcarving. The woods available in the camp locality will govern the material for beginning steps; wood for advanced projects may need to be purchased from craft supply houses or cabinet makers. Staff who do some exploring before the camp season begins can find various woods available in the forest, in nearby orchards and groves, or from sawmills, carpenters, and cabinetmakers. Scrap wood is usually plentiful and available for the asking. Carpenters and cabinetmakers should be asked for advice and help on local woods or on scrap wood that may be available. Fruit trees need to be pruned and thinned, and seasoned wood from most fruit trees is good for pins, buckles, and so forth. When land is being cleared near the camp, there may be a fine supply of logs for many projects.

Wood, in general, is divided into softwoods and hardwoods. The definitions for these vary with foresters and lumbermen and in different parts of the country. For beginners, a firm, fine-grained wood without knots or pitch is the best; northern white pine and red cedar are favorites with whittlers. Red cedar may be found locally or may be purchased in fence posts, or in planks, or scraps from boards for cedar-lined chests and closets may be available. Redwood is another wood of good color; this may be purchased in almost any locality, though it is found in the natural state only in the West. No list is complete for every section of the country, but the following are woods that are found in a wide area, and that are good for whittling: white pine, basswood, red cedar, cherry, apple, white ash, redwood, sycamore, and red (soft) maple. Oak and hard maple are good for advanced carvers.

Wood for whittling should be seasoned. Dead wood picked up in the open will be good for whittling if it is good for firewood. Green wood should dry for at least a year. Gather it one summer for the next year.

TERMS USED IN WOODWORKING AND CARVING

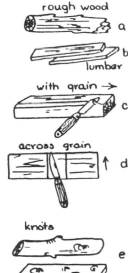

rough wood a

lumber b

with grain → c

across grain d

knots e

burl f

heartwood g

sapwood h

—*Rough wood:* wood as picked up in the open: twigs, sticks, logs, etc. (*a*)

—*Slabs* are boards with bark still on the wood.

—*Green wood:* wood that still has sap in it, not dried; it is easy to carve, but may split or check when dry.

—*Seasoned wood:* wood that has dried, either naturally in the open, or in kilns. Seasoned wood is necessary for whittling and woodcarving.

—*Lumber:* boards of varying sizes, sawed from logs (*b*). Dressed or finished lumber has been smooth and sanded, ready to use. *Timber* is another term generally used in the same way as *lumber.*

—*Softwood*—wood that is soft, light in weight.

—*Hardwood:* wood that is firm, dense, heavier in weight than softwood.

—*Grain:* the fibers which form the substance of wood—with the grain, along the length of the piece (*c*); against the grain, across the width of the piece (*d*).

—*Knot:* a hard spot at the point where a branch grew from the trunk or limb; valued in whittling, to make interesting contrast of color and texture (*e*). A *burl* is a protuberance on a tree where some injury has taken place, and the bark has grown over the knot or spot (*f*). Valued for bowls and noggins.

—*Heartwood (g):* the central part of tree trunk; usually darker and denser than outer part of *sapwood (h)*. The heartwood section is used for whittling and carving.

—*Low relief:* background cut down, leaving design at level of wood. Parts of the design may be flattened or rounded (*i*).

—*High relief:* background cut deeper than above, with more of the depth of the design exposed (*i*).

—*Intaglio:* carving into the wood, leaving the background raised (*k*).

—*In the round:* sculpture; free standing forms, with wood cut away on all sides, leaving object (*l*).

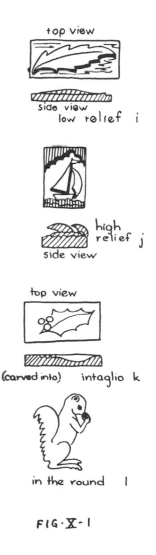

top view

side view
low relief i

high relief j
side view

top view

(carved into) intaglio k

in the round l

FIG·X·1

PLATE X

TECHNIQUES IN USING A KNIFE

A camper will usually begin whittling with the jackknife that is part of his camping equipment. If this knife has a small blade, he will have an easy time starting whittling projects, but if it has only the large utilitarian blade found in the common pocket knife, he will have difficulty going beyond the first steps. As he progresses, he will feel the need of a knife with smaller blades for fine work. The first steps, however, will come with his own tool, so the counselor will need to start there to help him to get the knife in good condition, to learn to use it, and to know what he can expect to accomplish with it.

To Sharpen a Knife

Since sharpening the blade is so important to whittling, the steps are given here. Even a new knife needs this attention before it can be used successfully. Standard equipment in a camp living group should include several sharpening stones, oil, and steel wool for cleaning blades. Many sharpening stones have two coarsenesses of material; at least one such stone should be availabe for use on knives that have somehow developed nicks in the blades. Eventually each whittler will want his own pocket stone to carry with him; as he learns to use a good sharp knife, he will find constant use for his own stone.

There are innumerable theories on the way to sharpen tools. In general, one method rotates the blade on the stone, the other uses a back-and-forth motion. For beginners, the rotating method seems safer, but as the camper progresses in skill, he will find his own most satisfactory way.

Steps

1. Lay stone on flat surface, or hold between thumb and forefinger (be sure they are below surface of stone). Lay knife on surface (Figure X-2 *a*).
2. Rotate knife with back edge flat, making stroke toward back edge. Turn and reverse motion (2 *b*). Repeat many times. Or, draw knife across stone, along edge, then turn and repeat on other side (2 *c*).
3. Clean rust, dirt, or pitch off blade (not edge) with piece of steel wool or oiled rag (2 *d*).
4. Finish on piece of leather (strop) fastened to block for fine edge (2 *e*).
5. If there is a nick, use coarse stone first, raising back edge of knife, and wearing entire edge of blade away until nick disappears (2 *f*).
6. Try it out on a piece of wood to see if it is sharp. Keep working at it and repeat often (2 *g*).
7. Oil hinges with machine oil for easy opening and closing (2 *h*).

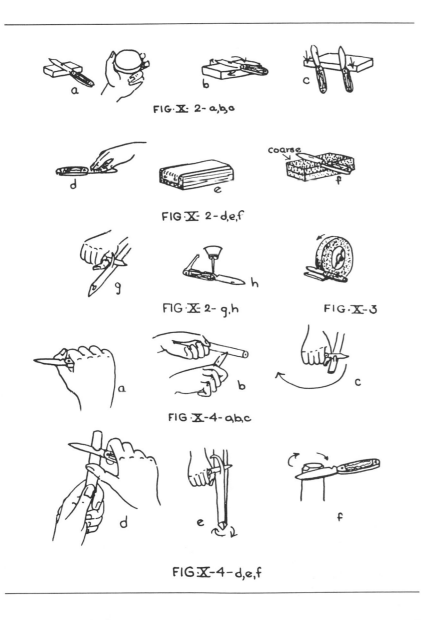

FIG. X: 2-a,b,c

FIG. X: 2-d,e,f

FIG. X: 2-g,h   FIG. X-3

FIG. X-4-a,b,c

FIG. X-4-d,e,f

To Handle a Knife

Skill in using a knife comes only with practice, but a few hints on how to start will give a camper confidence. All beginners need supervision at this stage. The group should not be too large, so that the counselor can keep an eye on each knife wielder. Pieces of soft wood such as pine (box ends or kindling without knots) should be provided for each camper for practice on cuts and strokes—and on keeping the knife sharp. Beginners usually start with pointing sticks or making shavings and are taught to whittle away from the body or against a whittling board (Figure X-6).

Steps

1. Grasp knife firmly in hand, thumb curled around handle (Figure X-4 *a*).
2. Cut away from hand holding stick (Figure X-4 *b*).
3. Be sure nothing is in the path of the knife, if it should slip (Figure X-4 *c*). When a whittler progresses to cutting a notch, make a pin or buckle, the motion of the knife is controlled by small cuts, holding wood with one hand close to the cutting.
4. To make a cut, brace wood and knife with thumbs, and cut in a *V*, taking out a chip. Cut small bits (Figure X-4 *d*).
5. To round, cut with the grain, turning stick as you go (Figure X-4 *e*).

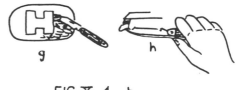

FIG. X-4-g,h

6. To round end, cut at angle, turning stick (Figure X-4 *f*).
7. To decorate, mark lightly with pencil; make a "stopper" cut, and then cut away small bits until design is accomplished (4 *g*).
8. Hold thumbs, behind hinge joint—don't push blade with thumb (Figure X-4 *h*).

TECHNIQUES IN FINISHING WOOD

With Sandpaper

Get the article as smooth as possible with knife or other tools. Then use medium sandpaper (#1). If the piece is straight, as a peg, wrap small piece of sandpaper around the stick, and rub up and down the length of the stick, sanding whole peg at once (Figure X-5 *a*). If piece is smaller, or flat, rub flat piece of sandpaper up and down with the grain. Avoid using circular motion, as the marks of the sandpaper will show, requiring more sanding (Figure X-5 *b*). For designs, use small folded bits of sandpaper to reach small crevices (Figure X-5 *c*).

To sand rounded ends, hold sandpaper in palm of hand, and rub ends in the paper (Figure X-5 *d*).

Finish with very fine sandpaper. Do not use knife after sandpaper has been used as fine particles of sand will be imbedded in wood, and these will dull the knife blade.

With Oil, Wax, etc.

When the piece is well sanded, paste wax may be rubbed into the wood with cloth or fingers. Let wax dry, then polish with soft cloth. The wax will bring out some color in the wood. Repeat several times for hard finish.

Wax shoe polish will give a stain and a polish. Let dry, and add plain wax for good polish.

Wood may be stained with linseed oil or wood stains, to bring out the grain of the wood or to add color. Rub well into wood, let it dry, and then wax and polish.

PROJECTS

Rounding a Stick for a Peg—a Practice Project

Learning to round a stick is a good project to help campers get the feel of whittling and finishing. Scrap pine from box ends or lumber or kindling wood may be used, with the camper's jackknife as the only tool. Pegs may be used in cabins, washrooms, dining halls, or wherever pegs are needed.

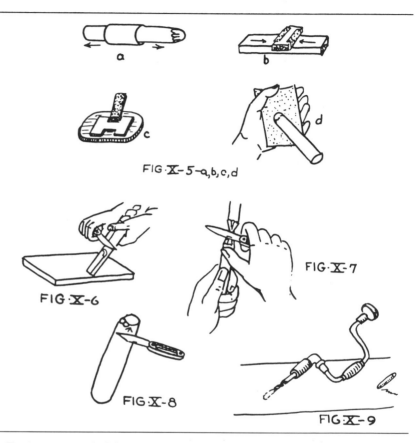

FIG·X-5-a,b,c,d

FIG·X-6

FIG·X-7

FIG·X-8

FIG·X-9

Equipment needed: jackknife (sharp, of course); whittling board; sandpaper; wax; bit and brace for hole in wall; plastic wood.

Materials needed: piece of straight soft wood, such as pine, about 9 inches to ten inches long, without knots.

Steps

1. Use whittling board on bench or floor, to steady piece of wood. Hold stick at one end, other end on board, and cut down the stick, cutting slivers or shavings. Cut squared edges first, turning stick as work progresses until it begins to be rounded (Figure X-6).

2. Continue cutting, turning stick until desired size for most of length. Then turn stick around, and cut other end to match. Look at stick to see where more cutting is needed, and round it evenly. Take off small amounts rather than big shavings. Make desired thickness. Make as smooth as possible with knife.
3. A long stick is easier to work with, but if short pegs are desired, cut in two by cutting at angles (Figure X-7), bracing with thumbs.
4. Trim off ends, cutting away small bits as stick is turned (Figure X-8).
5. Sand as in Figure X-5 and wax.
6. To insert in wall: drill hole with bit and brace at slight angle (Figure X-9). Make hole just smaller than peg, then whittle end of peg to fit snugly. Put bit of plastic wood in hole, then hammer in peg.

Simplest Activities in Whittling

First steps in woodworking will be with the jackknife. The camper will gain confidence, appreciation, and skill as he makes the simplest articles for camp living or begins the first craft article from wood. Many of these projects will be from wood picked up on the campsite. Good conservation practices are important; even when wood is plentiful, campers should learn to select and use wood carefully. An appreciation of the beauty of wood will be developed as campers sand and wax small pieces of wood for pins, belt buckles, or buttons. Good craftsmanship will come in the trimming of ends of sticks used for gadgets, lashed articles.

Equipment needed: jackknife; egg-beater drill; sharpening tools; saw; vise; sandpaper; wax; linseed oil or stain.

Materials needed: twigs, sticks, etc., found on site; safety pins or pin-backs; plastic wood or household cement.

— *Sticks for cooking*—from green sticks (Figure X-10); cut carefully where stick will not be missed; trim ends; make broilers, toasters.
— *Cooking helps* (Figure X-11): pot hooks; shavings and fuzz sticks (see Figure XII-6.); cranes, tripods.
— *Pegs and hooks* (Figure X-12): forked sticks—trim off back for flat surface to fit against wall, tree, or tent pole; drill holes with egg-beater drill if hook will be screwed to wall.
— *Pins, buttons, toggles, belts:* find interesting bits of wood; saw slices from branches; polish to bring out beauty of the grain; oil and wax (Figure X-13). Carve initials or leaves or simple designs

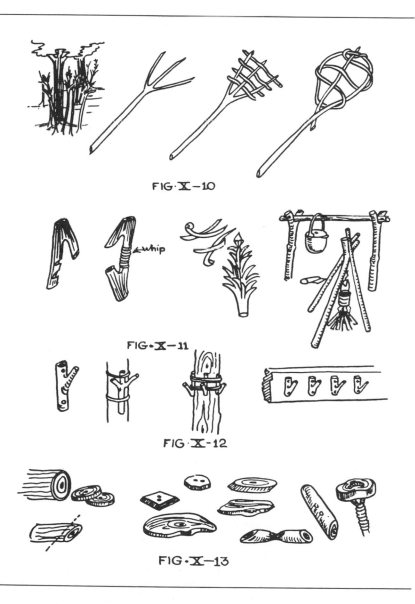

FIG·X—10

FIG·X—11

FIG·X—12

FIG·X—13

(Figure X-14). Make belts from interesting pieces of various kinds of wood, polished to show grain. Trim edges, drill holes for thong with egg-beater drill (Figure X-15).

—*Letter openers, butter or cheese knives* (Figure X-16): select a stick big around as thumb; look for interesting knots and curves. Decide on length of handle and leave bark on this end, or peel and carve design on handle. On blade end, draw the blade down the center of the stick (Figure X-16 *a*). Whittle wood away from both sides of this line, so the blade of knife is in the center of the handle. Make cutting edge of knife and point thinner than top edge. Sand and wax letter openers. Sand butter or cheese knives, and oil with vegetable oil.

—*To drill holes in buttons and toggles* (Figure X-17): place on whittling board or in vise; mark places for hole with pencil; use egg-beater drill; hold straight; press down *lightly* on handle.

—*To make groove in toggles, etc.* (Figure X-18): mark place with pencil; cut carefully all around.

—*To put pins on backs of wooden pins* (Figure X-19): gouge out small groove in back of pin; sand; put in small safety pin with small amount of plastic wood; smooth and take off excess plastic wood. Or, use commercial type pin-back with household cement; let dry for an hour or more.

Place pin above center line to make it hang correctly without tipping forward when pinned in place. Place so that the pin point is used from right to left (for right-handed use), or vice versa.

Progressive Steps in Whittling

From simple steps in trimming edges and smoothing surfaces, the whittler can progess to carving in low or high relief, in intaglio, or in the round (see Figure X-1). Equipment will be much the same as for first steps in whittling, except that a small-bladed knife will be essential. Beginner's wood-carving tools, or knife sets such as X-acto knives with varying shaped blades, may also be used at this stage.

—*Buttons, pins, buckles, in relief or in intaglio:* draw design lightly on wood; cut stopper cuts at edges of design; make small cuts away from the design edge; work against the grain to avoid splintering on stopper

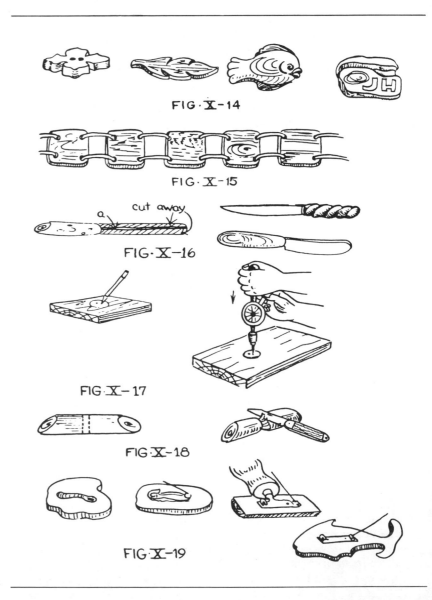

FIG·X-14

FIG·X-15

cut away

FIG·X-16

FIG·X-17

FIG·X-18

FIG·X-19

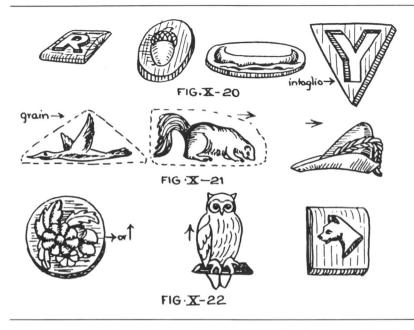

FIG·X-20

FIG·X-21

FIG·X-22

cut (Figure X-20). Cut out shapes of leaves, animals, etc.; make veins, features, etc., with knife cuts. Sometimes a coping saw is used to cut outline (Figure X-21). Make heads, ships, animals, etc., in relief or intaglio (Figure X-22).

Carving in the Round

—*Letter openers, knives, with carved handles* (Figure X-23): make blade as in Figure X-16; wrap narrow strip of paper around handle, and trace edges with pencil. Cut away 1/4 inch between marks. Smooth with knife, rounding edges. Sand well and polish.
—*Forks, spoons* (Figure X-24): start with block of wood; draw shape on sides, bottom, and top. Cut away in small bits, shaping handle and bowl as you go. Scrape and shape as desired. Sand well, then polish.
—*Animals, figures:* figures in the round stand free; they may be carved on a base, may be attached to a base, or may stand by themselves. Start with a piece of wood that suggests something, and go from there

(Figure X-25). Perhaps it makes you think of a horse. Carve around his nose and mouth, mane, then make ears last.

Select a piece of wood for size, length, thickness, width (Figure X-26). Mark off shape on three sides, two ends. Start by nicking shape on opposite sides, then connect on top by a groove. When a leg comes in front of body, cut body down slightly (shaded area above). Start with crouching or sitting figures rather than those that stand on legs.

Totems and Katchina dolls are good projects (Figure X-27). Wings are added by cutting slots, and inserting tab left on wing.

Balls in boxes and chains are "trick" whittling for the advanced craftsman (Figure X-28).

TECHNIQUES IN USING CARPENTRY TOOLS

A few carpentry tools will add to the possibilities for wood projects. These can be used with a good sturdy working space to give practice in handling and caring for basic tools.

—*Crosscut saw*—cuts across the grain of wood (Figure X-29 *a*).
—*Rip saw*—cuts with the grain of wood (Figure X-29 *b*).

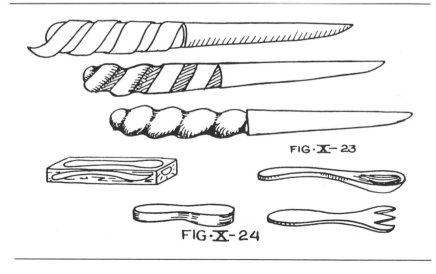

FIG·X-23

FIG·X-24

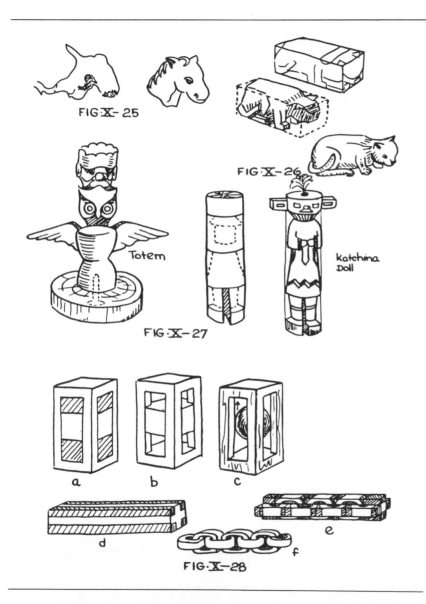

FIG X- 25

FIG X- 26

Totem

FIG X- 27

Katchina Doll

a   b   c

d   e

f

FIG X- 28

—*To saw*—hold board steady, braced close to place for cut. Follow a pencil line. Use steady, long strokes (Figure X-29 *c*).

—*Coping saw*—used for fine work. Hold wood on edge of bench, and saw straight up and down (Figure X-29 *d*).

—*Wood file*—use with steady strokes away from you (Figure X-30 *a*).

—*Vise and woodclamps*—used to hold wood while sawing, etc. (Figure X-30 *b*).

—*Plane and draw knife*—used to smooth wood (Figure X-30 *c* and *d*).

—*Bit and brace* (Figure X-31 *a*) and *Egg-beater drill* (Figure X-31 *b*)— used to make holes. Hold steady, and straight. Make a small depression in which to place tip of drill, to keep it from slipping.

—*Hammers*—hold at end of handle; strike sharp blows (Figure X-31 *c*).

—*Screwdriver*—hold straight; steady end of screw with one hand (Figure X-31 *d*).

PROJECTS USING CARPENTRY TOOLS

Candlesticks of Logs

Natural wood candlesticks may add just the right touch for decorations at special events or for mantels in cabins and other camp buildings. Wood from the woodpile or wood from dead-and-down trees may be used. Avoid using green wood.

Equipment needed: 3/4-inch bit and brace; vise; crosscut saw; sandpaper.

Materials needed: wood as desired; small nails or screws or glue.

Steps

1. Choose pieces of wood; saw in desired lengths, leaving bark on. Add feet (Figure X-32 *b*) if desired.
2. Mark places for candles, make small dent with nail, and bore 3/4-inch holes. Hold log in vise for boring holes (Figure X-32 *a*).
3. Nail or glue bases or feet to tops for steadiness.

Wooden Book Cover

Book covers may be used for memory or log books and for albums. The wood may be decorated in a variety of ways—with raised figures or letters, with paints, with burning or carving. Hinges may be of leather or

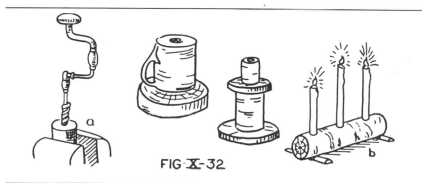

FIG·X-32

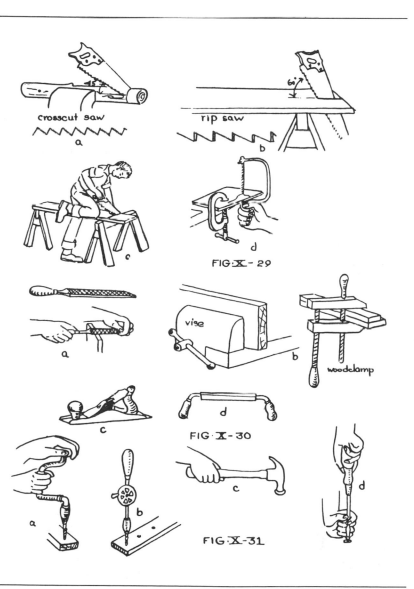

crosscut saw

a

rip saw

b

FIG·X-29

vise

woodclamp

a

b

c

d

FIG·X-30

a

b

c

d

FIG·X-31

of strips of copper or brass, or they may be purchased ready to screw in place. The book may be tied together with a leather thong.

Equipment needed: crosscut saw; sandpaper; egg-beater drill; wax and other finishing equipment; ruler and pencil; tools for decorating.

Materials needed: two pieces wood the desired size—plywood is good, or other thin wood; hinges and screws or brads; thong to tie; paper.

Steps

1. Plan size of book. This will be guided by the purpose and by paper to be used. Draw lines with ruler (Figure X-33 *a*).
2. Cut two pieces the desired size, keeping edges square.
3. From one piece (front) cut hinge piece (Figure X-33 *a*). Make this in good proportion to the cover. There are now two pieces for the front, one piece for the back.
4. Sand all edges and sides (follow grain of wood).
5. Mark places for hinges and for holes for thong (Figure X-33 *b*).

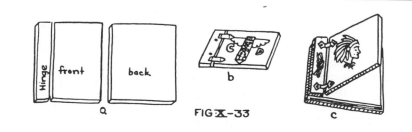

Hinge front back

a

b

c

FIG·X-33

6. Bore holes. Sand.
7. Decorate as desired. Consider the hinges and the thong in planning any decoration.
8. Place hinges.
9. Insert paper punched to match holes. Thread thong through back cover, paper, and front cover. Tie with square knot on top (Figure X-33 c).

Stools

Stools for cabins, tents, or campfire seats are good projects if rough wood is plentiful, and if a few carpentering tools are available. Logs from the woodpile, cross sections or slabs from sawmills may be used for the seat; legs are rough sticks from the woods or the woodpile.

Equipment needed: knife; crosscut saw; clamps; bit and brace with 1-inch bit; plane or drawknife; wood glue; sandpaper; ruler; oil and wax.

Materials needed: slab of wood as smooth as possible on top—pine is best for beginners, 14 inches by 8 inches is a good size; four sticks for legs, about 12 inches long 1½ inch thick.

Steps

1. Select logs and sticks. Leave bark on underside of seat and on legs for rustic appearance, if desired.
2. Smooth top with plane or drawknife (Figure X-34). Sand or leave tool marks.
3. Mark places for holes, placing them at equal distances from the corners (Figure X-35 *a*) on underside. Make holes with bit and brace, using a jig (Figure X-35 *b*); this consists of a board nailed to a base at desired angle. The bit rests against this angle to ensure each hole being drilled at same angle. Holes may be bored all the way through or only three-quarters of the way.
4. Whittle end of each leg to fit hole snugly. If holes do not go all the way through seat, put a little glue in hole; and hammer leg in place (Figure X-36 *a*). If holes go all the way through, fit wedge into leg at top (Figure X-36 *b*) and saw off any part of wedge that protrudes.
5. Even off legs at floor, so that stool stands evenly.
6. Finish top by sanding and waxing, or by oiling, as desired.

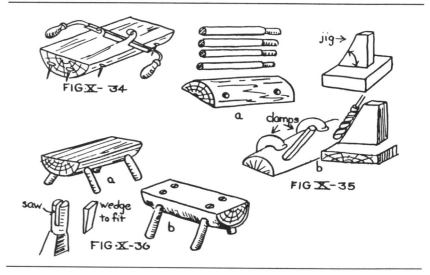

FIG X-34

FIG X-35

FIG X-36

Variations: Make seat from a thick cross section of log with three legs (Figure X-37).

Use slabs to make a Paul Bunyan campfire seat (Figure X-38).

Signs

Signs for tents and cabins, route signs on roads and paths, and signs leading to and designating special points of interest are all needed in camps, and the camper-craftsman can make them look rustic and out-of-

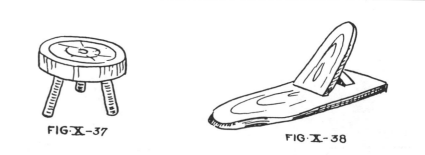

FIG X-37

FIG X-38

the-ordinary with twig or block letters, roughhewn or natural backgrounds, and so forth.

The first requisite of a sign is legibility; this is obtained by contrast in color, by size and shape of letters, and by selection of the appropriate materials for the sign. Letters may be painted, sawed out of blocks, or wood, constructed of twigs, or written in rope. An arrow may be added to help in showing direction. Capital letters are easier to make and to read than small letters. Signs used on trees should be hung from branches or lashed in place instead of being nailed to tree.

Signs made of unfinished wood will weather and grow dark. A stained, dark background, used with shellacked or varnished letters, will stay more legible than one that is not finished with some protective material.

Equipment needed: saws—crosscut and coping; jackknife; egg-beater drill; hammer or screwdriver; sandpaper; glue, finishing equipment—wax, shellac, stain, etc.

Materials needed: boards, slabs, logs, as needed; twigs, finished wood, rope for letters; brads, double pointed tacks, screws.

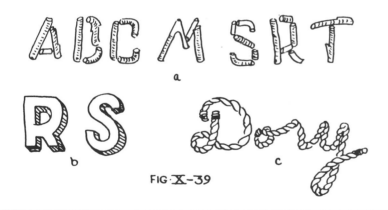

FIG·X–39

FIG·X–40

Steps

1. Make a plan and design for the sign. Make a paper pattern of letters, blocking in to be sure of good proportion, good spacing, good legibility. Make letters large enough to be seen easily from distance.

Letters may be made of twigs (Figure X-39 *a*), or of blocks cut from outdoor plywood or 1/2-inch plank (Figure X-39 *a*). Sand and varnish well before nailing or screwing to signs. They may be made of rope—using script (Figure X-39 *c*). Or, they may be carved out of the background (Figure X-40 *b*) by intaglio; stenciled (see Chapter VII on Printing and Stenciling); or painted free hand—block in first in pencil.

Backgrounds may be made of a single plank or slab or half-log (Figure X-40, *a, b, c, d*). They may be made of plank cut in specific shapes (Figure X-40 *e, f*); or of two or three planks held together by lashed or nailed frame (Figure X-40 *g, h*) or by cleats on back of sign, if back will not be seen (Figure X-40 *i*).

Frames or posts for hanging signs may be nailed, screwed, bolted (Figure X-40 *e*) or lashed (Figure X-40 *g*) together.

2. Complete background piece—cut it out, sand it, get hangers ready, etc.
3. Make letters, using paper letters to check spacing. Drill tiny holes for brads in block or twig letters, putting two or more holes in each letter or twig. Whip ends of ropes. Fasten letters or paint or carve. Use small brads for block or twig letters, double pointed tacks to straddle the rope for rope letters. A spot of wood glue on the back of the letters or rope helps hold them in place.
4. Varnish whole sign for outdoor use, or paint as desired. If background and letters are painted in contrasting colors, the painting should be done separately, and the pieces allowed to dry completely before assembling.

Frame for Bulletin Board, Picture, or Mirror

The project described here is a group project for an inside bulletin board. It is made of rough sticks with square lashing as the binding (see any campcraft book for lashing). Lashing is a campcraft skill which can also be an art if the lashing is done with fine cord, if the sticks are trimmed well, and if great care is exercised in making the lashing.

Equipment needed: rip saw and crosscut saw; knife; wood chisel; mallet; screwdriver; vise and wedge; egg-beater drill; yardstick and pencil.

Materials needed: piece of wallboard of desired size (be sure thumbtacks will go in the board easily); two sticks 3/4-inch thick for the frame, one for the length, one for the sides; wood for pegs; cord for lashing; eight small screws.

Steps

1. Cut wallboard, if necessary, to desired size, being sure sides are straight.
2. Measure and cut the long stick, so it is about 2 inches longer than the board on both sides. Measure and cut short stick, so it is the same at top and bottom (Figure X-41 *a*).

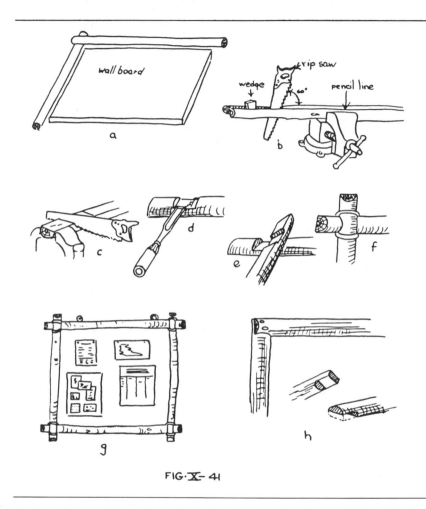

FIG·X- 41

3. Put short stick in vise; draw line lengthwise down middle of stick (Figure X-41 *b*). Cut in two, along line, with rip saw. Keep moving stick in vise, so the cutting edge of saw is near part of stick held by vise. Put small wedge in the sawed cut, to spring the two pieces apart. Do the same with the longer stick (this will take two or three people). You will now have two long and two short half-round pieces.

4. Place wallboard on floor; measure the sticks, determining best place to cross them at corners. Mark these places for notches.
5. With crosscut saw, cut 1/4 inch to 1/2 inch into back of top sticks, and into front of under sticks (Figure X-41 *c*). With knife or chisel, chip out the wood between cuts, and make notch smooth. Do not make notch too big (Figure X-41 *d*).
6. Trim ends of sticks with knife for beveled appearance (Figure X-41 *g*).
7. Fit together, and drill a small hole in back of each joint, through under stick, and into top stick about half the thickness of the stick. Whittle small pegs, and peg the frame together from the back. Put a drop of glue into each hole before driving in the peg. Let dry, and trim off tops of peg, if necessary.
8. Fasten joints with square lashing (Figure X-41 *g*).
9. Fasten screw rings to top stick for hanging (Figure X-41 *g*).
10. Screw wallboard to back of frame with at least two screws on each side.

Variation: Finished boards for frame will have less rustic appearance but may fit into some buildings better than a rough stick frame. The notching for this type of wood may be made with overlapping corners (Figure X-41 *h*). Mark places for cuts, saw through wood, chip out with wood chisel, and fit together. Drill two holes with small drill for each corner; whittle pegs to fit; insert with bit of glue on pegs, and clamp corners together to dry.

Birdhouses

A good group project in preparation for spring use is to make birdhouses to attract birds to the campsite. This is a fine project for small groups which will be camping during week ends the year round; the houses may be made in town during the winter, and the purpose of a spring week end will be to erect them where birds can be watched during the nesting season.

Equipment needed: crosscut saw; hammer and small nails or screwdriver and screws; paint, stain, etc.; brushes; bit and brace.

Materials needed: six pieces wood—fininshed or with bark on; twig for "doorstep;" ring for hanging.

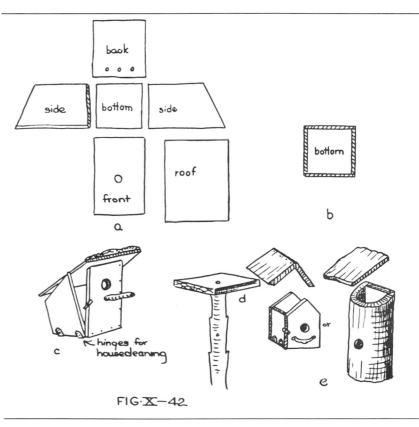

FIG·X—42

Steps

1. Check a book that gives more detail about birdhouses, and decide on type to make. Different types of houses are built for different types of birds; the example given here is for a bluebird home.
2. Cut wood so that there are six pieces, four for sides, one for roof, one for floor (Figure X-42 *a*).
3. Sand edges, fit together (Figure X-42 *b*).
4. Cut opening in front piece.
5. Nail or screw together. Make side so that it can be removed easily, for cleaning out house (Figure X-42 *c*).

6. Place twig near opening for doorstep.
7. Stain or paint green or brown, to make inconspicuous, unless the wood has natural bark on it or is weathered.
8. Put ring or hook on back or top to fasten house to tree or make pole with platform to screw to bottom of house (Figure X-42 *d*).

Variations: Make birdhouses of different shapes and sizes (Figure X-42 *e*).

PROJECTS USING WOODCARVING TOOLS

Woodcarving tools consist of gouges and chisels or firmers with handles that fit into the palm of the hand or with handles that are used with mallets. The shape of the metal end determines the type of cut that can be made. Gouges make curved and *V*-shaped cuts; chisels make straight cuts. For the first steps, the tools that have handles that fit in palm of the hand are good; these are similar to linoleum cutting tools. Sets of tools usually have ''slips''—shaped sharpening stones to aid in keeping the tools sharp. Woodcarving firmers are different from carpenter's chisels because they have blades that are sharp on both sides of the blade, as contrasted with the carpenter's chisel which is sharpened on only one side. There are many shapes and sizes of these gouges and chisels; a small woodcarving set gives the basic tools and is adequate for camper projects (Figure X-43). A bench block (Figure X-44) is an essential piece of equipment in using woodcarving tools.

Dishes, Bowls, Plates

All kinds of wooden utensils can be made from pieces of scrap lumber that are free from knots and cracks or from interesting natural pieces. These are products of pioneer crafts for such utensils were used in the daily living of pioneers and early settlers. One American song tells of the girl who was ready to marry for, among other things, she had ''a spoon and a cup and a trencher.''

Equipment needed: crosscut saw; gouges; jackknife; bench block; coping saw; finishing equipment—sandpaper, etc.

Materials needed: blocks of wood as desired—for a small plate, about 8 inches by 8 inches by 3/4 inch; for a bowl, about 4 inches by 4 inches by 4 inches.

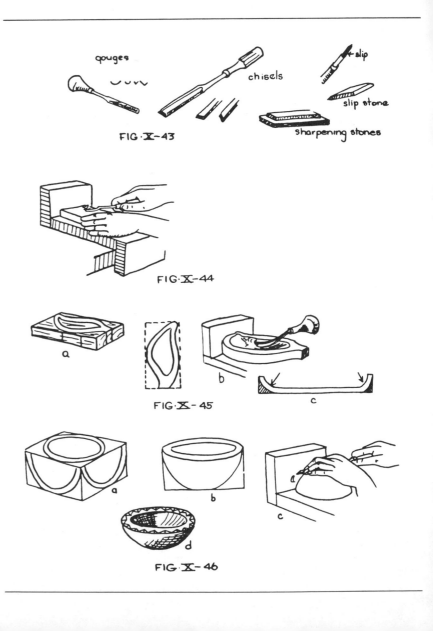

FIG·X-43

FIG·X-44

FIG·X-45

FIG·X-46

Steps

1. Plan shape of utensil. Draw on all sides of block to be used (Figure X-45 *a*). For a plate, the bottom may be cut out in a desired shape, the bowl of the plate conforming with the outside shape.
2. Saw off excess wood with coping saw, leaving 1/2-inch to 3/4-inch margin outside pencil marks of pattern. With jackknife, continue trimming and beveling until edges are as desired. Take off small bits of wood, using stopper cuts to prevent long splinters (Figure X-45 *b*).
3. Use gouges to dig out bowl; cut with the grain as much as possible. Turn the piece and go in opposite direction when the curve of side is reached. Make gradual deepenings, rather than sharp angles, and proceed slowly (Figure X-45 *c*).
4. Finish by sandpapering until satin smooth. Stain, if desired, and wax or shellac when dry. Rub down with very fine sandpaper, and wax or shellac again. Repeat several times. For salad dishes, use vegetable oil rather than shellac on inside surfaces.

A *bowl* is made in similar fashion to the plate, but the starting piece of wood is deeper, and the gouging of the inside of the bowl is more difficult (Figure X-46). Simple carving on the rim of the bowl makes the project more interesting to advanced craftsmen.

A Noggin or Hike Cup

Hike cups may be made from blocks of wood, in same manner as a bowl, but with a handle (Figure X-47). Noggin is the name given to a cup made from a burl of a tree. The burl is a protuberance where there has been some injury to the tree which has healed over completely, so there is bark all over it. The burl can be sawed from the tree in the same manner as removing a limb. The spot on the tree should be painted to prevent rotting. It is easier to make noggins from *green* wood, since the burl is a knot, and therefore very hard (Figure X-48). Gouge out with wood gouge. Sand and finish as desired.

Using Driftwood, "Character" Wood, Cypress Knees, etc.

There are many interesting forms in driftwood, roots, and other pieces of wood found in the open. Sometimes these suggest a use, as a lamp

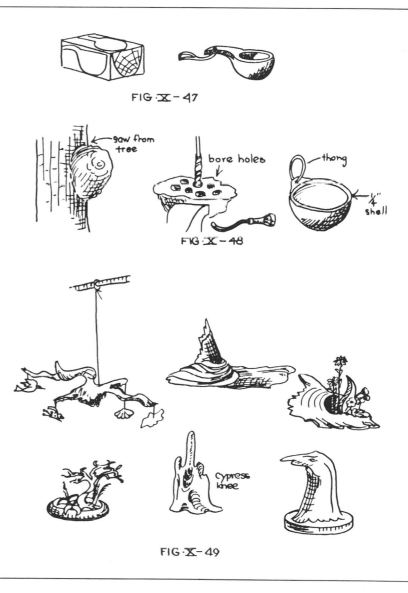

FIG X-47

FIG X-48

FIG X-49

base or a flower holder; sometimes they are beautiful in themselves or in some flower arrangement. The camper with an appreciative eye will soon find small and large pieces of wood that resemble something or that suggest beauty.

Some of these will have spots of rotted material in them; some will be enhanced by scraping or by sanding; many will be useful or beautiful as they are. A jackknife to dig out crevices, a bit of sandpaper and some steel wool, and wax to bring out the beauty will be the only tools needed.

Hang some pieces to resemble birds in flight, or make mobiles of other interesting nature objects. Put some on mantels with candles or flowers. Use some as bases for candles or lamps. There are many possibilities.

Chip Carving

This is a form of carving in geometric designs cut with a single-edge razor blade or stencil knife on a flat surface, such as a pin blank, box, or notebook cover. It is a good step in progression in working with wood, but is not a craft directly related to out-of-door living.

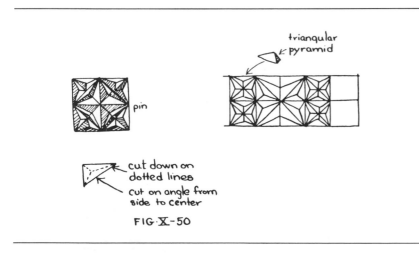

triangular pyramid

pin

cut down on dotted lines

cut on angle from side to center

FIG·X-50

Bulletins, Exhibits, Signs, Newspapers

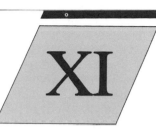

—On bulletin boards or group notices, use colored paper for background.
—Make it so interesting that everyone must stop to read!

Bulletin Boards
FIG · XI - 1A

Every camp has some use for bulletin boards, notices, signs, exhibits, and similar means of giving information, pointing directions, outlining step-by-step projects, interesting campers and staff, and so forth. Good arrangement of such notices and directions will result in more attention to the particular item, and use of visual aids, color, interesting printing, and pictures will help to catch the eye and tell the story. Too often a bulletin board is so cluttered with bits of paper that no one bothers to look at any of them; sometimes a nature trail is carefully laid, but the signs are so difficult to read that no one takes time to read them; the camp newspaper may be full of well-written news items, but unless the pages are attractive and interesting and well arranged, few will ever know what is in them. So an arts and crafts point of view may well go hand in hand with the interest that lays out the nature trail, the interest that fosters creative writing for the camp newspaper, or the interest that calls for posters for Saturday's special activities. The craftsmen of the camp may wish to have an exhibit for Visitors' Day; the photographers may sponsor a snapshot contest; the campcraft counselors may be encouraging a campcraft area where anyone who wanders may learn by reading and looking.

A few general hints will help in arrangement and planning any visual aid:

—Be brief—be clear.
—Use sketches, pictures, cutouts, colored paper to highlight.
—Plan the poster, exhibit, etc., before making final copy.
—Make the message fit the size and shape of the background.

Posters

FIG·XI-1B

will also have an effect on the degree of use. Bulletins that are on the beaten paths will be read more than those tucked away in some poorly lighted, out-of-the-way corner. Posters that spotlight a special event are most effective when they appear in unexpected places—where there usually are no such notices.

In the counselors' room, in unit huts, at the waterfront, in the campcraft supply hut, at the craft workshop, in the office, or in the infirmary, there may be bulletin boards that need constant care to make them do the job for which they were intended and to bring about the results hoped for by some staff members or campers. (See also chapter on Photography, Figures XXI-1 and 2.)

EXHIBITS

Exhibits may be displayed in many different areas of the camp. They may be changed or added to by individuals or groups as the days progress; they may be set up for a special occasion, such as Visitors' Day or the joint campfire of two units or cabins. Some exhibits take place out-of-doors, as in the campcraft area (Figures IX-2).

For craft exhibits, it is well to have dark paper or cloth to put under the articles. Exhibits need good signs which tell the story without further explanation. One should avoid cluttering up the exhibit with too many articles. But it is also important to exhibit the work of all grades of craftsmen, not just those who excel. Age, experience, and new interests all serve to make a craft article interesting to the viewer, and such details should be included in the identification when there is such a label.

BULLETIN BOARDS

It is important that some one person (or group) be responsible for each bulletin board (see Chapter X for making bulletin boards), to keep it up-to-date, to remove out-of-date notices, to group items together, to present special, interest-catching items that will make people come to read. Bulletin boards need constant "editing" to keep people coming to read them. They are of little use, no matter how important the messages, unless the groups for whom they are intended read them. Interest, color, highlights, legibility of notices, and brevity all contribute to reader participation (Figures XI-1 A and B). The place where the bulletin is hung

LABELS, NOTICES, SIGNS

In the nature den, the camp library, the craft workshop, the campcraft storeroom, at the waterfront, or almost anywhere in camp, there is need for labels and notices and signs. Since the purpose of these is to give information, to call attention, or to give directions, it is important that they be neat, well lettered, attractive, interest-catching. Good printing and margins produce legibility that puts over the message; pictures and sketches lighten the subject matter, and colors attract the eye. Labels, notices, and signs may be made of cardboard or paper, tin or other metals, or of wood.

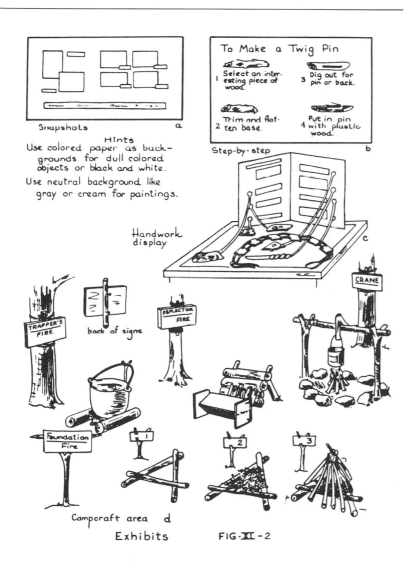

Snapshots   a

Hints
Use colored paper as backgrounds for dull colored objects or black and white.

Use neutral background like gray or cream for paintings.

To Make a Twig Pin

1 Select an interesting piece of wood.

2 Trim and flatten base.

3 Dig out for pin or back.

4 Put in pin with plastic wood.

Step-by-step   b

Handwork display   c

TRAPPER'S FIRE

back of signs

REFLECTOR FIRE

CRANE

Foundation Fire

1

2

3

Campcraft area   d

Exhibits   FIG·XI-2

Cardboard or Paper Labels, Signs, Notices

Equipment needed: lettering pens and brushes, felt-tip markers, ruler and pencil.

Materials needed: light cardboard, drawing, construction, or typing paper (white and colored); poster and watercolor paints, crayons, India ink (black and in colors); paint, clear and masking tape, whiteout fluid.

Tin or Metal Labels

Equipment needed: tin shears; files; drill or punch; paint brushes; permanent felt marking pens.

Materials needed: ends of tin cans; sheets of metal (see Chapter VI); wire or binder twine; enamel paint.

Wooden Signs

Equipment needed: woodcarving or woodburning tools; sandpaper; saw; brushes.

Materials needed: wood scraps; wire or binder twine; paint or varnish or shellac.

Here are some hints for sign or label making:

—Make a rough sketch on paper—actual size.
—Fit message to size and shape of paper. Keep it brief. Don't crowd it. Keep it clear. Make it interesting.
—Draw guide lines for lettering to keep it straight.
—Use large letters for important words, smaller letters for explanatory matter.
—Use twig letters sometimes.
—Add a sketch or a picture cut out of a magazine or a silhouette for eye appeal and to help tell the story.
—Use the question technique sometimes.
—Use good combinations of colors—dark letters on light background, light or white on dark background.
—For metal labels, use enamel paint and/or cutouts; permanent felt markers.
—Make rustic holders for cards.

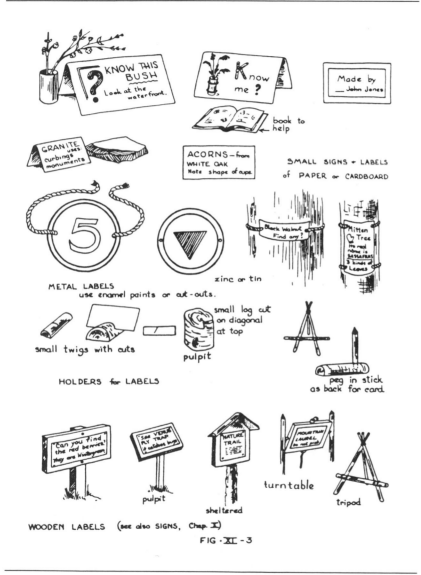

FIG · XI - 3

FIG · XI -4

—For cards that hold articles, use round elastic to hold articles, tie in back with square knot (see Chapter II, Figure II-16).
—Use borders of paint, ink, tape, etc.
—Varnish or spray with plastic all signs to be used out-of-doors, to make them waterproof.

CAMP NEWSPAPER LAYOUT

Although the writing of items for the camp newspaper may fall in departments other than the arts and crafts department, the layout and design of the paper will fall into the art field. Many of the suggestions for signs and bulletins will guide the editors and layout chairmen. Dummies help in good arrangement. Clear-cut headings and key letters, and occasional sketches will make the pages more interesting and readable. White space on each page will make for more attractive pages as well. If the paper is to be mimeographed by the campers, the job of cutting the stencils should be done by someone who knows how to do it. A good working space for the printers should be arranged and carried out. Good workmanship habits can be learned by the committee in charge of printing and a well-done page turned out to the satisfaction of producers and readers.

Correlation with Campcraft

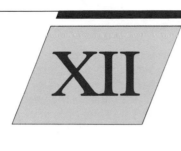

XII

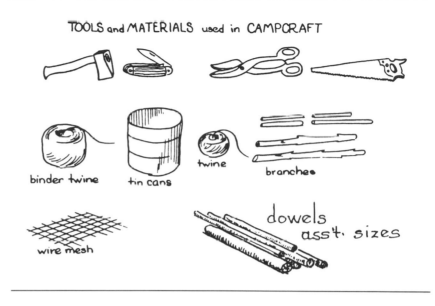

TOOLS and MATERIALS used in CAMPCRAFT

binder twine   tin cans   twine   branches

wire mesh   dowels asst. sizes

Campcraft is the term generally used to describe the skills needed for comfortable living out-of-doors. These skills usually include outdoor cooking, fireplace and fire building, ropework, toolcraft, trailing, using compasses and mapping, and the erecting or building of shelters. These skills and the activities that grow from them are the basis of a good camping program, when the emphasis is on learning to know and to use and to enjoy the out-of-doors. Learning to live with the woods as well as in the woods means that a good camper is a good woodsman, a good cook and fire builder, a good conservationist. This book is written to help integrate arts and crafts into all parts of this living in the out-of-doors. Here we will deal mainly with the craftsmanship that may grow with progressive steps in the various skills.

The camper brings good craft techniques into his camping when he learns to make a fuzz stick for his firebuilding, or when he makes a well finished article of camp furniture with his lashing. As he uses his imagination and craft skills to make a better design or a more beautiful article, he has become a craftsman as well as a camper. Good workmanship and good use of tools and materials will spell the difference between a beginner's project and a craftsman's article.

The chapters on Knotting and Braiding, on Whittling and Woodwork, on Mapping, and on Indian and Pioneer Crafts all present projects that may grow from a campcraft skill. This chapter presents some additional projects. *The Campcraft Book,* published by American Camping Association, will provide material for learning the basic skills of knot tying, lashing, use of knife, fire building, cooking, compass work, and so forth.[1]

LASHING

Lashing is a method of binding sticks together with cord, twine, or rope. Sticks used may be dried branches, dowels (purchased from a lumber company), broom handles, bamboo, or plastic pipes of various circumferences (used by plumbers). Lashing is used to make camp furnishings, temporary construction, and small craft articles (see any campcraft book). A piece of equipment will hold together and serve a utilitarian purpose if not neat and trimmed, but it takes on the quality of a craft project when these details are made part of the activity. The appearance of the article is measurably improved if the ends of wood are sawed or trimmed with a knife, and if the lashing is well done, with ends tucked underneath the windings. Pieces will hold together better when the joining parts are notched and fitted. Good planning for the particular piece with much imagination and creativity in making use of what is at hand to develop a one-of-a-kind piece and to add ingenious touches will make the project more satisfying and more interesting (Figure XII-1).

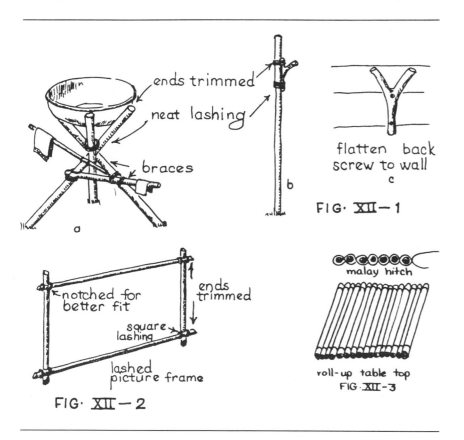

ends trimmed

neat lashing

braces

a

flatten back
screw to wall
c

b

FIG. XII—1

notched for
better fit

ends
trimmed

square
lashing

lashed
picture frame

FIG. XII—2

malay hitch

roll-up table top
FIG. XII-3

Picture Frame

This is made with four sticks, lashed with square lashing at the corners. Measure picture, with mat if desired, and cut sticks to overlap about 1 inch at corners. Notch sticks where they join, so they will fit firmly. Lash with hard-finished cord, such as Derrycord or Belfast cord. Cut ends to slant, to show grain of wood, or trim with knife. Small picture frames for postcards or photographs may be made with twigs and string (Figure XII-2).

Roll-up Table Top

This is made with a series of very fine straight sticks, held together with the Malay hitch—see Figure XII-3. Measure sticks for table top, and collect very fine shoots, rushes, cane, or bamboo about the thickness of a pencil. Trim ends so they are of same length and smooth at ends, and bind with fine cord with Malay hitch (Figure XII-3). Fasten end of cord with square knots, leaving enough cord to tie around roll for transportation. Make table frame as desired with lashed sticks.

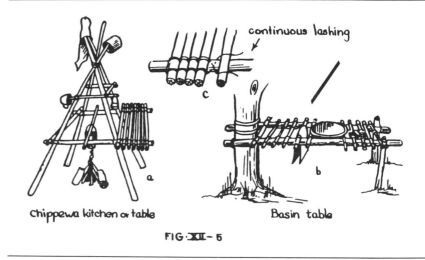

continuous lashing

c

a

Chippewa kitchen or table

b

Basin table

FIG. XII-5

Chippewa and Other Tables

The Chippewa type table is a special lashed table that is a whole kitchen in itself (Figure XII-4 *a*). It may be made in different ways with a series of table tops or with a fire in the center and pots hung from cranes crossing the frame.

A table may be made between two trees with spaces left for dishpans or basins (Figure XII-4 *b*). Posts may be placed in the ground where trees are not available in convenient spots though tables lashed to trees are sturdier than others.

KNIFE CRAFT

A good sharp knife and skill in handling it will make a camper's life easier—and more fun. Making shavings and fuzz sticks for starting fires is a test of both skill and knife care. Shavings may be made from any stick picked up at the cook-out site to make the simplest, most effective tinder. When shavings are left on the stick the product is called a *fuzz stick*. Small fuzz sticks (Figure XII-5 *a*) are made from short pieces, with five to ten shavings made on one side; the small fuzz sticks are piled one on top of another to make the base of a fire. A craftsman's fuzz stick will be larger (Figures XII-5 *b, c*) with shavings on the stick all around and a pointed end to stand the fuzz stick in the ground. With kindling piled around the fuzz stick, fire building is simple. Fuzz sticks are especially good to make when wood is damp or wet, as the inside of the stick is always drier than the outside. See Figure XII-5.

Fuzz Stick

Equipment needed: sharp knife; working surface.

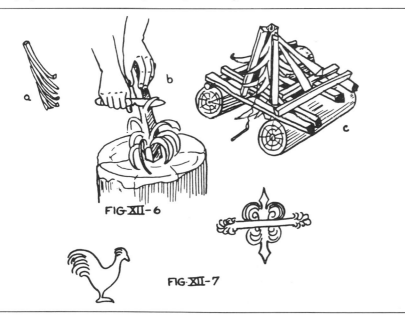

FIG·XII-6

FIG·XII-7

Material needed: piece softwood (pine kindling, etc.) about 10 inches long, 1 inch thick, without knots in it.

Steps

1. Hold stick at top with one hand, with stick braced on bench, stump, or whittling board. (Figure XII-5 *b*).
2. Cut long, slim shavings down the stick (avoid short, thick ones, starting at top, and making shavings as long as possible. Cut into wood at bottom, to keep from cutting shavings off, and draw knife out at bottom of stroke (Figure XII-5 *b*).
3. Turn stick as work progresses, making shavings even on all sides.
4. Point end of top of stick so it will stand in ground (Figure XII-5 *c*).

Swedish craftsmen use this technique in making intricate trees, crosses, and animals for Christmas decorations. Southern mountain craftsmen make roosters of twigs, making the tails like a fuzz stick. Camp craftsmen can explore these same activities for favors or ornaments.

Broilers

Broilers and toasters for cooking (Figure XII-7) are made from *green* wood (cut with care, of course!). A search will disclose the right stick with thumb-thick handle and the desired type of fork or forks. With a long end and green weaving shoots, a woven broiler may be made. If there is a straight stick in the middle, small green sticks may be woven across the rim. Small peg-like crosspieces may be inserted in a fork by digging small holes inside the fork and by placing the pointed sticks or pegs across the opening.

Pot Hooks

Pot hooks are made of forked sticks and are used to hang pots on a crane over a fire. The sticks used should be hard and firm, at least 1 inch thick. The notch for the bail of the kettle should be on the same side as the fork, for balance (Figure XII-8 *a*). Sometimes two notches are made, so the pot can be raised or lowered. Sticks with forks going both ways are rare (but they have been found!), so it is good to join two forked sticks (Figure XII-8 *b*). Cut ends of the sticks to fit together, and bind with whipping (see chapter on Braiding and Knotting, Figures II-10-14).

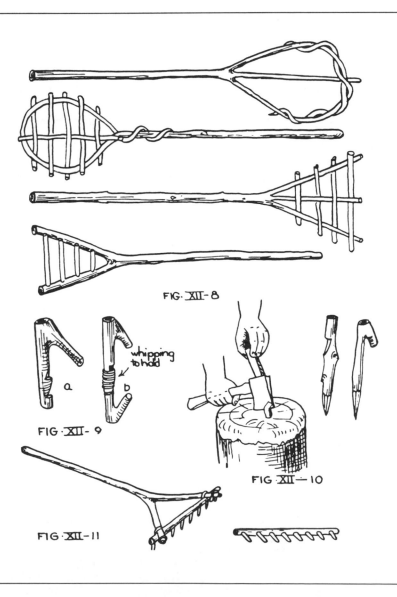

FIG. XII-8

FIG. XII-9

a

b

whipping to hold

FIG. XII-10

FIG. XII-11

Tent Pegs

Handmade tent pegs are often a necessity when pegs break or when there is a short supply for the primitive camp. A handmade set of pegs for a special tent will add to the rustic appearance of the setup. A sharp knife, a hand ax, and a small saw will soon turn a supply of dried hardwood sticks into tent pegs. The sticks should be about 10 inches long, 1 inch or more thick, and of sound maple, oak, or similar wood. Point one end, using knife or ax, with long, not too sharp point. Hold on stump or chopping block, turning peg for each stroke of ax or knife (Figure XII-9). Make a notch for tent rope, about 1 inch down from top of peg. Make straight cut into stick, then slanting cut toward it. A small saw will help make the first cut, and a knife will finish the cutting. Square off top of peg, rounding slightly with knife for finish. A forked stick also can be used.

Outdoor Rake

For an advanced project in knife craft, try a rake made of sticks and twigs.

Equipment needed: jackknife; egg-beater drill and 1/2-inch drill; vise; sandpaper; ruler and pencil; wood glue.

Materials needed: one forked stick, 5 feet long, 1 inch thick; one stick 12 inches to 18 inches long, 1 inch thick; six to ten sticks for pegs, 3/8 inch thick, 4 inches long; cord or twine for lashing.

Steps

1. Trim ends of all sticks neatly and evenly. Leave bark on or peel, as desired.
2. Place 12-inch stick in vise, and draw line through center, lengthwise.
3. Measure and bore series of holes for pegs on the line, beginning 1 inch from end and placing about 2 inches apart.
4. Whittle and sand pegs. Fit into holes with tight fit.
5. Put drop of glue in each hole, and twist peg firmly in place. Tap with hammer to make very secure. Let dry for several hours.
6. Notch forks of long sticks and crosspiece so that handle fits crosspiece (Figure XII-10). Lash with square lashing (see any campcraft book), putting a bit of glue where the sticks join and under the lashing.

Cup Tree, Pan Tree, or Clothes Rack

A small dead evergreen tree makes a good place to hang cups, pans, or clothes. Trim branches short and sandpaper ends. Make a ridge around top, and tie cord with clove hitch (see Figure II-19 or any campcraft book). Throw cord over branch or frame (Figure XII-11 *a*). Use taut-line hitch to lower or raise (see any campcraft book). A coat hanger may be made from a forked stick and branch. Cut all knots smooth, trim ends, and notch where joint will be made. Join with square lashing (Figure XII-12).

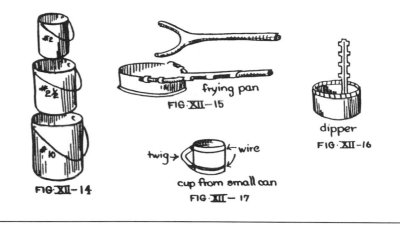

FIG XII-14

frying pan
FIG XII-15

dipper
FIG XII-16

twig → cup from small can ← wire
FIG XII-17

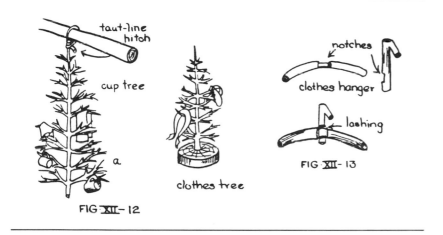

taut-line hitch

cup tree

clothes tree

notches

clothes hanger

lashing

FIG XII-13

a

FIG XII-12

TIN UTENSILS

Refer to Chapter VI on Metalwork for techniques in handling metal and for many additional suggestions. The following projects require less skill and may be used for quick projects. Tin cans must be scrubbed clean, especially at bottom seam, and must be free from rust before being used for cooking utensils. It is important that they be cleaned *thoroughly* after each use if they are to be used again for cooking as food that lodges in the crevice of the seam can easily become contaminated. Work gloves should be worn by campers when working with metal.

Nest of Kettles

Nested kettles may be made from #10, #2½, #2 cans (Figure XII-13). Punch holes in sides for wire handles. Make denim ditty bag (see chapter on Equipment Making, Figures XVI-24-30) for carrying the set.

Frying Pan

A serviceable frying pan can be made from a #10 can and a small forked stick for a handle (Figure XII-14). Mark height of pan around the can, and mark lines 1 inch from seam on each side of seam. Cut down the sides of seam and around the can. Cut small *V*-shaped pieces out of the top edge for turning edge. Be sure to match the cuts with strips on side of seam. Make the handle to fit, trimming smooth on ends. Make a few tabs on the seam to roll around handle. Fasten handle to pan, and turn out top edge of pan so there is no sharp edge.

Dipper

A dipper may be made in a fashion similar to that of the frying pan, using a #5 juice can or a tall cookie can. The handle can be all metal, using the seam as the center and bending 1/2 inch back against the seam (Figure XII-15).

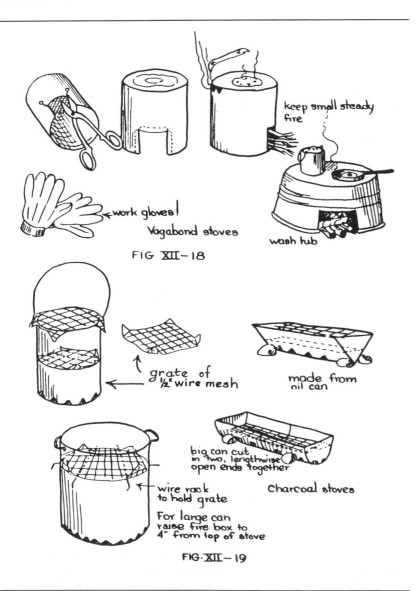

keep small steady fire

←work gloves!

Vagabond stoves

wash tub

FIG XII-18

grate of ½" wire mesh →

made from oil can

big can cut in two, lengthwise open ends together

Charcoal stoves

wire rack to hold grate

For large can raise fire box to 4" from top of stove

FIG·XII-19

Cup

A cup can be made from a small can, using a forked stick, wired on, as the handle (Figure XII-16).

Tin Can Stove

Vagabond or charcoal stoves may be made from #10 cans or from any size can up to wash tubs; 25 lb. and 50 lb. shortening cans are easily obtained from bakeries, and these make good stoves for group use. The smaller cans are good for two-camper cooking.

—*Vagabond stoves* have fires inside them, and the tops of the cans are used for frying. Larger stoves may be used for direct frying, or pots and pans may be used on them (Figure XII-17).

—*Charcoal* stoves need grates to hold the charcoal and are open at the top. They may be used with pots and pans on grills or for broiling and toasting. Much ingenuity can be shown in making and using these stoves which are especially useful where the wood supply is limited or where the fire hazard is great (Figure XII-19).

See *The Campcraft Book*[1] published by American Camping Association for details on how to make and use tin can stoves.

---

1. Hammett, Catherine T. *The Campcraft Book*. Martinsville, IN: American Camping Association, 1987.

Correlation with Dramatics

XIII

Camp dramatics are usually rather simple and informal, making great use of the imagination and ingenuity of the campers in the use of materials found in camp for costumes, props, and scenery. Dramatic efforts will be included in costuming for special events when each camper makes his or her own costume, as well as having the fun of making decorations, posters, or invitations for the affair. Creativity and ingenuity are great assets in fashioning all the paraphernalia that makes for good dramatic presentations. Arts and crafts are so much a part of all these activities that it is not possible (or desirable) to separate them. A good craft point of view will add a workmanlike touch to the costume or to the jewels of a princess, or to the rags and beard of the old man of the ballad. Good standards of crafts will help to make the costume-making enjoyable and imaginative, but the product will not be cheap, in poor taste, or ludicrous, nor will it come apart at the wrong moment. Good carpentry will assure the staunchness of the scenery, while good art will make it just right for the background.

The making of costumes, scenery, and props may provide an outlet for the shy campers who are not yet ready to take part in the actual play or ballad. The camper with craft skills will find his own place and satisfaction in the costume wardrobe or the scenery wing. Recognition of his contribution will be important, too.

Puppets and masks give an opportunity for another type of expression, especially for the shy camper who can more easily lose himself in another character when he has made that character and speaks his lines for him.

The use of natural materials will be part of the fun, and campers and staff concerned with conservation will be careful what they cut and use, as in all use of natural resources. Sheets and berets, bathrobes and jackets, socks and boots will also be the basis of costumes. Here again, guidance in good use of such materials will result in well-turned costumes rather than something that looks somewhat like the desired results.

Use of books for dramatic possibilities, and for help in making the costumes, props, and scenery authentic will provide a different approach to books for many campers. A good library of resource books of stories, ballads, and costumes may well be part of the craft workshop's library. Use of the equipment and material in the craft workshop will link the dramatic activities more closely with arts and crafts, and avoid duplication.

A scrapbook of pictures of costumes and props will be a good project for some group of campers to make and to keep in good order through the years. The photographers may add to the camp record of interesting scenery, costumes, and props with pictures in such a book.

A good supply of materials and equipment with which to fashion the need of the moment will do much to stimulate ingenuity and creativity in dramatic presentations.

Equipment needed: carpentry tools; metal working tools; poster or powder paints and brushes; enamel paints and brushes; crayons; stapler and staples; needles and thread; twine and cord; household cement; thumbtacks and paper clips; clamps; gummed tape.

Materials needed: big sheets or rolls of paper; paper bags (all sizes); cartons (all sizes); wood or bamboo for braces; nuts, bolts, hinges, screws, nails, and brads; dyes; aluminum foil, tin cans, etc.

A few suggestions of possibilities for props and costumes are shown in Figure XIII-1.

SCENERY

The use of large cardboard cartons will simplify scenery problems. They may be used as boxes, with the scenery fastened on the front; or the boxes may be cut open and spread out for wide pieces of scenery like a Viking ship. Carton cardboard may be used as the base of scenes that are painted on the cardboard, as a rock wall, or may be the base on which paper scenery is pasted or stapled. Sometimes easels will be needed to hold up

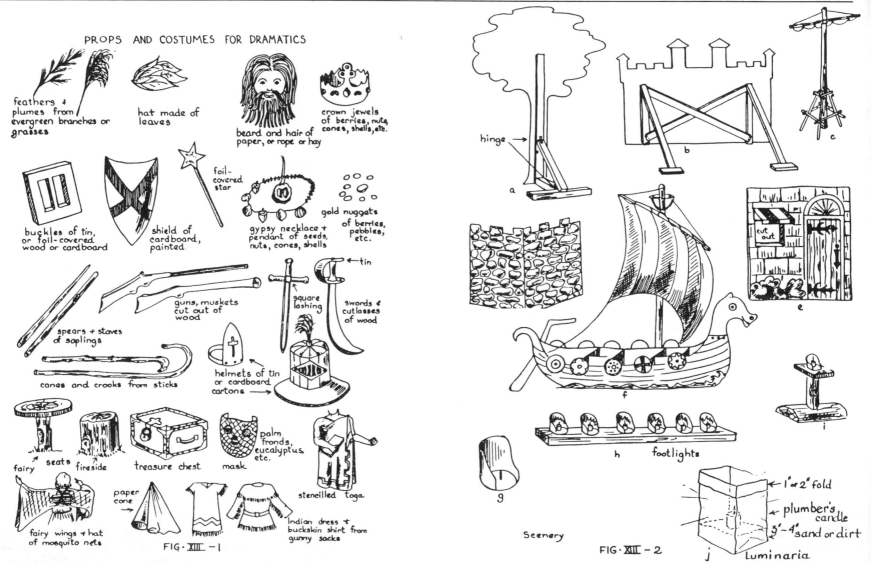

PROPS AND COSTUMES FOR DRAMATICS

feathers & plumes from evergreen branches or grasses

hat made of leaves

beard and hair of paper, or rope or hay

crown jewels of berries, nuts, cones, shells, etc.

buckles of tin, or foil-covered wood or cardboard

shield of cardboard, painted

foil-covered star

gypsy necklace + pendant of seeds, nuts, cones, shells

gold nuggets of berries, pebbles, etc.

spears + staves of saplings

guns, muskets cut out of wood

square lashing

tin

swords & cutlasses of wood

canes and crooks from sticks

helmets of tin or cardboard cartons

fairy seats   fireside

treasure chest

mask

palm fronds, eucalyptus, etc.

stencilled toga

fairy wings + hat of mosquito nets

paper cone

Indian dress + buckskin shirt from gunny sacks

FIG · XIII - I

hinge

a   b   c

cut out

e

f

g   h   footlights   i

Scenery

FIG · XIII - 2

1" or 2" fold

plumber's candle

3'-4" sand or dirt

j   Luminaria

the castle wall or a house frame. Doorways or the frame of a ship may be nailed to orange crates. Masts and trees may be lashed to tripods. Lashing is a convenient skill to use in making frames and bases for scenery. For more permanent use, and for easy storage, a series of braces can be made with nuts and bolts, with holes drilled in several places for adjustment and hinged for folding.

FOOTLIGHTS

Tin cans, size #10, make good candle footlights (Figures XIII-2 *g* and *h*). They may be nailed to a board so several may be focused as needed, or they may be single units. A nail in the bottom of the can holds the candle firm. Posts to raise one or two lights may be made from logs and sticks and a board for the platform (Figure XIII-2 *i*). Making candles for these lights may add extra interest to the planning; old candle ends or paraffin wax may be used. See Chapter VI for use of metal tools.

CEREMONY LUMINARIA

On a path to a special ceremony or to a campfire circle, luminaria will lend an air of enchantment and will serve to light the way, eliminating flashlights.

Use brown paper bags about 10-12 inches high with square bottoms. Put an inch or more of sand or dirt in the bottom. Place a sturdy plumber's or emergency candle firmly in the middle of the sand or dirt. (See Figure XIII-2 *j*.)

PUPPETRY

The making of puppets is a craft that adds a new dimension to dramatics. There are many types of puppets, from the simplest hand puppets to marionettes that dance from strings. Planning for a puppet show and making of simple puppets and stages provide a great opportunity for originality and creativeness. Characters from familiar tales and ballads, such as Paul Bunyan and his Ox, Pinnochio, or Young Lochinvar may be portrayed, or campers may create their own plays and characters. Nature legends may be developed, and puppets may be used to tell the history of the camp or to present some of the camp activities in an unusual way at the first night's campfire. The simplest types of hand puppets, such as may be developed for campfires, rainy day activities or other short-term projects, are described here.

Paper Bag Puppets

These are made by stuffing a small paper bag for the head, adding features with crayons or paints.

Equipment needed: scissors; paint and brushes or crayons; paste and glue; pencil.

Materials needed: paper bags—any size (5-8 lb. recommended); string; cardboard; construction paper; material for stuffing.

Steps

1. Make a plan for the head, and sketch in roughly (Figure XIII-3). Divide bag in thirds, horizontally: top for hair, middle for face, lower part for shoulders.
2. Draw or paint eyes, nose, mouth, eyebrows. Make features exaggerated, even caricatured. Hair may be drawn, painted, or made from colored paper, raveled rope, or grass. Curly hair is made from long strips of paper curled over the blade of scissors, and pasted to the head. Moustaches and beards are made in similar fashion. A nose that sticks out from the face is made by folding a triangle and pasting it in place. Ears are cut out, and pasted or stapled by the edges to sides of head (Figures XIII-3 *a, b, c*).
3. Stuff head with crushed newspaper, grass, etc. Tie string around under chin (Figure XIII-3 *b*).
4. To use the puppet, insert forefinger in neck (Figure XIII-3 *b*).
5. Cut slits in bag at shoulders for "arms." The operator's thumb and middle finger make the arm action. Paste cardboard hands on sides, if desired (Figure XIII-3 *c*).

Variation: Use a larger (10-12 lb.) bag, making head of one third of the bag, the rest of the bag as costume, painted or colored with crayons (Figure XIII-3 *c*).

Vegetable Puppets

Carrots, potatoes, apples may suggest faces and bodies of people or animals. With the aid of paint, paper, thumbtacks, yarn, rope, and a bandana or handkerchief, the vegetables will become puppets. These are not good for long-term use, as the vegetable or fruit dries out and the features change.

FIG · XIII-3

Steps

1. Choose an interesting vegetable or fruit with possibilities for nose, ears, facial expression. (Figures XIII-3 *d* and *e*).
2. With a jackknife, hollow a space big enough for the forefinger to fit in.

3. Paint additional features, add hair. Sometimes another vegetable or seed pod or nut can be added for a grotesque nose (Figure XIII-3 *e*). Eye and mouth can be cut, jack-o-lantern style. Little cones and berries can be the eyes and ears.
4. Fasten kerchief or handkerchief to finger with elastic band, for costumes (Figure XIII-3 *d*).

Modeled heads for puppets may be made from clay or from papier-mache. See Chapter IV on Ceramics, and Chapter XX for making papier-mache.

Sock Puppets

Stuff grass into the toes of a sock, to the instep. Tie string around at instep, leaving space for forefinger. Make features with washable paint, scraps of cloth, berries, bits of wood. Make hair and clothes as above.

To make animal puppets, use the foot of the sock, and make ears, tongue, and mane from red flannel and rope. (Figures XIII-3 *f* and *g*).

Finger Puppets

Little faces may be drawn be drawn on the finger or made of gummed paper and stuck to the finger with handkerchief or scrap of cloth as the costume. This is fun for informal play for little campers on rainy days or in bed in the infirmary. (Figures XIII-3 *h* and *i*).

Shadow Puppets

These are flat silhouettes cut from thin cardboard (file folders or shirt cardboards). They are attached to sticks for handles (Figure XIII-3 *j*) and are used against a sheet screen with light coming from the back, so the puppet casts a shadow on the screen (Figure XIII-4 *c*).

It is necessary to exaggerate details to give puppets character. Make body front view, with hands, arms, and legs side view, or make all in profile (Figure XIII-3 *j*).

Colored cellophane paper may be inserted in the figures, to make colored shadows. Paper fasteners at shoulders and hips will make the puppets mobile; threads tied to the arms and legs may be worked by one camper, while another works the stick handle.

Such simple puppets as are described here will be good starting points, and as campers gain in skill, they may progress to other types.

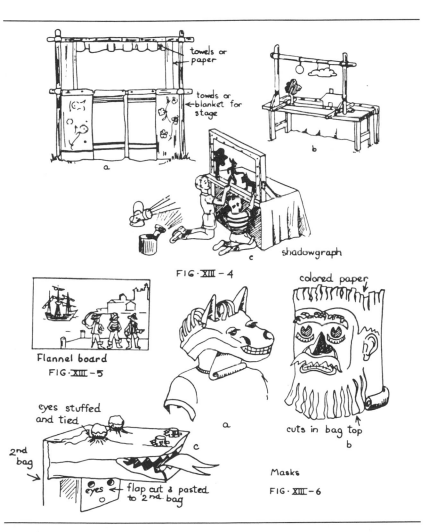

towels or paper

towels or blanket for stage

shadowgraph

FIG·XIII-4

colored paper

cuts in bag top

b

Flannel board
FIG·XIII-5

eyes stuffed and tied

2nd bag

eyes → flap cut & pasted to 2nd bag

a

c

Masks
FIG·XIII-6

Puppet Stages

A frame for showing puppets of all kinds may be made by lashing or nailing notched sticks or dowels in desired size (Figure XIII-4). Feet fastened across the bottom will help the frame stand on a bench or table,

or the frame may be made with legs that stick in the ground, holding the frame at the right height for the campers operating the puppets to sit behind the curtain (Figure XIII-4 *a* and *b*).

For shadow puppets, a screen is thumbtacked across a frame (Figure XIII-4 *c*). The frame should be high enough for campers to sit on floor or ground, and lights should be arranged so that the shadows of the campers do not show on the screen.

Scenery may be thumbtacked to bottom and sides of screen frame, for permanent scenery. For changes of scene, large slides of silhouettes may be tacked in place. Birds may be hung from a thread on end of stick, and waved about for flight. Curtains at the sides may be of blankets or other dark materials. A curtain at the top of the screen helps give the feeling of a stage, with puppets as the players.

FLANNEL BOARDS

A very simple method of illustrating stories and acting out plays is to use the flannel board idea. The characters and scenery pieces are cut out and decorated as desired, and a small piece of outing flannel or similar material or sandpaper is pasted on the back. A blanket, piece of felt, or piece of cotton flannel is stretched on the wall or on an easel (it is best to have bottom edge at a slight angle, so flannel figures will stay in place). The figures are just pressed against the blanket or other background and will stay in place, or may be moved at will.

Flannel boards are a good device to use for nature study activities, for instance, learning about various habitats. Lenore Miller, in her book, *The Nature Specialist,*[1] describes the possibilities in Chapter III.

ANIMAL HEADS AND MASKS

Heads for animals may be made from paper bags large enough to fit over the head of camper (Figure XIII-6). Cut along two folds for half the length of the bag. The front part will go under the chin. Decorate top and sides as desired. Pin or paste on eyes, ears, hair, mane, etc., or paint features. Cover the rest of the body with appropriate costumes.

Heads for people may be made in the same manner. *Masks* may be made from clay or papier-mache (see Chapters IV and XX).

1. Miller, Lenore H. *The Nature Specialist.* Martinsville, IN: American Camping Association, 1986.

Correlation with Music

XIV

Music hath charms of its own, as a creative expression and as a specific camp activity, but it also has a close relationship with such other camp activities as dramatics and arts and crafts. Many projects in the crafts field will help campers enjoy music activities. Simple instruments for rhythm bands, for Indian ceremonials, and for campfire music can be made by campers. Many dramatic presentations call for music; and musical presentations call for scenery, props, and costumes when ballads, action songs, and singing games are presented. Puppets and shadowgraphs will be fun to use to illustrate favorite songs. Some instruments can be made by campers, and cases for such instruments may be part of the project.

The camp's library of sheet music, song books, and records can be protected with books, folders, or special files made and decorated with craft skills.

Music is a good accompaniment to some activities; finger painting, for example, may be helped by the rhythm of a smooth-flowing tune and may reflect in color and design the feeling of the music. Murals for the library or activity rooms may well depict characters and scenes from folk songs, especially those of Indian or pioneer origin. Folk songs that tell the story of those who lived out-of-doors, like gypsies, cowboys, or sailors, are good ones for camps, and with Indian and pioneer songs, provide background for special events that call for posters, invitations, or decorations (see Chapter XVII).

MOUNTING AND PRESERVING SONG SHEETS AND RECORDS

Books or sheets to preserve copies of camp songs, or to keep the camp's collection of original songs can be made in the same manner as logbooks (see Chapters V and X) with leather or wood covers.

The books may be bound, but loose-leaf books are better for changes and additions as the years pass. For easy identification, single songs can be mounted on colored construction paper; sea songs might be on blue, nature songs on green, hiking songs on brown, and so forth. Library files for such song sheets can be made from cardboard boxes. Files for records, cassettes, or tapes may be edged in different colored tapes for ease in sorting and identifying. Such files and folders for songs or records can be decorated with stencils, prints, or sketches (see Chapters VII and VIII). Covers for the camp's song books can be made and stenciled with the camp symbol, and mending or re-covering such books can be a fine rainy day service project for campers.

DRAMATIC ACTIVITIES WITH MUSIC

Ballads and action songs call for scenery, costumes, and props. Many folk songs and action songs will lend themselves to shadowgraphs, puppet shows, and flannel boards, as campers illustrate their singing at campfires or on rainy days (see Chapter XIII). Costuming for singing games and for square and other dances will be part of the campfires that include such activities.

INSTRUMENTS

Rhythm Sticks, Sand Blocks, Rattles for Rhythm Bands

Rhythm Sticks are about 12 inches long, 1/2 inch thick. They are sanded and shellacked or varnished and are used as drumsticks or to click together. Plain sticks do not have the ring that shellacked sticks have. Sticks can be decorated before finishing (Figure XIV-3 *a*).

Sand blocks are made of blocks of wood, about 4 inches long, 3 inches wide, and 5/8 inch deep, with coarse sandpaper glued or tacked on the bottom. Handles of leather or cloth or small pieces of wood help in handling the blocks. The blocks should be well sanded, and decorated (Figures XIV-3 *b*).

FIG·XIV—1

Costumes for folk dances

a

Shadowgraph "Louisiana Lullaby"

b

Puppet show "Soldier, soldier"

c

Flannel board — "Spin, Spin"

e

Costumes for ballads

d

FIG·XIV—2

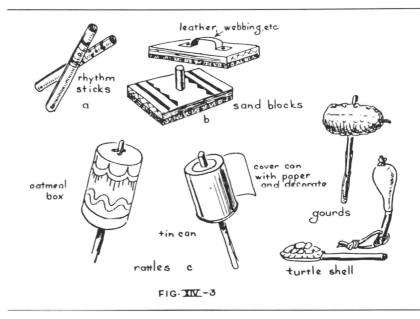

FIG·XIV—3

Rattles are made of gourds, tin cans, cardboard or wooden boxes, and so forth. They may be decorated in many ways, either in a free hand or in a stylized manner. Pebbles, seeds, tiny shells, small nuts, and similar hard objects may be used to make the rattle inside the case. Handles may be made of whittled sticks inserted in the case. Experimentation will produce variety in sound from the different sizes, shapes, and materials used inside the rattles. Hawaiian and Mexican rattles sometimes have feather trimmings. Rattles are important accessories in Indian dancing (Figure XIV-3 *c*).

Tom-toms, Drums, and Tambourines

These are all made in similar fashion: a piece of material is stretched over a round case of wood, metal, or some natural object such as a gourd or cross section of a hollow log. The stretched material may be unbleached muslin, sailcloth, rubber, leather, or oiled paper. Cloth such as unbleached muslin can be treated with shellac or airplane cement to stiffen it; oiled paper may be obtained by rubbing melted wax into heavy brown wrapping

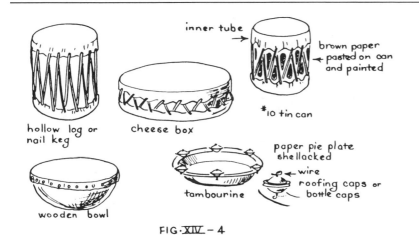

inner tube

brown paper pasted on can and painted

#10 tin can

hollow log or nail keg

cheese box

paper pie plate shellacked

wire

roofing caps or bottle caps

tambourine

wooden bowl

FIG·XIV–4

paper. Material is stretched tightly over the head of the drum or tom-tom, and held in place with rubber bands, tacks, or lacing that holds the top and bottom pieces together. Material treated after being stretched into place will shrink in drying. Heads and sides of the instruments can be decorated in many ways (Figure XIV-4).

Box Instruments

Older campers who are interested in music may enjoy making instruments such as cigar box banjos and fiddles. (Figure XIV-6.) Many other ethnic instruments make interesting projects. One from Africa is the Thumb Piano, made of wood and metal strips, and played by plucking the strips with both thumbs. These are sold in some music stores, and are played by black musicians. (Figures XIV-5).

Marimbas or Xylophones

These instruments may be made with graduated pieces of wood that ring when tapped with a small wooden hammer. The crosspieces are sanded and polished, and graduated on a base (Figure XIV-7). A small hammer may be made by whittling a ball, and inserting a small stick for a handle. Experimentation is needed to catch the right tone of the wooden

AFRICAN THUMB PIANO

May be constructed of 2 pieces of wood, glued/screwed together

Hard wood, preferably

$6" \times 2\frac{1}{4}" \times \frac{1}{4}"$

$1\frac{3}{4}" \times \frac{3}{4}" \times \frac{5}{8}"$

Keys – flattened nails or coathanger wire $1\frac{3}{8}"$ to $2\frac{1}{8}"$ made $\frac{1}{64}"/.015"$ thick

steel

$4\frac{3}{4}" \times \frac{5}{8}"$

$7 - \frac{1}{8}"$ holes

Adjust by pulling or pushing for different notes, scales, etc.

Pluck with thumbnail

Geometric designs, burned or carved

5" coat hanger wire

double strand copper wire - 22 gauge

FIG· XIV–5

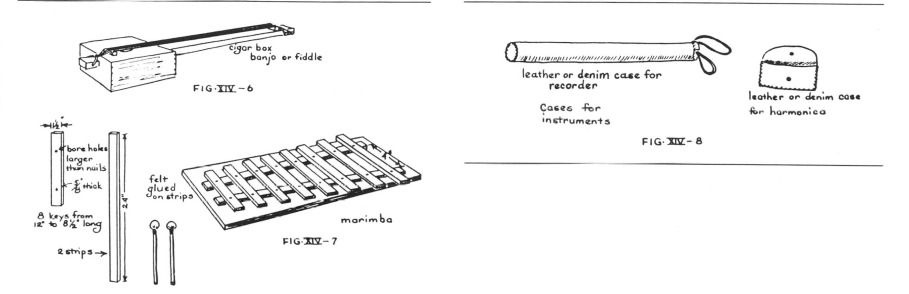

FIG·XIV-6

cigar box
banjo or fiddle

bore holes
larger
than nails

⅝" thick

8 keys from
12" to 8½" long

24"

2 strips →

felt
glued
on strips

marimba

FIG·XIV-7

leather or denim case for
recorder

Cases for
instruments

leather or denim case
for harmonica

FIG·XIV-8

crosspieces, but an octave of eight notes can be made by placing graduated pieces of wood—longest piece is about 12 inches long, 1½ inches wide, 5/8 inch thick. A strip of felt is placed on the base sticks, and small holes drilled in the crosspieces, to be fastened with a small brad (Figure XIV-7).

Case for Instruments

Cases can be made by following the general directions for making patterns and cases in Chapter V. Leather or cloth cases for recorders, for harmonicas, and for other instruments will be valued by those who own such instruments. Methods of decoration suitable to the material used will individualize the cases (Figure XIV-8).

Correlation with Nature

Living out-of-doors and living with nature are the same. One cannot live happily out-of-doors without knowing the ways of nature, without knowing what resources can be used, and without an awareness of the wonders of the universe. It is impossible to go camping without being a part of nature; it is impossible to "do" nature without going out-of-doors, at least some of the time. Nature and outdoor activities are so closely related that this book, written about arts and crafts in camping, also includes much about nature. Knowledge and enjoyment of the out-of-doors is one of the objectives of camping, and the more one sees, hears, smells, feels, and touches, the more he learns to know and to use the out-of-doors, and the more happily he lives with and in it. With that enjoyment and that living goes a responsibility for the out-of-doors, a responsibility to use materials wisely, to conserve, and to help increase the resources. Appreciation and knowledge help us to understand the necessity for preserving our natural resources; low impact camping practices and good outdoor citizenship ensure camping places for generations to come.

As the chapters of this book have been compiled with these aims in view, activities and projects that are correlated with nature are found in any chapter. This particular chapter will serve to point out those arts and crafts activities that may be part of the specific nature program in the camp, that will help campers to know more of the creatures and things of nature and to gain an appreciation of nature's treasures.

Nature study is an activity that may be a special activity area in a camp program. With so much that is fascinating in the world of nature, a whole summer is not enough time to spend on getting acquainted with cardinal flowers or cardinal birds, pine or palm trees, walking sticks or mud dab- bers, turtles or tadpoles, pebbles or crystals, clouds or sunsets. Often the way of catching the first interest of campers is to help them make something that will aid in nature study—an animal "tourist home" (for just a night!); a chart for recording birds seen in the camp; or a place for animals to walk at night so casts can be made of the footprints and tracks. Crafts help in this discovery of the world around campers. From the nature angle, they should help campers to know more of the wonder of the out-of-doors; from the craft angle, they should make use of craft fields and techniques to make individual, well-fashioned articles.

Since the preservation of our natural resources and respect for the woods and the bounty found in them are such important facets of crafts in the nature program, a close tie-in with low impact use of the outdoors is important. Slogans and pledges may be used to help instill good citizenship practices in campers. Two such pledges are:

I give my pledge as an American to save and faithfully to defend from waste, the natural resources of my country, its soils and minerals, its forests, waters, and wildlife.

As a good citizen, I pledge myself to try in every way I can to protect my country's soil, water, plants, and wildlife from harm and waste, and to try to increase their abundance.

Such pledges may be attractively presented on posters and displayed in lashed frames in the nature shack, the craft shop, and around camp.

In general, in using natural materials for crafts or other activities, it is wise to seek the advice of the nature counselor or local authorities. Materials that are found in abundance in the camp locality may generally be safely used. A good rule is to leave more than one takes, and to be sure that seed plants are left for the future. Service projects to protect or to plant willow groves, brush straw, honeysuckle vines, and similar materials usuable in crafts will make fine activities for campers and provide good co-operative ventures for the nature and craft counselors.

PROJECTS

Of the many projects that make use of crafts in relation to nature activities, a few have been worked out in detail in this chapter; many others are found in the other chapters in the book. (See Figure XV-1 for ideas.)

Boxes for collections of rocks and shells.

Homes for animals and insects

Collections of wood samples

Books for mounting bird sketches, flowers, leaves, ferns

Water scopes

Bags and cases for collecting, for magnifying lens, etc.

Nets for insect or water life

Display board for shells, rocks, fossils

Carved or modeled animals or birds, or made of paper or cardboard

Birdhouses, feeders, baths

Dippers and shakers from nuts and gourds

Signs for trails and exhibits (see Chap. XI)

Buttons, toggles, buckles from natural materials

Candles from bayberry wax

FIG. XV -1

Nature Prints

Leaves, grasses, seed pods, and similar nature objects may be used to make a variety of prints. Two such processes, *spatter printing* and *blueprinting* are described in Chapter VII. Some other very simple processes are included here, for use in making nature records. Prints of leaves or flowers may be made for personal nature-lore books, or for a record of trees, ferns, etc., found on the campsite. Such a record would be for the use of the whole camp. Prints may also be used for invitations, end papers, covers, writing paper, and similar craft projects.

Good craftsmanship in tidy work, color combinations, and interesting arrangements will make the project a good craft venture. It is also important for the camper to progress from the making of a print to the identification of and interest in the trees, bushes, and plants from which the leaves are obtained.

In general, it is good to press grasses, ferns, and flowers before printing with them, but most leaves may be used as they are picked. When picking a leaf, do it carefully, so as not to injure next year's leaf bud.

Mobiles

A mobile is a hanging, moving, three dimensional design in space. A stabile is similar, but is fixed at the base; some of its parts may move in the wind.

Equipment needed: scissors, coping saw, wire cutters, clear glue, nylon fish line, clear thread, wire.

Materials needed: dry branches (from downed material on ground), dowels, bamboo, or driftwood; natural objects such as shells, nuts, cones, rocks, pressed leaves;

Steps

1. Attach at least 6 inches of nylon fish line to two objects.
2. Fasten one object to each end of smallest section of wood—this makes one unit.
3. Balance over finger, so the wood is horizontal, and attach fish line at this point.
4. Attach the unit to one end of the next larger piece of wood and also attach a single object or another unit to the end.

5. Balance this over finger, and attach fish line at this point.
6. Continue working from bottom to top until desired length and width of design is achieved.
7. Drops of clear glue will secure lines to objects.
8. Hang completed mobile in area where it can rotate in breezes.

Crayon Prints

Equipment and materials needed: wax or pencil crayons; soft paper, such as mimeograph or typing paper; construction paper for mounting; scissors; rubber cement; newspapers; leaves, etc., as desired.

Steps

1. Press specimen, if necessary.
2. Place a pad of newspapers on working surface. Put leaf on pad, top surface down, and cover with piece of plain paper.
3. Hold paper firmly with one hand, and color paper over the leaf with parallel strokes of the crayon, using flattened end or side. The veins and stem of the leaf will stand out darker than the background.
4. Cut out the shape of the leaf from the paper, to eliminate the marks that ran over the edge.
5. Mount cutout leaf on paper of contrasting color, using rubber cement. Make good arrangement of one or several leaves.
6. Press until dry.

Ink Prints

Equipment needed: two rollers, one for ink, one for pressing; piece of glass; hard working surface; newspapers; kerosene; mineral spirits or kerosene; rags; putting knife.

Materials needed: printer's ink; paper—mimeograph or construction; leaves, ferns.

Steps

1. Arrange a work area for efficient use by placing glass and ink on left, inking pad of newspaper next to the right, then newspaper on which is placed the paper to be printed (Figure XV-3). Cut sheets of newspaper into quarters.

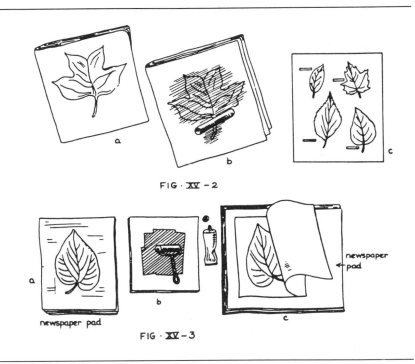

FIG · XV - 2

FIG · XV - 3

2. Squeeze out about 1/2 inch of ink on glass, and roll out evenly with ink roller. Use a drop of kerosene to thin, if necessary.
3. Lay leaf or fern *vein side up* on the inking pad. Roll inked roller over it, covering with ink evenly.
4. Pick up inked leaf by stem and lay it *inked side down* on the paper to be printed, placing as desired. Mark this spot before beginning inking, so leaf will be placed accurately.
5. Cover the leaf with a piece of paper, and roll with the clean roller, or with the heel of the hand or the bowl of a tablespoon.
6. Remove top paper, then remove the leaf carefully. Print will be on the lower paper (Figure XV-3). Let dry.
7. Throw away the top piece of paper on the inking pad, so clean sheet is ready for next inking.
8. Same leaf may be used again and again for printing.

9 When finished with one color of ink, clean roller with newspaper, then mineral spirits. Scrape extra ink from glass with putty knife, and clean it with mineral spirits and rag.

Ink pad or carbon prints are made in similar fashion, but the leaf is placed *vein side down* on the ink pad or carbon, a piece of paper is placed over it, and the paper is rubbed with fingers or bowl of a spoon. The inked side of the leaf is placed *vein side down* on paper to be printed, covered with another paper, and rubbed as above.

Smoke prints are made in a fashion similar to that used for ink pad prints, but the ink is made by holding a piece of greased brown wrapping paper over a candle flame. The paper is moved constantly over the flame, so the smoke of the flame is caught on the greased portion, forming carbon. The paper is then used as in the carbon or ink pad printing above.

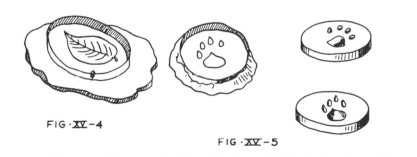

FIG · XV -4

FIG · XV - 5

Plaster Casts

Plaster casts make a permanent record of leaves, ferns, animal tracks, seed pods, seeds, and so forth. Casts may be used in such articles as dishes and trays, or may be made into plaques for wall decoration. A series of plaques showing interesting nature finds might be a frieze around the dining hall or camp house.

Equipment needed: water, tin can, and stick for mixing; poster or watercolor paint and brushes; shellac and brush; talcum powder and vaseline; newspaper or oil paper; paper clips; sandpaper; roller.

Materials needed: plaster of Paris; plasticene or modeling clay; thin cardboard (file folders); wire; coloring, if desired.

Steps to make casts of leaves, ferns

1. On newspaper, roll out a piece of plasticene or clay to flat pad larger than the desired object, with dowel, roller, or heel of hand.
2. Place leaf on clay pad, and impress it into clay with fingers (Figure XV-4). Remove carefully.
3. Make a collar of a 2-inch strip of cardboard, and press around the imprint of a leaf, overlapping ends and joining with paper clips (Figure XV-4).
4. Mix plaster of Paris; put enough water in can to fill the mold to a depth of 3/4 inch. Put in plaster until it forms a mound and comes to the surface. Stir gently so there are no lumps and the mixture is the consistency of heavy cream.
5. Pour mixture into mold slowly and carefully, so there will be no air bubbles.
6. Let plaster set, then remove collar and cast from mold.
7. Sandpaper edges, paint in colors, and shellac as desired.
8. If the cast is to be hung as a plaque, put small loop of wire in plaster in proper place when the plaster is partially set.
9. Plaster, while it is still liquid, may be colored with poster paints.

Steps to make casts of animal tracks

If tracks are in mud or firm soil, make a collar around the track by pressing cardboard or tin strip into soil, building a wall of soil around the cardboard collar, if necessary. Let it harden before pouring cast mixture into mold. From there:

1. Shake talcum powder into track.
2. Mix plaster of Paris, and pour carefully as above.
3. Let plaster set, remove collar, and take cast from mold. This makes a positive mold, that is, the track will be raised.
4. To get a cast like the track in the ground, it is necessary to make a negative mold. (If these steps are used, it is wise to color the plaster for the positive mold lightly with a little poster paint, so the two parts may be easily distinguished.)
5. Coat the positive cast generously with vaseline.
6. Make a collar of cardboard around the positive mold, and make a wall of clay or plasticene outside the collar, to hold it firmly in place.

7. Mix plaster and pour into mold. Let plaster set.
8. Place wire loop for hanging, if desired, when plaster is partially set.
9. Remove collar, and separate the cast from the mold (Figure XV-5).

Cast from mushroom or similar round object: making plaster models of mushrooms (or similar objects) will be an interesting project, one that will help in learning to identify them. Using modeling wax, make a copy of the mushroom. Then make a plaster cast of the model. Coat the model with vaseline, and pour liquid plaster over it in a thin coat. Repeat when this plaster is hard. When the plaster is about 1/4 inch thick, cut through the plaster all around, so that the mold can be removed in two pieces (*do this carefully*). Take one half off, then lift out the model. Line the cast with vaseline, and pour liquid plaster in both sides; let set a little, then put both sides together and hold them tight with rubber bands. Let harden, then take the cast away. The model will need sanding and decorating to look like the original (see Chapter IV).

Bark Articles

When such trees as white birch are already cut and down for some other purpose, it may be possible to use the bark to make boxes, baskets, and similar objects. Many articles can be made from birch or other supple bark because they can be cut and stitched, using leatherwork techniques (see Chapter V).

Great care should be taken to practice good conservation in the use of bark, and campers should have it impressed upon them that cutting bark from a live tree is not only injurious to the tree but also leaves it unsightly. For this reason, many camps discourage bark crafts. It is possible, however, to train campers to have respect for living trees; and, as part of the nature program, it is wise to help them know what they can use from the woods and what precautions they must take as good outdoor citizens. Sawmills that handle logs of birch and similar thin-barked trees may be willing to save pieces of bark for campers to use.

Bark should be soaked in hot water before using so that it will not crack. For baskets, boxes, drinking cups, carrying cases, picture frames, make paper patterns and staple the pieces together (see Chapter V). Punch holes with awl or spring punch, and lace with leather, raffia, or similar material, or stitch with large needle and string. Strengthen tops of baskets and boxes with a green shoot, overcast around top (Figure XV-6).

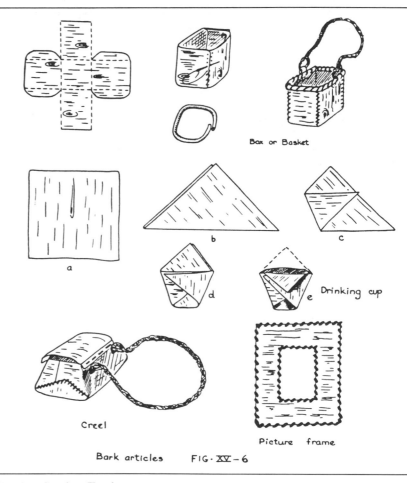

Box or Basket

Drinking cup

Creel

Picture frame

Bark articles   FIG. XV-6

Weather Station Equipment

Weather flags, barometers, bulletin boards, cloud charts, and wind vanes are projects that can be carried out in establishing and maintaining a weather station. Wind vanes of wood or metal are also good craft projects for decorative use on camp buildings. They use tools and techniques as described in Chapters VI and X.

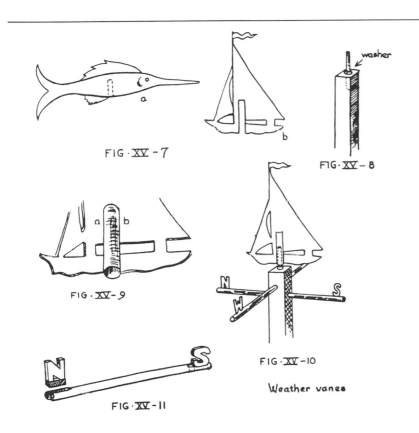

FIG·XV-7

FIG·XV-8

FIG·XV-9

FIG·XV-10

Weather vanes

FIG·XV-11

Weather Vanes

Equipment needed: tools (see Chapter VI or X); drill and bit; wood glue or plastic wood; compass.

Materials needed: wood—1/2-inch pine or outdoor plywood, or something similar; metal—10 or 12 gauge copper, or two pieces of lighter gauge, riveted or soldered together; 1/4-inch wood dowels, or hollow tube; 1/8-inch rod or spike; two 9-inch by 1-inch sticks or dowels, or one 18-inch; post; washer.

Steps for a wooden vane

1. Make a design: in general, plan a design that will catch the wind, such as a boat, fish, or scene. Be sure it has a definite pointer (Figure XV-7). Make on paper first.
2. Cut design from wood with coping saw.
3. Find center point by balancing vane across a dowel stick.
4. Bore 3/16-inch hole just in front of this spot, to within 1 inch of top of vane (Figure XV-7 *a*).
5. Insert a 1/8-inch rod or 1/8-inch spike with head cut off into hole.
6. Finish by sanding, painting, or varnishing, as desired.
7. Bore hole in post and insert rod in post (Figure XV-8), with washer.
8. Put vane on post, adjusting so it will swing easily on post.

For a *metal vane,* follow same general steps of design, cutting out with jeweler's saw (Figure XV-7 *b*). At step 3, find balancing center point, and cut out a strip or slot in the vane (Figure XV-9) 3/16-inch or 1/4-inch wide, halfway into design. Insert a hollow tube the same length as the slot, and solder in place in slot, on line *a* and *b* (Figure XVI-9). This is to hold the rod in the post for swinging. Bore hole in post, and insert 1/8-inch rod. Put washer over rod, and insert rod into soldered tube in vane, to swing freely (Figure XV-10).

Steps for markers

Markers for north, east, south, and west may be cut from 1/2-inch wood or from metal (Figure XV-10).

1. Make an extra foot on each letter, for attaching to dowel (Figure XV-11).
2. Cut stick or dowel in half, making two 9-inch pieces.
3. In both ends of stick, cut slot wide enough to take the foot of the letters (Figure XV-11). Sand wooden letters and slots.
4. Drill 1-inch holes through post, and place sticks in place at right angles to each other, using wood glue or plastic wood to secure (Figure XV-10).
5. Glue letters in place on ends of sticks (Figure XV-10).
6. Place post so that the markers are fixed with points of compass.
7. Finish as desired.

Dyeing with Natural Dyes

Many lovely colors may be obtained for craft articles by using dyes from natural materials. Discovering these colors holds great fascination for campers. The colors from natural dyes are not as brilliant as those of chemical dyes, but they are as soft and lovely as any piece of homespun. Basket material, costume material, camp unit ties, or bandanas are some of the possibilities for dyeing with natural dyes. This craft makes use of local plants; natural history museums and state libraries will have information about such resources in specific localities.

To make the dye, berries, bark, vegetable juices, seeds, roots, and blossoms are crushed or broken into bits; after soaking overnight they are brought to a boil, then simmered for an hour or more. The color of the dye bath should be more intense than the desired finish shade, as it is concentrated at this stage.

Natural dyes do not hold their color unless the material is treated with a mordant that helps to fix or change the color, impregnating the fibers. For wool or silk (animal fibers) the mordant is made of water and alum (one ounce of alum to a gallon of water) plus one-fourth ounce cream of tartar. For cotton, linen, or rayon (vegetable fibers) one-fourth ounce of plain washing soda should be added to the alum and water. The material should be boiled in the mordant bath for one hour, rinsed well, and then immersed in the dye bath.

The container for the dye bath should be enamel or copper ware and should be large enough to hold the material without crowding. In general, materials should be simmered in the bath for one-half hour to one hour or until desired shade is obtained (shade will be darker when wet). Add salt or vinegar to the dye bath, and simmer for ten minutes or so.

Dioramas and Habitat Boxes

These are miniature scenes in three dimensions. Sometimes they are used as centerpieces, sometimes as arrangements for a flower show, sometimes as exhibits to show habitats of animals that live in camp, sometimes as part of relief maps (see Chapter XX). One type is constructed to be viewed from all four sides, while another has a background on three sides and is viewed from the front and top.

Equipment needed: scissors and knife; stapler and staples; string and thread; glue or household cement; poster paints and brush.

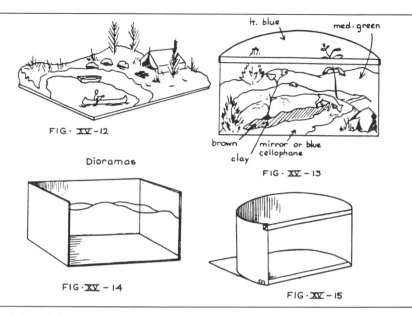

FIG · XV – 12

Dioramas

FIG · XV – 13

FIG · XV – 14

FIG · XV – 15

Materials needed: mosses, grasses, small plants, twigs; mirror or cellophane; colored paper; cardboard or carton; sand or dirt, papier-mache or plaster of Paris; cloth or canvas; plasticene.

Steps for centerpiece (viewed on all sides).

1. Make a plan on paper, deciding on content, size, and arrangement in general; 12 inches by 18 inches or 18 inches by 24 inches are good starting sizes (Figures XV-12 and 13). Gather together materials to make the diorama.
2. If water is to be included in the scene, place mirror or blue cellophane or blue paper covered with clear cellophane on base.
3. Build up land with sand, dirt, pebbles, or one of the materials described in Chapter XX, to reproduce the topography of the spot.
4. Place twigs for trees, small plants and grasses for bushes, moss for grass (Figure XV-12).
5. Make buildings, tents, boats from colored paper or thin cardboard painted or colored with crayons, or from bits of cloth (see Chapter XVII).

6. For a camp scene, make tiny lashings of twigs for construction, boats and canoes from paper or bark (see Chapter XVII).
7. Model animals from plasticene (see Chapter IV).

Steps for diorama with background (viewed from front).

1. Make a plan on paper, as above (Figure XV-13), planning the piece to fit cardboard carton (Figure XV-14) or similar container. For rounded container (Figure XV-15), use thin cardboard secured in position with staples and with strips 1 inch wide across front.
2. Paint the back and sides on inside with poster paint to suggest sky, skyline, mountains, etc. Paint outside as desired.
3. Assemble as above.

Star Boxes and Projectors

Viewers or projectors for star constellation slides may be made from shoe or oatmeal boxes. They are useful in star study groups, and for individual use and enjoyment.

Equipment needed: paper punch (with star shaped punch, if possible); scissors; poster paint; star chart and book.

Materials needed: box—oatmeal, shoe, etc.; thin cardboard (file folders) or file cards; flashlight; construction paper or paint for covering.

Steps

1. Cut rectangular window in end of box (Figures XV-16 *a* or *b*). At the four corners, cut diagonal slits about 1/4 inch long.
2. At other end, make a hole to hold the light end of flashlight, or a peep-hole about 1 inch in diameter (Figures XV-17 and 18).
3. Paint outside of box with poster paint, or cover with construction paper as desired.
4. To make slides: cut thin cardboard or file cards into rectangle 1/2 inch wider than the height of the window and longer than the width of the box. With help of star observation, star charts, etc., plan the positions of stars in several constellations, one to each card or a grouping of constellations on a card. Mark place for stars. Punch holes with paper punch.
5. To use: place slide in front of window, and hold toward light to view (Figure XV-17), or hold flashlight in the end, and flash stars on screen, wall, or ceiling. Several campers may flash constellations in proper groupings at one time, to give a segment of the sky.

Star Dome or Planetarium

This is a good group project, especially for a group interested in star gazing, or for an older camper group interested in a service project for

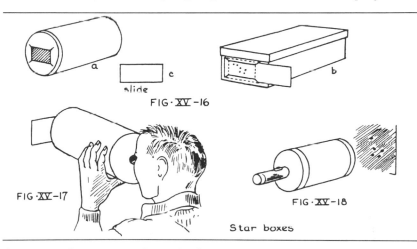

FIG·XV–16

FIG·XV–17

FIG·XV–18

slide

Star boxes

the nature department. Once the frame has been made by campcrafters, different groups may make linings to show the stars at different times of the year.

Equipment needed: hammer; poster paints and brushes; scissors; stapler and staples or thumb tacks; crayons and pencils; glue; compass; water and container; star books and charts.

Materials needed: supple shoots or wood pieces for spokes and rim; lashing cord or fine wire; wrapping paper in big sheets or cloth; yellow colored paper or gummed gold stars.

Steps

1. Select a central point in a large open clearing. This may be a flag pole or a stake set in the ground.
2. Find North with compass, and have one camper lie down with head at pole or stake, feet pointing north.
3. With binder twine, mark a circle with circumference at the feet of this

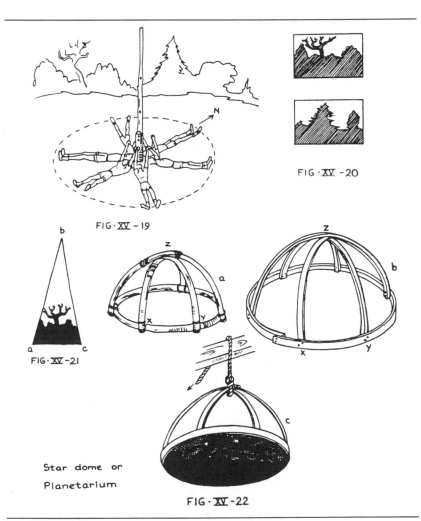

FIG · XV - 20

FIG · XV - 19

FIG · XV - 21

Star dome or
Planetarium

FIG · XV - 22

one camper's hands is the segment for which he is responsible. Each camper makes a rough sketch of his segment of skyline.

5. To construct framework: soak willow shoots or strips of wood until pliable, and bend into circle, overlapping ends and lashing or nailing together (Figure XV-22).

Use radius of circle as a measure to mark out six equal spaces around circumference.

Soak shoots or strips for ribs, and when pliable, fasten across the circle, making a dome. Notch at rim and at joining spots. If short shoots or strips are used, join at side of center crossing spot with sheer lashing (see any campcraft book for lashings) with cord or wire. (Figures XV-22 *a* and *b*). Use small brads or glue to hold ribs to rim. Let dry.

6. To make liner: measure distance from middle of each rib to middle of next (Figure XV-22 *x-y)*, and measure length of ribs from circumference to top of dome (*x-z*). Cut segments of wrapping paper by these dimensions, allowing a little on edges for overlap and for fastening. Try for fit.

Have each camper sketch his segment of skyline from his small, rough sketch, on a piece of wrapping paper (see Chapter XX for how to enlarge). Be sure adjoining edges coincide. Do not try to reproduce the skyline in detail, but pick out the outstanding features, such as buildings, trees, hills (Figures XV-20 and 21). Orient and mark with compass points.

Paint the upper part of the segments dark blue, the lower outlines in black, showing skyline in silhouette. Fasten segments on underneath sides of ribs with staples or thumbtacks or glue, touching up the metal with paint, if needed. Locate major stars and constellations in pencil, and cut stars in three sizes from yellow paper (or use gummed stars), and place in proper places on inside of dome with glue.

7. To hang: hang dome with rope, tie with bowline knot and attach to rafters overhead (Figure XV-22).

Variations: Segments may be made of cloth (such as unbleached muslin or pieces of an old sheet) stitched together. This is a better plan if several different liners are to be used. The cloth liner may then be thumbtacked in place.

If the size chosen is over 5 feet in diameter, it will be better to have 12 segments of skyline, using 12 campers around the center pole or stakes, and 12 ribs.

camper, mark off the six equal spaces on circumference, and have five other campers lie down with heads at stake, feet at the points on circumference (Figure XV-19).

4. Have campers reach out and clasp hands with neighbors, holding hands high (Figure XV-19). The segment of skyline viewed between

Equipment Making

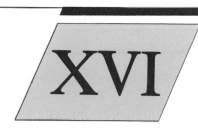

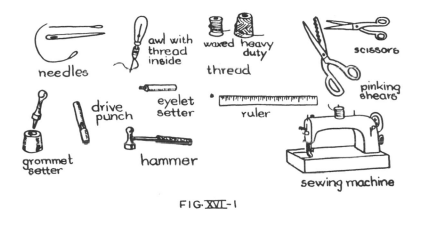

TOOLS FOR MAKING EQUIPMENT OF CLOTH

needles — awl with thread inside — waxed heavy duty thread — scissors — pinking shears — drive punch — eyelet setter — ruler — grommet setter — hammer — sewing machine

FIG·XVI-1

Do-it-yourself enthusiasts are found in the realm of camping gear and equipment, as they are in many other fields these days. Campers can have gear that is right, at lower cost, by making their own. Satisfactions and learnings are an important part of equipment-making activity, which calls for ingenuity, resourcefulness, and good craftsmanship in the use of many craft techniques. Leatherworking, woodworking, and metalworking skills are put to good use as equipment is developed. Planning the article, making a pattern, adding an individualized symbol, creating just the right features to make it a one-of-a-kind object—all these mark equipment making as a good craft for campers.

Some gear is individual; some is for groups. When a group works together to make a food box or a tent, good teamwork results, and there is real anticipation for the outings ahead. A group project is often a progressive step toward making individual or family gear. Progression, too, will come in making more complicated articles, and also in the use of heavier materials or new tools, and in the use of different techniques.

This chapter gives some techniques in working with cloth; other chapters, such as those on Leatherwork (V), Woodwork (X), and Metalwork (VI) give techniques in those areas.

MATERIALS USED

Material used in making cloth gear is usually firmly woven, such as unbleached muslin, denim, awning cloth, duck, or lightweight canvas, or very finely woven material such as balloon cloth, Egyptian cotton, or a type of material known as "typewriter ribbon cloth." The finer the weave, the better the cloth is for lightweight articles, but the more expensive it is, too. Plastics, waterproofed materials, and nylon may also be used. Denim comes in two weights. The lighter denim, which may be had in many plain colors and also in stripes and plaids, is especially good for beginners' projects. Remnants of denim or awning cloth are often obtainable at little or no cost.

TOOLS USED

Tools used in making equipment with cloth are the sewing tools, such as needles, and waxed or other heavy thread. Curved needles for canvas, square needles for leather, a sailor's palm, and an awl with thread in the handle and an eye in the point all help to simplify the stitching. A sewing machine is a must for big equipment, such as a tarp or tent, but many articles can be stitched by hand, using leather or canvas stitching methods (Figure XVI-1).

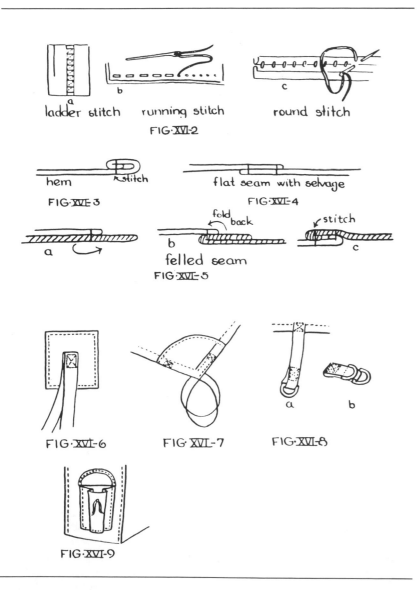

ladder stitch   running stitch   round stitch

FIG·XVI·2

hem   ^stitch   flat seam with selvage

FIG·XVI·3   FIG·XVI·4

fold back   stitch

a   b   c

felled seam

FIG·XVI·5

FIG·XVI·6   FIG·XVI·7   a   b   FIG·XVI·8

FIG·XVI·9

TECHNIQUES IN HANDLING CLOTH

Stitches, Hems, and Seams

Stitches used in hand-stitching cloth are, in general, the stitches used in leatherwork (see chapter on Leatherwork, Figures V-22-31). A few canvas stitches are shown here; the ladder stitch is often used where a broad, flat seam is needed, as on the side of a ditty bag (Figure XVI-2).

Hems are made in the conventional manner. If a selvage edge can be used, only one fold is needed. In places that will have strain, double stitching gives added strength (Figure XVI-3).

Seams are also made in the conventional manner. Flat seams are usual in heavy material. If two selvages made the seam, the edges are overlapped and stitched flat, without turning (Figure XVI-4). If raw edges are to be used, a felled seam is best; all raw edges are concealed (Figure XVI-5). Stitch seams twice for strength.

Sewing Patches and Tapes

Patches of the material are stitched in places where there will be extra pull, as on the corner of a tent, or where tapes will be sewed. Double the material, turn raw edges in, and pin patch in place. If tape is needed, pin it in place. Stitch the patch with two rows of stitching at edges, and with crisscross stitching from corner to corner.

Tapes may be sewed on for ties, for holding rings or D-rings, or to give strength where there will be pull. If the tape is single, turn one end in and stitch this double end to the main material; if the tape is doubled, as for D-rings, turn ends under, stitch along the edges, and crisscross through the middle (Figure XVI-6). Use plenty of tape and plenty of stitching. If tape is sewed on a patch, pin in place, and stitch it and the patch at the same time, or stitch tape to patch before putting patch in place. Loops may be made for ground pegs or guy ropes by looping the tapes and securing them along the sides of the article (Figure XVI-7).

Rings or D-rings for straps and guy lines are held in place by tape, using a 3-inch loop (Figure XVI-8 *a*). Crisscross the stitching where the tape is sewed to the article and at the ring. Two rings are fastened in a fold of tape (Figure XVI-8 *b*) to make an adjustable strap fastening.

Patch pockets may be planned for packs and hike kits; they are cut, edges are turned in, and the pockets pinned in place, then stitched with the same stitching used in making the pack. A pleat or bellows to give extra room is made by pleating the material on both sides of the center line and stitching the pleat across the bottom, leaving fullness at top (Figure XVI-9).

Setting Grommets

Metal rings, called grommets, are used in many pieces of equipment where rope or thong will be tied or inserted as a drawstring, or where a spike will be used, as on a tent pole. Eaves of tents, tops of duffle bags, corners of tarps, and similar places on articles made of cloth may require grommets. Grommets, with the die and punch to set them, may be purchased from tent-making or canvas-working establishments.

Equipment needed: grommet setting die and punch (see Figure XVI-1); drive punch or sharp pointed scissors; metal hammer; grommets—in two sections (Figures XVI-10 *a* and *b*).

Steps

1. Punch hole in material, using two or more thicknesses, as in a corner or hem; use drive punch or pointed scissors (Figure XVI-11). If scissors are used, make a small hole, then cut four cuts at right angles from center. For added strength, insert a bit of material in fold or hem where grommet is to be set.
2. Push *a* section of grommet up through hole, fitting material snugly around the collar. Trim off extra material, but be careful to have it fit tightly rather than loosely (Figure XVI-12).
3. Place the *a* section, with material on it, in the groove in the die (Figure XVI-13).
4. Place pronged section of grommet (*b*) over the collar and material.
5. Place pointed punch through center of assembled grommet (Figure XVI-14).
6. Hold punch upright; strike it with several sharp blows of a metal hammer.
7. Remove punch. The grommet sections will have been forced together to make a smooth ring set in material.

Smaller metal rings are usually called *eyelets;* these are used on small articles, such as food bags and hike kits. Eyelets may be purchased at

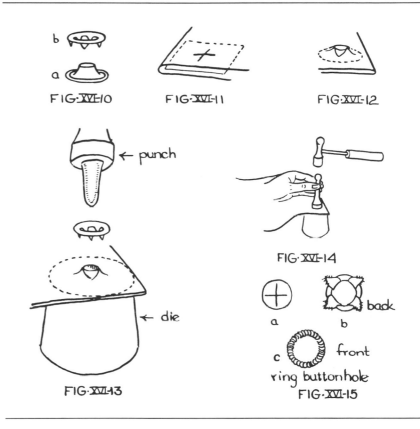

FIG·XVI·10

FIG·XVI·11

FIG·XVI·12

← punch

← die

FIG·XVI·13

FIG·XVI·14

a   b   back

c   front

ring   buttonhole

FIG·XVI·15

notions counters in department stores. The set will include a small tool for setting; directions for setting, to be found in the package, will be similar to those for setting grommets.

Buttonholes

Buttonholes, or handmade grommets, are sometimes more practical than metal grommets because they call for little equipment and can be made easily in camp. Some craftsmen prefer small rings and buttonholing to make grommets in fine material, such as is used in lightweight tents.

It is important to decide where buttonholes will be placed before stitching hems. Sometimes the buttonhole is made on the outside of the drawstring hem before the cloth is turned under and stitched; sometimes the buttonhole is made through the double thickness of the hem after it is finished.

Steps

1. Cut two small cross slits in material at places for buttonhole (Figure XVI-15 *a*).
2. Put ring on underside; turn back the tabs made by the slits (Figure XVI-15 *b*).
3. Stitch the ring in place with a few overcast stitches, then cover these stitches and the ring with buttonhole stitches (Figure XVI-15 *c*).

Waterproofing

Packs, groundsheets, tents, and tarps will need to be processed to make them shed water. *Waterproofing* means that no water can go through the material, as in rubberized or plastic material; *water repellent* means that the material will shed water, as an umbrella does. Waterproofed material does not breathe; tents and similar articles are made water repellent because it is important that they do breathe, or have air circulating through the threads. The process of making an article water repellent is to coat the threads of the cloth so that when the threads are wet, air bubbles form, causing the water to run off. If these bubbles are broken, the cloth will leak at the point of contact. It is common to use the term waterproofing for any method used in making canvas and cloth articles rain repellent.

There are many excellent commercial liquids for waterproofing large areas, such as tents tarps. For small articles, paraffin can be used.

Wax: small flat articles (or the material to make them) may be waterproofed by spreading the cloth on a table, thumbtacking it smooth, and rubbing it with paraffin. The wax is scrubbed thoroughly and evenly into all parts of the cloth. The cloth is then placed between sheets of plain paper and pressed with a warm iron; the heat melts the wax, and helps it impregnate each thread.

Waterproofing calls for some experimentation; it is well to seek the help of someone with experience. An alternative is to purchase a commercial product and follow its instructions for application.

PROJECTS

Simple Hike Kit or Pouch Bag

This is one of the simplest types of hike kits for younger campers. It is a good beginning step in making one's own hiking gear that will be just right for a lunch, for treasures collected on the way, or for the group's first aid kit. The kit becomes individualized by stenciling or block printing (see Chapter VII) on solid colored materials. The stitching may be done by any of the usual leather stitches.

Equipment needed: large-eyed needle; colored string or crochet cotton for stitching and for whipping ends of cord; pinking shears or scissors.

Materials needed: square of cloth, approximately 18 inches square—or any desired size of lightweight material (bandanas, kerchiefs, old sheets to be dyed); about 2 yards small cord.

Steps

1. Trim edges of square with pinking shears, or make 1/4-inch hem, using running stitch (see stitching techniques in Chapter V on Leatherwork).
2. Fold corners back (Figure XVI-16).
3. Make hems at folds, wide enough to carry two thicknesses of the cord (Figure XVI-17).
4. Cut cord in two pieces and insert as drawstrings, so ends of ropes are on opposite sides of bag (Figure XVI-18).
5. Join ends of rope with square knot or fisherman's knot; whip ends with same string used for stitching (see chapter on Braiding and Knotting, Figures II-10-14).
6. Pull cords in opposite directions, to make pouch (Figures XVI-19).
7. Wear over shoulder or on belt.

Simple Backpack

This pack presents a progressive step in equipment making. It is worn on the back, with two straps over the shoulders, and is a good pack for day hikes, overnights, or skiing trips. The project involves planning to meet individual desires; special pockets and fastenings make the project more interesting.

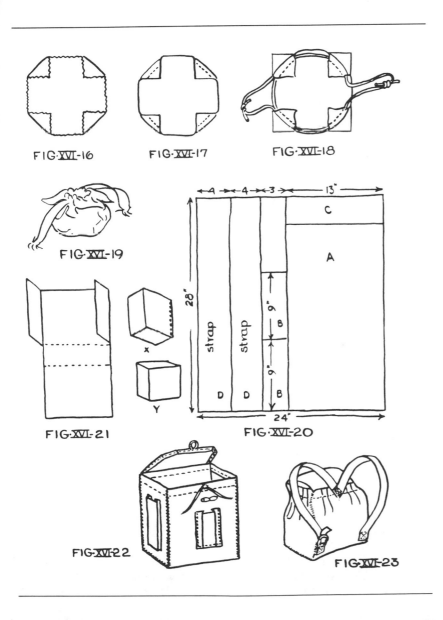

FIG·XVI-16   FIG·XVI-17   FIG·XVI-18

FIG·XVI-19

FIG·XVI-21   FIG·XVI-20

FIG·XVI-22   FIG·XVI-23

Equipment needed: pinking shears—for best results; large-eyed needle; string or warp or heavy thread; grommet setting tools, if desired; paper and pins for pattern; stapler.

Materials needed: 2/3 yard 10 oz. denim, or similar firm material; about 40 inches small cord or thong; 4 D-rings, if desired.

Steps

1. Make a pattern; staple together to test for size and fit. Adjust as needed (Figure XVI-20).
2. Take pattern apart; cut material from it (Figure XVI-21).
3. Sew the *B* pieces to *A* piece, using overcast stitching (for stitching techniques, see Leatherwork, Chapter V). Sew bottom edges to fold of *A* piece, pinning in place before stitching (Figures XVI-21 *x* and *y*).
4. Mark place for grommet or ring or buttonhole for cord in top of front of *A*; insert grommet, attach ring, or make buttonhole (see preceding pages in this chapter) before sewing hem.
5. Turn hem at top, allowing room for the cord to pass through easily. Stitch with running or cobbler's stitch.
6. Turn 1/4-inch hem on all sides of *C* pieces, for flap. Stitch with running stitch or cobbler's stitch, as used for hem on *A*. Stitch to back (Figure XVI-22).
7. Make one or two buttonholes; or sew a piece of thong for attaching flap to *A* piece (Figure XVI-22).
8. Turn 1/4-inch folds on sides and ends of straps *D*. Adjust to individual size by pinning in place at center back and at lower corners of pack. Stitch edges with same type stitching used for pack.
9. Sew straps in place (Figure XVI-23). To make adjustable straps, use D-rings at bottom corners (see Figure XVI-8).
10. Insert cord for drawstring in top hem; whip ends (see chapter on Braiding and Knotting, Figures II-10-14). Gather top together (stuff paper in pack to fill it out); mark place for fastener(s) for flap.
11. Make toggle(s), pioneer button(s), or similar fastener(s), and secure in place (see Leatherwork or Woodworking chapters).
12. Waterproof flap, or spray whole pack with water repellent liquid.

Variations: To use identification marks: stencil, print, or paint identification mark on front of pack before assembling at step 3, above. Place this with reference to toggle(s) or button(s) for fastening flap.

Place patch pockets as desired, on front or sides, not on back (Figures XVI-9 and 22).

Advanced Packs

For older campers who are ready to make more advanced packs, there are many types from which to choose. Packs may have light wood or metal frames which may be made or purchased. The experienced camper designs his pack to his own need and fancy. Because these projects may be so varied and the details so extensive, it is not possible to give them here.

Ditty Bags

Bags with circular bottoms are usually referred to as ditty bags. They may be made in many sizes and are useful for personal gear, for food bags, for tent or sail bags. They are standard equipment for sailors. Small bags are made of lightweight material, such as unbleached muslin, balloon cloth, or plastic; duffle or sea bags are made of lightweight canvas or denim. Food bags are generally waxed; the flat bottom makes them easy to use out-of-doors, as they stand easily when full.

The directions given below are for a bag for small articles of personal gear. The size of the ditty bag may be varied for the desired article, as described at the end of the project. See preceding pages in this chapter for techniques.

Equipment needed: thimble or sailor's palm; sail or large-eyed needle; pinking shears; chalk; ruler and circle marker; paper, pins or staples for pattern.

Materials needed: unbleached muslin, plastic, balloon cloth, duck, denim, or sailcloth; heavy thread or string; grommets, eyelets, or rings; cord or rope for drawstring.

Steps

1. Make a circle marker: cut a strip of lightweight cardboard about 7 inches by 1 inch; 1 inch from one end, mark place for thumbtack. From this point, punch holes at two spots, one at one-half the diameter of the bottom of the bag, the other 1/2 inch beyond this spot; for example, for 8-inch bottom, at 4 inches and 4½ inches (Figure XVI-24).
2. Make a paper pattern: for the bottom X (Figure XVI-24), with thumbtack on circle marker at center spot of bottom, place chalk in

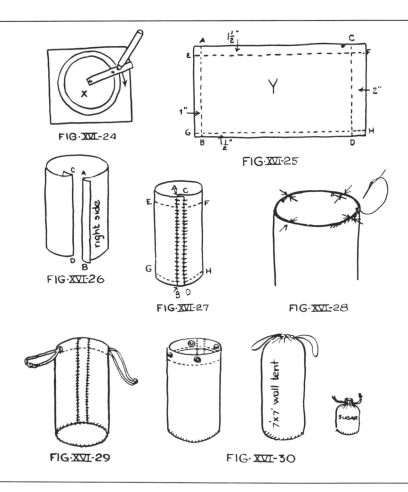

FIG·XVI-24

FIG·XVI-25

FIG·XVI-26

FIG·XVI-27

FIG·XVI-28

FIG·XVI-29

FIG·XVI-30

the other holes of marker, and draw two circles, one the size of the bottom (8 inches) and the other 1/2 inch larger all around (8½ inches).

For the length Y, cut length of bag 14 inches plus 1/2 inch at selvage (or plus 1 inch, if no selvage) and 1½ inch for top hem (16 inches in all). To determine the width of this piece, multiply the diameter by 3.1416 or 3-1/7 (for 8-inch bottom, this is 25 inches); add 3 inches for seams, 2 inches on one edge and 1 inch on the other (for 8-inch bottom, 25 inches plus 3 inches, or 28 inches total). Mark these lines with chalk—*A-B* and *C-D* (figure XVI-25). Pin or staple pattern together; adjust as needed.

3. Cut material from pattern. With chalk, mark line for bottom on right side of *X*; mark lines *A-B* and *C-D* on right sides of *Y*; mark lines *E-F* and *G-H* on right side of *Y* (Figure XVI-25).

4. To make side seam: fold at line *C-D*, wrong sides of material together, and place line *C-D* at line *A-B* on right side of material. Pin this side of seam in place. Turn inside out, and turn 1/4 inch at edge nearest *A-B*, right sides of material together. Pin this turned edge in place, making a flat seam (Figure XVI-26).

5. Sew length of *A-B* and *C-D*, working on right side; use ladder stitch. Space stitches evenly. Work on right side of material for second side of seam, feeling through material to be sure the stitching catches edge of seam; match stitches to first row (Figure XVI-27). (A chalk line 1/2 inch from edge of seam will guide the stitching.) Seam is flat, with two rows of stitching showing. The bottom of *Y* should be just the size of *X*, with edge turned in (8 inches).

6. Turn edge of *X* at chalked circle (8 inches), and turn bottom edge of *Y*.

7. With chalk, mark four evenly spaced points on right side of pieces *X* and *Y* (fold in half once, then again, to determine these points).

8. Pin pieces *X* and *Y* together at these points, right side of material out (Figure XVI-28). Pin in several more places, as needed.

9. Stitch *X* to *Y* with overcast stitch (see Chapter V on Leatherwork); there should be *no gathers* (Figure XVI-29).

10. Edge *G-H* may be stitched to piece *Y* with running stitch, for a better finish.

11. If drawstrings are to be used, insert grommets or eyelets on *front* of top hem before hemming; place two grommets at equal distances from center of side seam.

12. Turn hem at *E-F*, and stitch with running stitch (Figures XVI-27 and 29).

13. If drawstrings are *not* used, put an even number of grommets, eyelets, or buttonholes through both thicknesses of hem (Figure XVI-30).

14. Insert rope or cord for drawstring; whip ends of rope; tie ends together with square or fisherman's knot (see Chapter II on Braiding and Knotting).

Variations: Food bags—make of plastic or any firm cotton material. Mark bags (sugar, etc.) with felt marking pen before waterproofing. Waterproof before stitching. Bags for flour, sugar, and the like may have plastic linings; they should have an inner flap sewed at top hem, to keep food from falling out of bag. A single stitched seam may be used instead of the flat seam. Machine stitching is best for food bags. Cord attached on the outside, and tied with clove hitch or miller's knot, is more effective than a drawstring (Figure XVI-30).

Duffle or sea bag—use heavy material, such as sailcloth or denim. A sailor's palm and sail needle will be useful with light canvas. A good size for a duffle bag is from 10 inches to 16 inches for the bottom, and from 26 inches to 32 inches for the length. Duffle bags may be stenciled, or initials of cord may be sewed on the bag. Marlin, a tarred cord, is sometimes used by sailors for such decoration.

Tent bag—roll tent tightly, and tie with rope. Make bottom and length of bag fit the rolled tent (Figure XVI-30).

Collapsible Tent Poles

For trips or for storage, tent poles are easier to handle if they are collapsible. A good project for a trip group is to make compact sets from commercial poles or from saplings or dowels. Poles may also be made from the aluminum pipes used to house electric wiring or from strong lightweight plastic pipes used by plumbers. Ridge poles may be treated in similar fashion. This project is best for lightweight poles for small tents. The dimensions given here are for a pole 1½ inch in diameter.

Equipment needed: crosscut saw; vise; ruler and pencil; hammer; wood or rawhide mallet; tin shears; lightweight cardboard for pattern; sandpaper.

Materials needed: tent pole, or pole of needed length and diameter; galvanized metal, or tin from cans, to make two strips 5½ inches wide, long enough to go around pole, plus 1 inch; tacks.

Steps

1. Mark a 70 degree angle on tent pole. This angle is the diagonal on a 5 inch space (Figure XVI-31 *a*) on a 1½-inch pole. (Protractor may be used.)

2. Put pole in a vise, and saw on angle line; sand edges of cut (Figure XVI-31 *a*).

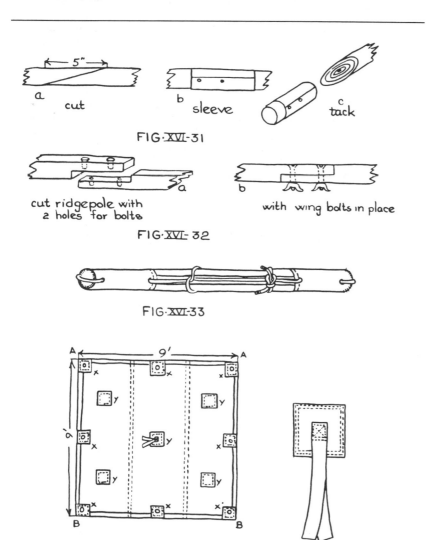

a cut

b sleeve

c tack

FIG·XVI-31

cut ridgepole with
2 holes for bolts

with wing bolts in place

FIG·XVI-32

FIG·XVI-33

FIG·XVI-34

FIG·XVI-34-a

3. Make a cardboard pattern of the metal sleeve to go around the pole with 1 inch overlap for seam. Make sleeve 5½ inches wide, allowing 1/4 inch to be folded back if using tin from a can; 5 inches is sufficient for galvanized sheet metal, if edges are smooth.
4. Make a tight joint (Figure XVI-31 b).
5. Transfer outline of pattern to metal; cut out with tin shears. If tin, turn top and bottom edges and flatten, to strengthen metal and to make edge smooth.
    (See Chapter VI on Metalwork for techniques in bending edges.)
6. Bend edges for seam (Figure XVI-31 b); flatten to make good fit.
7. Place on pole, both pieces of pole in place; hammer seam tight.
8. Remove one piece of pole; tack sleeve to other piece with tacks in two places (Figure XVI-31 c).

Collapsible Ridge Pole

Ridge poles may be made collapsible in the same manner as tent poles, if the ridge is lightweight. For heavier ridges, the pole should be cut and bolted as in Figure XVI-32 a; countersink the holes for the bolts; use wing nuts for the *under* side of the ridge pole (Figure XVI-32 b). It is important not to have anything such as the metal sleeve edge or a bolt head rubbing against the ridge of the tent.

Carrier for Poles

A simple device for carrying lightweight poles or sections of poles is the two-ended cloth carrier (Figure XVI-33). Use lightweight canvas or heavy denim. Make the ends round, and fit as in the ditty bag project in this chapter. Fasten cord to ends, allowing enough cord to wind around the poles and to tie in the middle of the bundle. This is a good device for keeping poles for a specific tent in one package. A bag for pegs, a bag for tent, and pole carriers may be made of similar materials, marked for easy identification.

A Tab Tarp

This is a good beginning step in tent making, especially for a group. A sewing machine is really essential in tent making, although it is conceivable that all stitching might be done by hand. This tarp may be used in a number of ways—as a shelter, a fly, a woodpile cover, etc. Grommets in the corners and on the edges of this tarp make it especially strong; tapes may be used instead of grommets, if desired. See preceding pages in this chapter for techniques.

Equipment needed: sewing machine or needle, thimble, etc.; grommet setting tools; pins; waterproofing equipment; heavy thread.

Materials needed: 9¼ yards material 39 inches wide—closely woven, firm material, such as duck, heavy muslin, sheeting, or balloon cloth; 10 yards cotton twill tape, 1 inch wide; grommets or rings.

Steps

1. Cut material into three strips, each 39 inches long.
2. Overlap center selvage edges 1½ inches, and stitch flat with two rows of stitching. Turn side selvage edges *A-B* 1½ inches, and stitch flat, using two rows of stitching (Figure XVI-34).
3. Turn ends *A-A* and *B-B* 1½ inches; pin tape across to bind this hem. (Tape may be used on selvage edges at sides, above, but is not necessary.) Or, turn regular hem across ends, and pin in place.
4. Cut thirteen patches each 3 inches square; turn edges in 3/4 inch, and baste in place as in Figure XVI-34—at the four corners (*x*), at the middle of the four sides (*x*) and in the places for the five tapes (*y*).
5. Stitch side hems of tarp, stitching corner and side patches at the same time. Stitch each row twice to be sure these are firmly stitched.
6. Stitch tape patches *y* in place with double rows of stitching.
7. Cut tapes 18 inches long; baste in place in center of *y* patches, as in Figure XVI-34 *a*; stitch through patch and tarp material on edges, and through center, crisscrossing for strength.
8. Set grommets or rings at corners and sides (*x* patches); or, sew tapes at these patches if preferred.
9. Waterproof as desired (see this chapter).

Rope Making

Rope may be made by a number of methods. Binder twine, used in lashing and other camp construction projects, is the usual base of rope that is handmade, although long vines, such as grapevine and fibers and inner strip of bark, may be used. Rope may be braided in a three-strand braid or twisted by hand. A good group project is to make a machine that will twist rope. The making of the machine described below calls for the aid of several campers. Once the machine is ready, it can be used indefinitely.

Equipment needed: bit and brace with 3/16-inch drill; pliers; screwdriver; crosscut saw; ruler and pencil; sandpaper; matches or lighter.

Materials needed: wood for machine as follows—1 piece 3/4 inch by 6 inches by 7½ inches for back, one piece 3/4 inch by 6 inches by 24 inches for base, one piece 1/4 inch by 1½ inches by 12 inces for paddle, one forked stick for beater about 5 inches by 1/2 inch with 2-inch fork; 24 inches of 12-gauge wire; two angle irons and four screws; binder twine, cotton cord, or similar material.

Steps to make machine

1. Drill three holes 2 inches apart, and 1¼ inch from top in backboard. Saw corners of board at top (Figure XVI-35).
2. Attach base to back with angle irons (Figure XVI-35).
3. Sand edges of paddle (whittle handle, if desired). Mark center line, and mark places for three holes, to correspond with those on the backboard (Figure XVI-35). Drill these holes.
4. Sand all edges.
5. Cut wire into three 8-inch pieces with cutting edge of pliers, and bend hook ends. Insert in holes from front, and finish as in Figure XVI-36.
6. Slip paddle on wires.
7. Make a beater from the forked stick; peel bark and sand smooth (Figure XVI-37).

Steps to make rope

1. Cut three lengths of twine or cord; measure each length twice as long as desired length of finished rope, plus about one-third length. There will be some "take-up" by the twisting.
2. Fold each strand in half, so there is a loop in center. Slip a loop over each metal hook, and have one person (No. 1) stretch the six lengths out, away from machine, tying together with an overhand knot (Figure XVI-38).
3. Another person (No. 2) sits on the baseboard, and is the operator of the paddle which turns the three wires (Figures XVI-39).
4. A third person (No. 3) uses the beater to keep the twine from becoming entangled (Figure XVI-39).

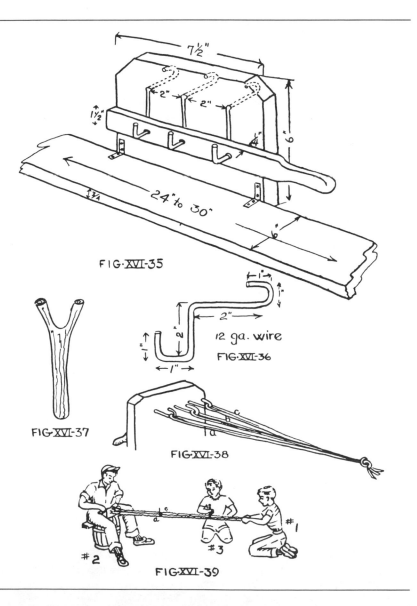

FIG·XVI-35

FIG·XVI-36

12 ga. wire

FIG·XVI-37

FIG·XVI-38

FIG·XVI-39

5. No. 1 holds bundle of twine strands out taut, as No. 2 pushes paddle around in a circle, making the strands *a-b-c* twist in three separate strands; as these strands are twisted tight, No. 3 moves the beater up and down length of strands, keeping the hairs of the twine from getting tangled, and also keeping the three strands separate. When the three strands are tightly twisted, No. 1 loosens hold on the end, and helps the rope twist evenly, in opposite direction from the twist of the individual strands. No. 3 uses beater to make the rope firm, pushing the beater against the three-stranded piece, as No. 1 guides the twisting. (Only practice will tell when to begin the rope-twisting.) The rope should be smooth, without little bumps of the smaller strands.
6. When rope is twisted all the way to the backboard, the loops are taken off the hooks, and the ends tied with an overhand knot, or whipped.
7. To remove hairs from the rope, singe with match or lighter, moving the flame under rope, and smoothing off with hand.
8. Roll under foot on board or floor, to make even.

Hanging Shelves

When an extra shelf is needed in a cabin or an outdoor kitchen, a simple one can be made of boards and rope. To make into a cooler or a dust-proof food box, just add heavy cotton material.

Equipment needed: brace and bit; sandpaper; crosscut saw.

Materials needed for shelf: three pieces of wood (ends of orange crates, outdoor plywood, 1/2-inch pine, etc.) desired size for shelves (for square food box, 12 inches is good size); four pieces of rope, 30 inches to 40 inches long, depending on distance between shelves. *For cooler,* add piece of cloth (heavy muslin, terry cloth, etc.; *not* cheesecloth; old turkish toweling is good; 4 feet 2 inches wide, long enough to reach above and below shelves (about the same length as one piece of rope); zipper for the length from top to bottom shelf; tacks or thumbtacks; pan for top.

Steps for hanging shelves

1. Bore holes in the corners of each board. Place these about 1 inch from corner; make size to allow rope to slip through easily.
2. Sand edges and corner holes.
3. Tie overhand knot (see chapter on Braiding and Knotting, Figure II-21) in end of one rope, and slip the rope through the hole in bottom shelf;

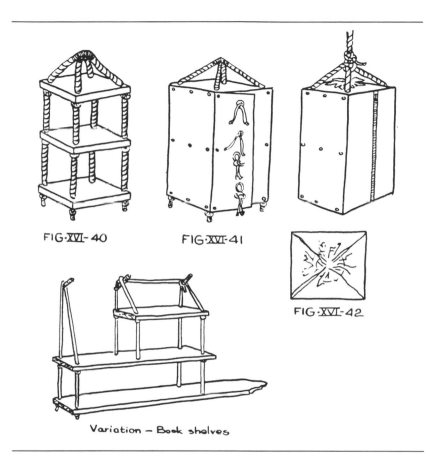

FIG·XVI-40   FIG·XVI-41

FIG·XVI-42

Variation — Book shelves

Steps for a food box (dry cache, Figure XVI-41)

1. Cut cloth size to stretch around top and bottom shelves, allowing for 1/2 inch to be turned under.
2. Sew in zipper in front, making a tube of cloth; or use without zipper, having an overlap in front, to be secured with snaps or ties.
3. Tack the cloth in place at the three shelves.

Steps for a cooler (wet cache, Figure XVI-42).

1. Cut cloth long enough to gather at the bottom of shelves, and to fold over the top of the top shelf; add zipper, snaps, or ties, as desired, and tack in place at the shelves.
2. Tie end of cloth under shelves in a loose overhand knot, or whip together loosely.
3. Place a shallow pan (such as a deep pie pan, or a 9-inch square cake pan) on top of cache. Slit the corners of the cloth at top, and place the pieces in the pan so they soak up the water.
4. Keep the pan filled with water; hang cooler in a dry, shady spot with good circulation. Wet sides of cloth, so that water drips off end. The cloth will keep wet, and evaporation of the water will keep contents cool. (This is not a refrigerator, however!)

Chest with Tray

This is a woodworking project, to be planned and carried out by an individual or by a group. A small box could be one camper's treasure chest, a larger one a food or kitchen equipment box, or a program supply or equipment box. The project is described with a tray, to indicate a step in progression.

Equipment needed: hammer; crosscut saw; ruler and square; reamer or countersink; screwdriver; bit and brace; sandpaper.

Materials needed: lumber as needed for specific box (read directions); nails, screws; hinges—metal or leather; rope for handles.

Steps

1. Decide on size of box, and on the lumber necessary. Plywood (use outdoor plywood, if box will be used outdoors) or scrap lumber can be used. Measurements will depend somewhat on wood available.

make another overhand knot just under place for second shelf; repeat for top shelf, and carry rope over to opposite corner of top shelf, allowing for loop to hang shelf (Figure XVI-40). Do same in opposite corner. Repeat on other two corners. Hang shelves on a tree limb, and adjust knots so shelves hang evenly. Knots may be adjusted without untying them. Ropes at top may be whipped together, and an additional piece of rope tied there to hang shelves to tree; or one length of rope may be used to go through first and second set of corners, and another length for third and fourth sets.

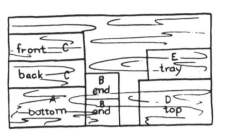

FIG·XVI-43

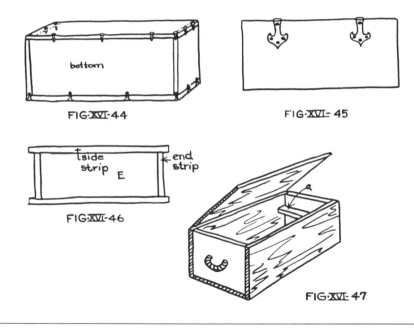

FIG·XVI-44

FIG·XVI-45

FIG·XVI-46

FIG·XVI-47

3. Assemble with screws or nails; screws make the box stronger, and must be used with plywood. Countersink holes before screwing. Fill holes with plastic wood, if desired.
4. Bore holes in ends for rope handles; tie ropes with overhand knots inside holes, or make ring grommets (see chapter on Braiding and Knotting, Figures II-105-107).
5. Sand all edges.
6. Attach metal hinges to cover and back, or make leather hinges tacked on with upholstery nails (Figure XVI-45).
7. To make removable tray Figure XVI-46 *E*: the bottom of tray may be wallboard, masonite, or 1/4-inch plywood; sides may be 1/2-inch pine strips or similar. Cut bottom of tray 2 inches shorter than inside length of chest. Cut side strips so they will slip in and out of chest easily. Cut end strips to fit inside the side strips on tray bottom. Nail or screw tray together at bottom, setting end strips inside side strips, at edges of bottom, so there are finger spaces between sides of tray and sides of box.
8. Screw two pieces 1-inch square strip on inside ends of chest, the desired height for the tray rests (Figure XVI-47 *a*).
9. To finish: sand edges; stain and rub with wax, or paint, or rub with linseed oil and polish with a cloth. Decorate as desired, with stencils, rope, etc.

Reflector Oven and Case

A collapsible reflector oven is a great addition to trip or primitive camping gear. The making of the oven utilizes some of the techniques of the chapter on metalwork, making of the case is similar to projects in this chapter. Both are good group projects. Sheet metal, cut to size, may be used instead of the cookie sheets used here; many individual variations are also possible. Aluminum sheets are lighter than tin and they are rust resistant, but they are more expensive.

Equipment needed for oven: egg-beater drill with metal drill or big nail and hammer; file. *For cover:* needle and thread; scissors or pinking shears; paper and stapler for pattern.

Materials needed for oven: four cookie sheets, two large, 2 small; the kind with edges on four sides is best; two stove bolts or 1/4-inch threaded steel rods, 1/2 inch longer than sheets—two wing nuts to fit; six 1/2-inch bolts and wingnuts. *For cover:* cloth and string.

2. Measure pieces and cut them to size. If material is mill cut, use side and one end as a corner (Figure XVI-43). There will be one bottom (*A*), two ends (*B*), front and back (*C*) and top (*D*). Top may be 1/2 inch wider and 1 inch longer than bottom (*A*) to give a fingerhold for lifting cover.

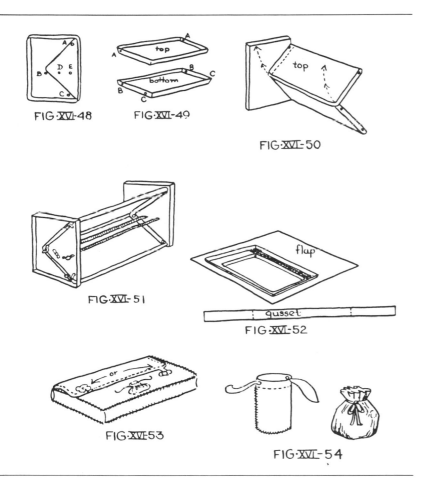

FIG·XVI-48   FIG·XVI-49

FIG·XVI-50

FIG·XVI-51

gusset
FIG·XVI-52

FIG·XVI-53

FIG·XVI-54

2. Bore holes in the top corners of sides of top sheet at *A* (Figure XVI-49) to correspond to holes on side sheets; bore holes on bottom sheet at *B* and *C* to correspond to *B* and *C* holes on side sheets. The top sheet has holes *only* at the top (*A*), so that the top sheet can pivot on the *A* bolts, making it possible to look at the food while it is cooking, without moving oven (see dotted lines, Figure XVI-50).
3. Assemble as in Figure XVI-51; put bolts in from inside out, with wing nuts on outside of oven. The bottom edge of the top sheet should rest on the top edge of the bottom sheet at back of oven, overlapping just a little. It may be necessary to bend edge with pliers, to make this possible.
4. Stove bolts or rods are inserted to make rack for pan; wing nuts are on outside of oven (Figures XVI-48 *D* and *E*; and 51).

Steps to make case.

1. Review techniques at beginning of this chapter, and see Leatherwork chapter, project on cases. Make a paper pattern first. Stack the pans together, with stove bolts inside top pan. Mark around the larger sheets, allowing space on ends and bottom for seams and hem, and adding flap on bottom pieces (Figure XVI-52). Cut top piece the same size, without flap. Cut gusset piece to go around sides and bottom, as wide as depth of the stacked pans. Allow for seams. Cut out pattern, staple or pin together, and try on; adjust as needed.
2. Cut cloth from pattern with pinking shears or scissors. Pin together.
3. Stitch with overcast or similar stitch (see Chapter V on Leatherwork, Figures V-22 and 30). Make hems on flap and top, using running or similar stitch.
4. Fasten flap with two buttonholes (see Figure XVI-15) and wooden buttons (see chapter on Woodworking); or make two loops of cord, and attach to toggles on case (Figure XVI-53).
5. Make a small drawstring bag for the bolts and nuts (Figure XVI-54) and stitch it on the outside of case below buttons. Make it big enough to hold the bolts and nuts and to slip them in and out easily.

Small Wall (three-sheet) Tent

Tent making is an advanced project for a group interested in lightweight equipment for trip or primitive camping. The making of the tent will

Steps to make oven.

1. Review techniques in Metalwork chapter. Mark off a right angle on the two small (end) sheets, as in Figure XVI-48; bore holes as indicated, at *A, B, C, D, E; D* and *E* should be parallel to the bottom of the sheet, spaced to hold rods for cooking pan.

probably be an in-town activity, in preparation for camping. When boys and girls have had experience in making group tents, they often become interested in making their own individual tents. As with other equipment-making projects, the basic plan should be altered to carry out individual desires and to meet particular needs. The project described here is for a two-person tent.

In making a tent, it is a good plan to make a small model, cut to scale and basted together; this helps in seeing how the tent will look and in planning stitching. When the actual tent material is cut, it is good to pin it together, and to insert patches, tapes, and other small pieces, so that one stitching will secure them into seams or hems as the sewing progresses. Planning and testing are essential parts of the procedure in making a large object such as a tent.

Equipment needed: scissors or pinking shears; large work space; sewing machine; pins; grommet setting tools; brush or spray for waterproofing.

Materials needed: three sheets of fine quality, 81 inches by 108 inches—irregulars or seconds serve very well—white, or colored as desired; or 7 yards of 81-inch unbleached muslin sheeting, or similar material; 19 feet 1-inch twill tape; 28 grommets or D-rings; heavy duty cotton thread cord for guy lines; dye, if desired; waterproofing material; material for poles and ridge.

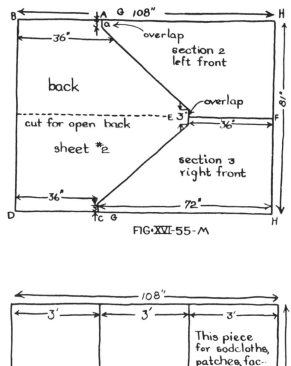

FIG·XVI-55-M

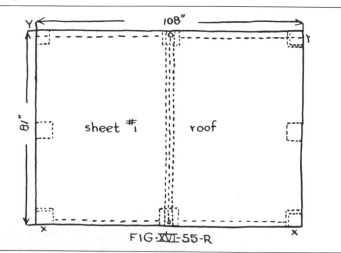

FIG·XVI-55-R

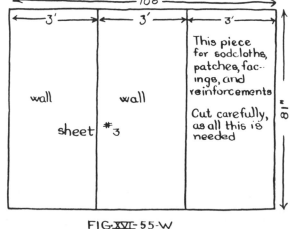

FIG·XVI-55-W

Steps

1. Read directions through first; think through the whole project; plan whether you want tapes, rings, grommets, sod cloth, overhang.

   Make a cloth model, one inch to a foot; baste it together; set it up to see how the tent will look. Check each detail.

2. If using sheets, take out hem; wash and press. If using new material, wash and dye before cutting, to shrink material and to remove sizing.

3. To cut (Figures XVI-55 *R, M,* and *W*):

   Sheet No. 1 makes the roof, as is.

   Sheet No. 2 (Figure XVI-55 *M*) is cut to make front and back pieces.

   Sheet No. 3 (Figure XVI-55 *W*) is cut in three strips each three feet; two of these strips are for the side walls; the other is for small pieces, such as patches and strips. Cut six pieces 5 inches by 10 inches to make 5-inch doubled squares for reinforcement patches. Cut a strip six inches by 72 inches to extend front flap at opening; cut a similar strip for back, if back is to be open.

4. To stitch:

   Roof: fold roof piece in half, through center for 81-inch ridge. Turn in edges of two patches and pin at each end of ridge, running selvage under 1/2 inch. Pin tape across ridge, turning under at ends, or extending to make loops or to hold D-rings for guy ropes. Stitch tape in three places—at edges and in middle. Stitch patches, criss-crossing stitching.

   Walls: turn 3-inch hem on sides of roof for eaves; turn 1/2-inch hem at top of wall pieces and pin into roof hem, so that there are overhangs or eaves of about 3 inches (Figure XVI-56 *x*). Insert tapes at middle of hem, for rolling up wall *y* (Figure XVI-57 *y*); half of tape inside, half outside tent.

   Front and back: double the 6-inch by 72-inch strip and turn edges in; stitch it to the left front section (*A-G*) to extend the 3-inch overlap provided (Figure XVI-55 *M A-a*). Do the same with the left section of back, if back is to be open. If back is not open, stitch tape across from corner at top of wall to opposite corner before seaming.

   Hem length of right-hand section(s) (Figure XVI-55 *M*) *G-H.*

   Pin front sections to roof, turning edges under, starting at *a* to *E,* and *c* to *E* (Figure XVI-55 *M*), making flat seam. Do same with back piece(s) (Figure XVI-58).

Insert tapes through corners so that half of each piece is on the outside of tent, half on the inside, to tie rolled flaps (Figure XVI-56 *E*).

Pin patches at corners of tent (Figure XVI-56); insert tapes and D-rings, if desired. (Put grommets in later.) Stitch all seams and patches.

Join corners at sides of wall and front and back with flat seams *A-B, C-D, E-F.* Or, these may be hemmed, and left open, with tapes to tie, or with grommets for lacing.

Turn hem all around the bottom of the tent, from front to back; insert tape for loops for ground pegs, or put grommets in later; stitch. If sod cloth is desired, stitch in with hem (see below). Stitch tapes in place in front (and back) opening(s), to tie overlap (Figure XVI-57).

5. *Grommets* may be placed at the spots where guy ropes will be used, for ground pegs at bottom hem and for tent pole spikes at ridge. Guy lines will go at the four corners, in the middle of the roof eaves, at peak of roof, front and back, if no ridge pole is planned. D-rings may be used instead of grommets. Handmade grommets are preferred by some for lightweight material; make with small ring and button-

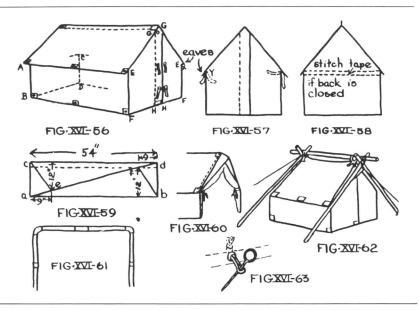

FIG·XVI-56   FIG·XVI-57   FIG·XVI-58

FIG·XVI-59   FIG·XVI-60   FIG·XVI-62

FIG·XVI-61   FIG·XVI-63

holing. (See techniques in this chapter for fastening patches, D-rings, grommets, etc.)

6. *Waterproof* as desired. It is easiest to waterproof a tent when it is standing; brush or spray the solution evenly and thoroughly. Let it dry thoroughly.

7. *Place guy ropes* as needed; a taut line hitch may be used to shorten ropes, or small wooden or metal runners may be used. Whip all ends.

8. *Desirable additions:*

   Sod cloth: a 6-inch to 10-inch strip may be sewed to bottom of walls and front and back pieces, making a sod cloth to go under a ground sheet. Stitch into bottom hems, and hem as needed. Place grommets in the four corners, inside the tent.

   Ground cloth: a ground cloth may be made of waterproofed material, such as plastic; make it the size of the floor of the tent; hem it all around; put grommets in the four corners, to correspond with grommets in the sod cloth, so the ground cloth can be pegged down through the sod cloth with skewer pegs.

   Overhangs: these may be made for the front and back openings; cut as in Figure XVI-59; hem edges; stitch to roof when front and back pieces are stitched (Figure XVI-60).

9. *Tent poles* (see Figures XVI-31 and 32): poles for the front and back of the tent should be 6 feet, with spike at top to go through grommet in ridge. Tent poles may be made of saplings, wooden poles, or of metal.

   A ridge pole stretches the length of the ridge, with holes in the end, through which the pole spikes are placed. Guy ropes at front and back overhangs or at ends of tent ridge will do away with need for a ridge and should be satisfactory in this small tent.

   Tapes on the outside of the tent ridge will make it possible to use an outside ridge pole, with shears for poles at front and back. This outside ridge may be suspended from a tree (Figure XVI-62).

   Electrician's thin wall conduits with couplings may be used to make collapsible poles and ridge. These are lightweight and rust resistant. They are used inside the tent without spikes, so no grommets are needed in ridge of tent (Figure XVI-61).

10. *Ropes for ground pegs:* small lengths of rope are put in the grommets in hem of tent, for pegging tent to ground. Put loop through grommet from inside of hem, and tie ends together with overhand knot—see Braiding and Knotting chapter, Figure II-21 (Figure XVI-63).

Decorations for Special Events

XVII

Camp parties, banquets, special days, campfires and other out-of-the-ordinary occasions call for special trimmings of decorations, favors, invitations, menus, or costumes. Such events will stimulate many activities as the entire program is planned and carried out by the campers. By no means the least of these activities will be those that call for ingenuity and creativity in making the color for the big event. The arrangements committee will find that there are ways to use techniques described in this book; imaginative use of materials found out-of-doors or in the craft supplies will produce all kinds of articles that will create the atmosphere for the occasion.

Real creativity will be the privilege of those who make the sample that will be used in fashioning a hundred favors, the backdrop for the banquet's head table, or the mobiles of natural objects that will twist in the breezes made by the square dancers, but there will also be fun and chances for individual expression for those who help to make all the decorations and favors.

Lesser events than the last night banquet or the all-camp barn dance will give many campers opportunities for similar projects. These may be invitations issued by one tent group for a special cook-out, name tag favors made by the oldest boys for those smallest campers who are joining their campfire, or handmade gifts fashioned by each girl in a cabin group for someone else at the last night's campfire. Such occasions give many campers chances to use their imagination in creating something worth giving away or worth saving a memento.

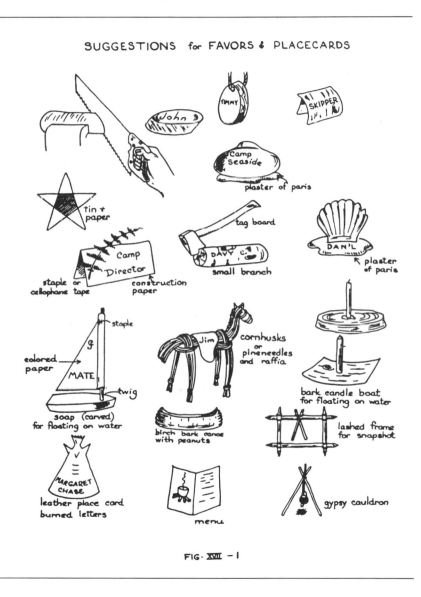

SUGGESTIONS for FAVORS & PLACECARDS

FIG. XVII - 1

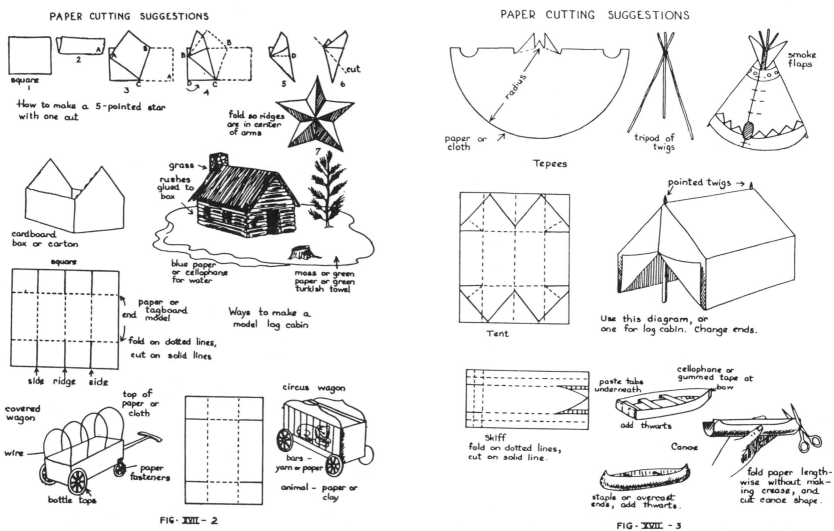

PAPER CUTTING SUGGESTIONS

square
1

2

A

3
B
C

4
B
B
C

5
D

6
cut

How to make a 5-pointed star with one cut

fold so ridges are in center of arms

7

cardboard box or carton

grass →
rushes glued to box

blue paper or cellophane for water

moss or green paper or green turkish towel

Ways to make a model log cabin

square

paper or tagboard model

fold on dotted lines, cut on solid lines

side ridge side

covered wagon

wire

top of paper or cloth

bottle tops

paper fasteners

circus wagon

bars – yarn or paper

animal – paper or clay

FIG· XVII – 2

PAPER CUTTING SUGGESTIONS

radius

paper or cloth →

Tepees

tripod of twigs

smoke flaps

Tent

pointed twigs →

Use this diagram, or one for log cabin. Change ends.

Skiff
fold on dotted lines, cut on solid line.

paste tabs underneath

add thwarts

cellophane or gummed tape at bow

Canoe

staple or overcast ends, add thwarts.

fold paper length-wise without mak-ing crease, and cut canoe shape

FIG· XVII – 3

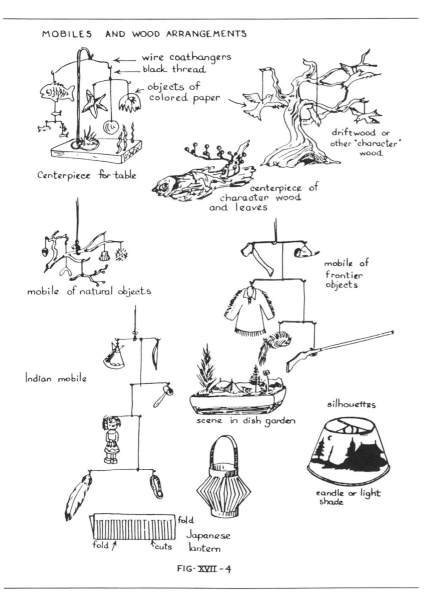

MOBILES AND WOOD ARRANGEMENTS

← wire coathangers
← black thread
objects of colored paper

Centerpiece for table

driftwood or other "character" wood

centerpiece of character wood and leaves

mobile of natural objects

mobile of frontier objects

Indian mobile

scene in dish garden

silhouettes

candle or light shade

fold
Japanese lantern
fold ↑   ↑cuts

FIG·XVII-4

Banquets and parties usually have a theme around which the decorations and favors are planned. The dining hall may be transformed into a gypsy camp, an underwater cave, or a pioneer village; the recreation hall may blossom with panels depicting the tales of Paul Bunyan or Hiawatha; the waterfront dock may be the throne from which Neptune views his subjects, or the landing place of the Vikings. There is so much in the lore of the early inhabitants who have lived in the various regions of our land that there seems no end to the possibiliteis for dressing up camp occasions. An appreciation of those who pioneered our country or a new view of the heroes of our folk tales may well be as much a result of the festivities as will be the development of initiative and resourcefulness and the use of the imagination. Good group activity is also a result.

If books, materials, and equipment are easily available to tent and cabin groups, and if counselors are quick to seize the opportunities to encourage campers to see the possibilities for creative activity, many fascinating projects will result. No two occasions will be the same in one summer, or even as the years pass—and this is good! Each camp group should be free to create its own special events, and the trimmings that make them memorable.

Pictured here are some ideas that have been used in camps. They are intended as suggestions only, to start campers along the trail of ingenious projects for their own special occasions.

EQUIPMENT AND MATERIALS

Equipment and materials needed cannot be listed completely, as they will vary with the specific projects, but this basic list may serve to point out the kind of equipment and material which will be most helpful if it is provided for each tent or cabin group, in the unit hut or the small camp's recreation center, making it simple to take advantage of the first glimmer of a good idea.

—*Equipment to put things together:* household cement; white glue; rubber cement and paste; staplers; Scotch tape and masking tape; fine wire and coat hangers; lacing; thong, string and twine; pins, clips, and paper fasteners; needles and thread.

—*Materials for making articles:* construction, wrapping, newsprint, and mimeograph paper; remnants of cloth and leather; aluminum foil and tin cans; natural objects found in camp—acorns, shells,

MURALS as BACKGROUNDS for BANQUETS

mural on brown
wrapping paper
with poster paint

Paul Bunyan
theme

head table

Pioneer Village

Signal Flags for nautical theme
authentic, or
colored paper

International theme,
flags from other countries
may be made of colored
paper or cloth.

pennants
colored paper or
crayon on cloth, ironed

FIG· XVII - 5

cones, wood, seed and seed pods, bark from dead-and-down trees.
—*Equipment for marking and decorating:* crayons, pencils, felt marking pens; all kinds of inks; poster or watercolor paints; brushes; wood burning tools.

PAPER CUTTING AND FOLDING

Paper cutting and folding is a craft that may be used in creating some of these articles. Once a procedure is worked out, it may be used over and over in the cutting and assembling of articles. Individual treatment of the basic design will provide opportunities for creative expression. Tents, tepees, log cabins, covered wagons, corrals, bunk houses, and stars may all be developed in this way (Figures XVII-2 and 3).

Check these chapters for further help: Chapter VII on Printing and Stenciling for suggestions for menus, inviations, and favors; Chapter XIII on Correlation with Dramatics for scenery, masks, etc.; Chapter XV on Correlation with Nature for conservation practices and suggestions for centerpieces and decorations; and Chapter XX on Map Making for table models and relief maps.

Games and Sports Equipment

XVIII

In the games and sports fields there are many areas in which campers can use arts and crafts techniques and media. Some of these areas have to do with creating equipment, and some with keeping equipment in good repair. Some are good for service projects for the camp by a group of campers, and some serve as individual projects for campers in making their own designs, adaptations, and decorations. Game sets for rainy-day use or for quiet periods, archery targets and tackle, waterfront equipment, Indian game materials, and board games with pegs or counters or men—all of these are possibilities for camper handcraft activities.

EQUIPMENT FOR INFORMAL GAMES

Games using boards, such as checkers, may be made on stumps or from pieces of interesting wood from lumber yards and cabinetmakers' shops. Natural objects, such as pebbles, acorns, seeds, can be used as men or counters. Boards may be carved or marked and counters made with a minimum of woodworking tools, such as jackknife, saw, chisel, drills, and finishing materials. Pegs for ring games can be whittled as beginning projects in woodworking. Old favorites take on new flavor when the equipment is made by the campers, or when ingenuity makes it easy to set up a game wherever campers may be. Handmade equipment is less expensive and often more durable than commercial game sets, and it gives the added satisfaction of a good craft project.

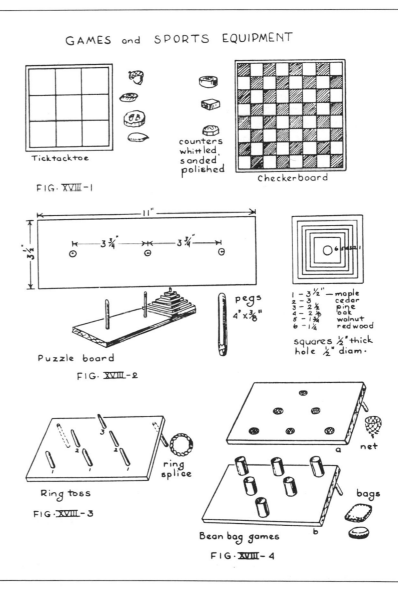

GAMES and SPORTS EQUIPMENT

Ticktacktoe

counters whittled, sanded, polished

Checkerboard

FIG. XVIII-1

Puzzle board

pegs 4" x ³⁄₈"

1 – 3½" – maple
2 – 3" – cedar
3 – 2½" – pine
4 – 2⅛" – oak
5 – 1¾" – walnut
6 – 1¼" – redwood

squares ½" thick
hole ½" diam.

FIG. XVIII-2

Ring toss

ring splice

FIG. XVIII-3

net

bags

Bean bag games

FIG. XVIII-4

—*Tick-tack-toe and checkerboards*—make wooden bases, using wood-carving tools to mark divisions. Sand well, and wax for durable finish, or paint. Make men from slices of wood or nuts, or from whittled or natural objects (Figure XVIII-1).

—*Puzzle boards* are fun for individual play. The one pictured is from the Kentucky Mountains. It has three whittled pegs set in a board, and six squares of wood (each a different wood) with a hole drilled in the center of each. Biggest is 3½ inches square, smallest 1¼ inches square, others in between. All should be well sanded and waxed. Puzzle is to move the pile of graduated squares, one move at a time, to other pegs, so the pile is finally on another peg, in same order (Figure XVIII-2). Time the operation for competition. More intricate puzzles are those where pieces of wood interlock.

—*Ring toss*—whittle pegs and drill holes in board to hold pegs. Put extra pegs at back for legs to hold board at slant. Use ring splice (see Figures II-105-107) to make the rings. Paint or tape a colored strip for scoring (Figure XVIII-3).

—*Bean bag games*—make bean bags of lightweight canvas, denim, leather scraps, etc., using leather stitches (see Chapter V). Use pebbles, coarse sand, dried corn or beans, for fillings. A board for bean bag toss can be made with holes sawed with compass saw (Figure XVIII-4 *a*). Nets (see Chapter II) can be made to tack in back of holes, to catch bags. Tin cans nailed to boards can be used instead of holes (Figure XVIII-4 *b*).

—*Skittles*—small wooden pegs and a throwing stick may be whittled from rough sticks, kindling, or broom handles (Figure XVIII-5). This is a Pioneer game.

Pins for *bowls* are longer—use with indoor baseballs.

GAMES WITH INDIVIDUAL EQUIPMENT

Many games can be played by two or more campers, using sticks and other handmade equipment. A few sets of such equipment, ready for introductory play, will stimulate campers to play the game, and eventually to make their own sets of equipment.

—*Toss and catch* is an Indian game of a stick and wooden, bone, or leather rings held by a thong (Figure XVIII-6).

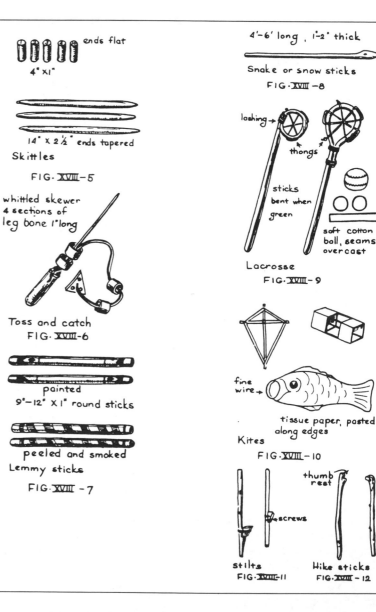

ends flat
4" x 1"

Skittles
FIG. XVIII—5

whittled skewer
4 sections of
leg bone 1"long

Toss and catch
FIG. XVIII-6

painted
9"-12" x 1" round sticks

peeled and smoked
Lemmy sticks
FIG. XVIII - 7

4'-6' long , 1-2" thick

Snake or snow sticks
FIG. XVIII —8

lashing

thongs

sticks bent when green

soft cotton ball, seams overcast

Lacrosse
FIG. XVIII - 9

fine wire

tissue paper, pasted along edges
Kites
FIG. XVIII - 10

thumb rest

screws

stilts
FIG. XVIII-11

Hike sticks
FIG. XVIII - 12

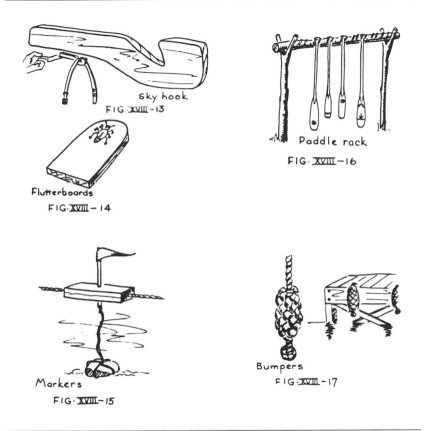

sky hook
FIG XVIII-13

Flutterboards
FIG XVIII-14

Paddle rack
FIG XVIII-16

Markers
FIG XVIII-15

Bumpers
FIG XVIII-17

—*Lemmy sticks or Maori sticks* are used in rhythmic tapping, tossing, and twirling by two (or four) players. Sticks are about 10 inches long and thick as a broom handle; they may be decorated by carving, painting, or staining (Figure XVIII-7).
—*Snake or snow sticks* are sticks that are hurled across ice, hard snow, or hard ground for distance and for accuracy. The bottom is flattened, and the end carved as a head (Figure XVIII-8).
—*Lacrosse sticks* are made of forked sticks and netting (Figure XVIII-9). They may be used informally for catch or in the game of lacrosse.

INDIVIDUAL PLAY EQUIPMENT

Some activities that are termed play activities may be enjoyed as individual or group activities. Kites, stilts, walking sticks, and tricks are typical equipment for such activities.

—*Kites*—for camps with open fields and windy days, this activity has wide scope for originality in design and construction. It is also a good international play activity (Figure XVIII-10).
—*Stilts* are fun for younger campers. The stilts can be made with rough sticks or finished lumber. A cutout on side of stick helps to hold the "step" with a screw or two and lashing (see any campcraft book) to fasten securely (Figure XVIII-11).
—*Hike or totem sticks*—these are staffs to help with climbing, with construction, or to tell a story. A stick that reaches in height to between shoulder and elbow is good. Mark in feet and inches for measuring heights and distances, or burn or carve "totem" signs to tell the history of the owner's adventures (Figure XVIII-12).
—*Sky hook*—this is a sort of trick game, using a wooden "hook" to balance a belt or similar object. Sky hooks are fun to make and to use. The one shown is about 3½ inches long, to be used with 1 inch belt. Trick is to balance the sky hook on the end of finger or table; it works only when a strap or something similar is hung on the hook (Figure XVIII-13).

WATERFRONT EQUIPMENT

On the waterfront there are many ways in which campers can make equipment to add to the fun in the water, or to the shipshape appearance of the setup. Well-whipped or spliced ends of rops and lines (see Chapter II) on boats and canoes, on markers for the swimming areas, or on the lines used with life preservers; bumpers made of braided rope; stenciled symbols and names on boats, canoes, paddles, oars: these are all good craft ventures for campers. Here are some suggestions:

—*Flutter boards*—make them smooth and colorful (Figure XVIII-14).
—*Markers for swimming areas*—floaters or flags (Figure XVIII-15).

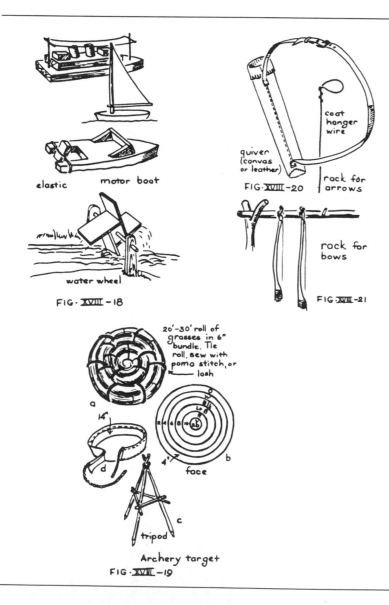

elastic   motor boat

water wheel

FIG · XVIII –18

20'-30' roll of grasses in 6" bundle. Tie roll, sew with poma stitch, or lash

a

14"

b
face

4"

d

c

tripod

Archery target

FIG · XVIII –19

quiver (convas or leather)

coat hanger wire

rack for arrows

FIG · XVIII –20

rack for bows

FIG · XVIII –21

—*Paddles and oars*—keep them in good condition, well-marked, well-sanded, colorful. Make a rack for them using lashing, or whittled pegs (Figure XVIII-16). Advanced campers may make their own paddles.

—*Bumpers for the docks*—(Figure XVIII-17). Also see chapter on Braiding and Knotting, Figures II-76-81.

Keeping boats and canoes in good condition is a craftsman's job, too. For shallow pools, brooks, creeks, etc., younger campers will like to make *boat models, water wheels, bridges* (Figure XVIII-18).

ARCHERY EQUIPMENT

Various pieces of archery equipment may be made. *Targets* can be made of grass or straw, using basketry coil techniques (Figure XVIII-19 a; also see Figure III-15 in chapter on Basketry). *Target faces* can be painted on oilcloth, lightweight canvas, or heavy paper (Figure XVIII-19 b). *Easels* for holding targets can be lashed (Figure XVIII-19 c). Other pieces to make are *leather tackle*—quivers, arm guards, etc. (see Chapter V on Leather); *wire racks* for arrows (Figure XVIII-20); *racks for bows,* using wooden pegs (Figure XVIII-21). For advanced archers, the making and repairing of arrows and bows is suggested.

OTHER SPORTS EQUIPMENT

Some things to do are illustrated in Figure XVIII-22: *bases* made of burlap or canvas, stuffed with straw or grass; *nets* for badminton, volley ball, tennis, etc.; *repairing* of leather balls and nets; improvised lacrosse and other sticks. (See chapters on Leatherwork, Braiding and Knotting.)

BOXES, BAGS, AND RACKS FOR EQUIPMENT

Make *pegs* with jackknife and wood scraps for hanging all kinds of equipment (see Chapter X). Make *boxes* with trays for storing games, sports equipment, etc. (see Chapter XVI). Make *bags* for toting and storing sails, balls, etc. (see Chapter XVI). Make *signs* for storage shelves, signing-out charts, etc. (see Chapter XI). Some of the articles that may be made are illustrated in Figure XVIII-23).

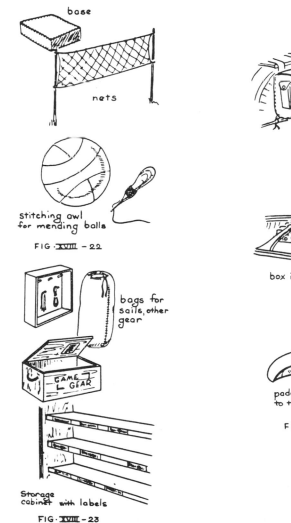

base

nets

stitching awl
for mending balls

FIG · XVIII - 22

bags for
sails, other
gear

GAME
GEAR

Storage
cabinet with labels

FIG · XVIII - 23

saddle bags

box in canoe

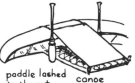

paddle lashed
to thwart

canoe
shelter

FIG · XVIII - 24

TRIP EQUIPMENT

Various items of trip equipment (Figure XVIII-24) may be made: *food bags;* *saddle bags* for bicycle or horseback; *shelters* for equipment; *first-aid kits* and *covers;* *baskets* or *chuck boxes* to fit into canoes or station wagons; waterproofed *covers* for packs. (See Leatherwork, Basketry and Equipment Making chapters.)

Indian and Pioneer Crafts

The campers in organized camps of today are probably as close as any present-day group to the living of the Indians and pioneers who were the earliest campers throughout our country. Campers are learning to live with as well as on the land, and most camp activities are rooted in the way of life of those early settlers. Basic camping skills grow from the everyday activities of making a home and a living from the resources of the land. Much of the color of our themes, special occasions, and background activities come from the history of these first campers. Many good camp crafts are based on fashioning useful and beautiful articles as did the Indians and the pioneers, using natural materials or designs from nature. A number of these crafts have been suggested in the chapters on various techniques in this book; this chapter will present some further suggestions of specific crafts that have come from these important groups in our country's folk lore.

INDIAN CRAFTS

Many camps are located in areas that are rich in Indian lore; there is no section of this country that cannot be linked with the history of some tribe. Many camps are in territory where Indians still live, either on reservations or in nearby communities. Some camps are privileged to have campers of Indian ancestry. Many camps have adopted an Indian name or tradition, and such camps make wide use of Indian lore in ceremonials, council fires, and camp traditions. As there is so much on this subject, it is impossible to do more than suggest some general possibilities. In all

INDIAN SYMBOLS   PLATE XIX

Indian activities, it is important to honor the true lore, and not to feel that the situation is well carried out by a feather in a headband or a blanket—any blanket—over a camper's shoulders. So much is authentic in the lore of the Indian, and this is so readily available in books that it is deplorable not to keep faith with the crafts, the costuming, and the customs which are truly part of our heritage.

INDIAN SYMBOLS

There are Indian symbols that may be used for decorations. Sometimes these are combined to make a stylized design; sometimes they tell a story. Colors, too, may be traditional in designs of Indian origin: blue for water and sky; white for sky and snow; green for earth and growing things; yellow for sun and light; black for outlines and for basic parts; red for animal tongues, bird feathers, etc.

A few of the traditional symbols that may be used in telling stories of camping are illustrated in Plate XIX.

For books giving more extensive material on symbols, see Books to Help at the end of this chapter.

CRAFT PROJECTS BASED ON INDIAN LORE

Ceremonial or dance equipment and costumes are illustrated in Figures XIX-1-9.

Craft articles are illustrated in Figures XIX-10-14.

Beaded articles are illustrated in Figures XIX-15 and 16.

Projects for group construction are illustrated in Figure XIX-17 *a-g*.

Decorations for special occasions are illustrated in Figure XIX-17 *h* and *i*. See also Chapter XVII on Favors and Decorations.

PIONEER CRAFTS

The crafts of the pioneers and early settlers are closely related to the crafts of the Indians. Throughout the Americas there is much fascinating lore of the Pilgrims, the covered wagon families, the settlers in the Midwest, the homesteaders in the Far West, the pioneers in Canada, and the Spanish settlers in the Southwest. All of these groups, and many more, contribute color as well as activities to a camping program. From their

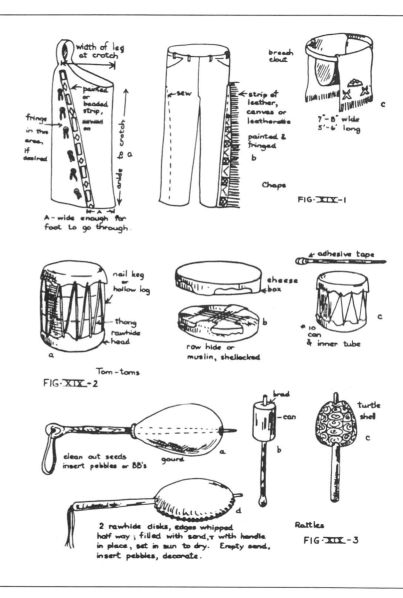

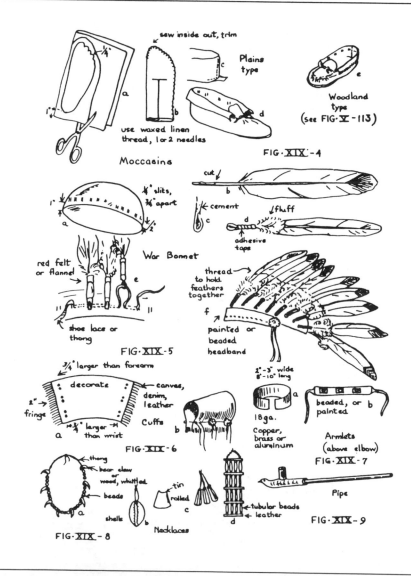

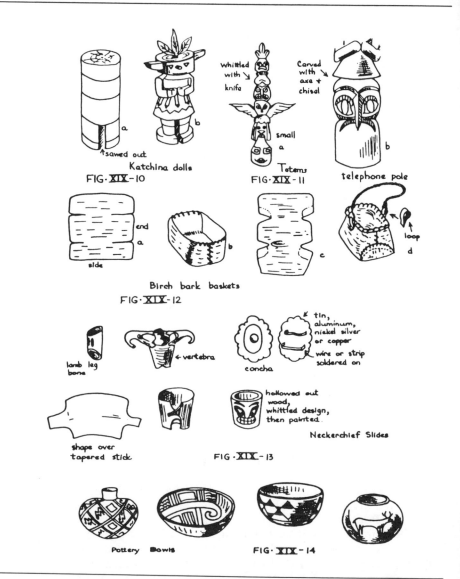

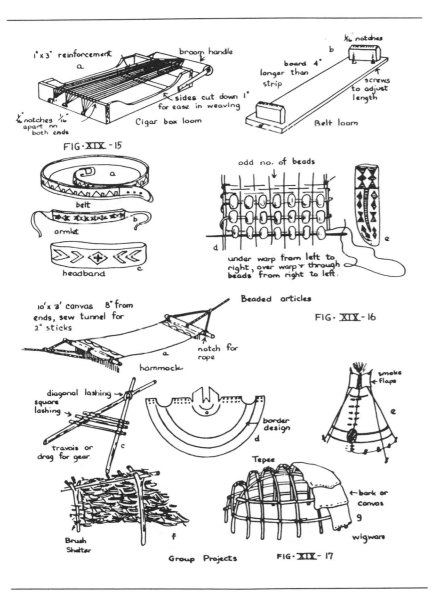

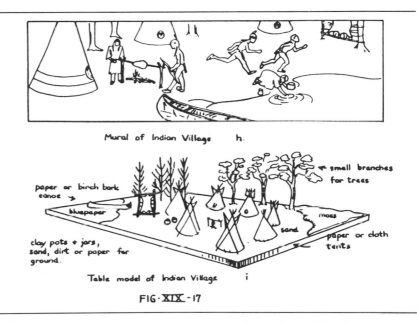

living stems much of the emphasis on simple outdoor living in our camping today. Appreciation of the courage and the hardihood required of those who pioneered or blazed new trails across the land comes to the camper who helps to establish a camp at an outpost, or to make a log cabin. Campers develop ingenuity and resourcefulness when they use what is at hand to make the camp more livable or more attractive, or to provide the materials for their own craft articles. Books that tell of the settling of any section where a camp is located will have pictures of the dwellings, the utensils and tools, and the toys that were developed and used by the early settlers; and from these books will come many camp program suggestions.

Pioneers and early settlers, of necessity, made great use of natural materials found near their homesites, and their utensils, tools, and wearing apparel were made with good, honest craftsmanship. The articles were utilitarian, but they had a rugged, homespun beauty. Wood, clay, leather, bark, bamboo, corn cobs and husks, shells, and gourds were commonly used as materials. A major part of this book develops such media, and because of this, much of the book is related to the crafts of pioneers.

Basic campcraft skills and the activities that grew out of them were stock in trade of the early settlers. Since the days of the pioneers, we have come to recognize the need of preserving our natural resources for future generations. Campers need to be reminded to leave more natural material than they use and to use only fallen or dried wood, not living trees. Reference should be made to the chapters on Basketry, Ceramics, Leather, Whittling, Correlation with Campcraft, and Correlation with Nature, in expanding the suggestions that are illustrated.

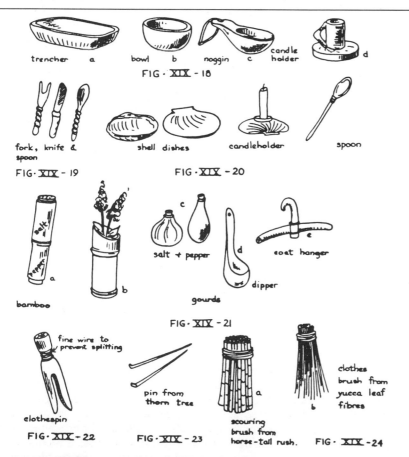

trencher   a   bowl   b   noggin   c   candle holder   d

FIG · XIX – 18

fork, knife & spoon

FIG · XIX – 19

shell dishes   candleholder   spoon

FIG · XIX – 20

bamboo   a   b   salt + pepper   c   d   dipper   coat hanger   e

gourds

FIG · XIX – 21

fine wire to prevent splitting

clothespin

FIG · XIX – 22

pin from thorn tree

FIG · XIX – 23

scouring brush from horse-tail rush.

clothes brush from yucca leaf fibres

FIG · XIX – 24

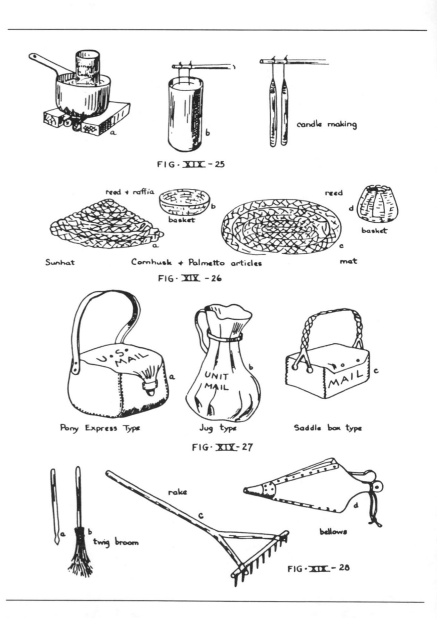

candle making

FIG · XIX – 25

reed + raffia   reed   d

Sunhat   basket   b   c   mat   basket

Cornhusk + Palmetto articles

FIG · XIX – 26

U·S· MAIL   a   UNIT MAIL   b   MAIL   c

Pony Express Type   Jug type   Saddle box type

FIG · XIX – 27

a   b   twig broom   rake   c   bellows   d

FIG · XIX – 28

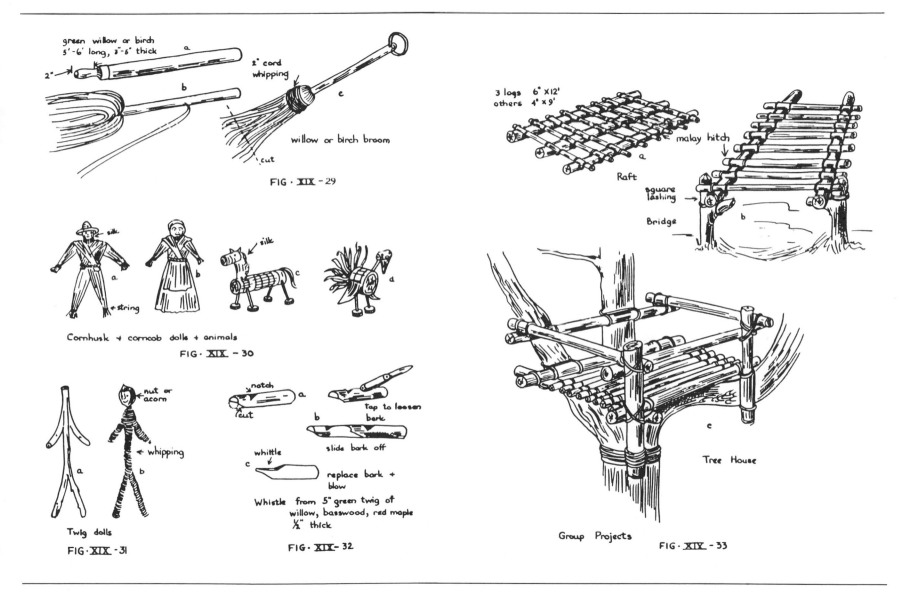

green willow or birch
5'-6' long, 3"-5" thick

a

2"

b

2" cord
whipping

c

cut

willow or birch broom

FIG · XIX - 29

silk

a

b

silk

c

d

+ string

Cornhusk + corncob dolls + animals

FIG · XIX - 30

nut or
acorn

a

b

← whipping

Twig dolls

FIG · XIX - 31

notch

a

cut

b

Tap to loosen
bark

slide bark off

whittle

c

replace bark +
blow

Whistle from 5" green twig of
willow, basswood, red maple
½" thick

FIG · XIX - 32

3 logs   6" X 12'
others 4" X 9'

malay hitch

a

Raft

square
lashing

Bridge

b

c

Tree House

Group Projects

FIG · XIX - 33

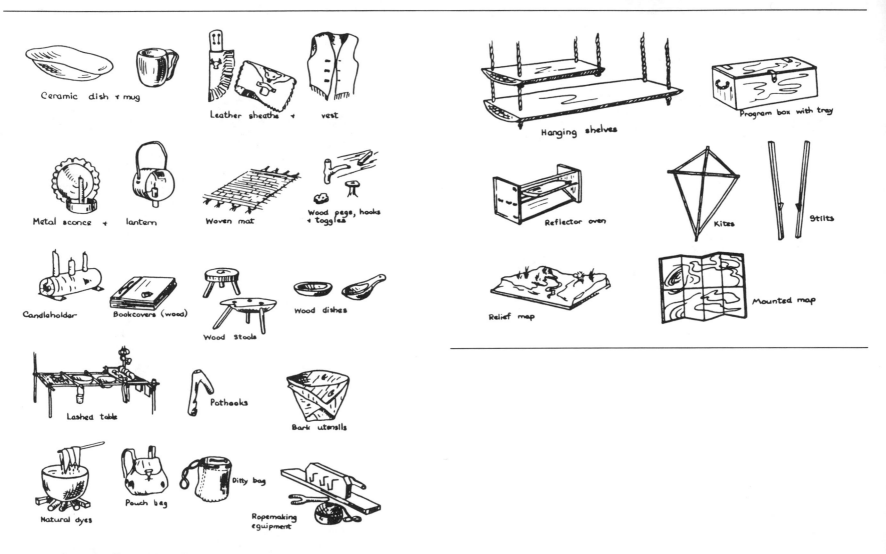

Ceramic dish + mug

Leather sheaths + vest

Metal sconce + lantern

Woven mat

Wood pegs, hooks + toggles

Candleholder

Bookcovers (wood)

Wood stools

Wood dishes

Lashed table

Potheoks

Bark utensils

Natural dyes

Pouch bag

Ditty bag

Ropemaking equipment

Hanging shelves

Program box with tray

Reflector oven

Kites

Stilts

Relief map

Mounted map

Suggested Projects from Other Chapters

Map Making

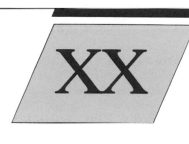

The making and using of maps is a good camping activity, involving compass work, cross-country travel, and exploration. These are basic campcraft activities, especially good for older campers. Map making is a good group project, beginning with simple sketch maps used for trails or explorations, or for giving simple directions, and extending to the making of detailed maps of the area. In the craft realm, such maps may be developed into pictorial maps, relief maps, or three-dimensional maps, or maps may be enlarged for use in orienteering or cross-country going.

Details on how to make sketch maps or more extensive maps can be found in specialized books dealing with orienteering or map making. This chapter will present map making from an arts and crafts point of view. For field use, a map must be very legible, accurate, and detailed, but for decorative use there is freedom in developing the map, using the basic scale and dimensions.

Any map should tell a story of a place, indicating directions, distances, or scale, designed to help the observer to find his way in the specific place. There are *sketch maps,* usually very simple in scope, *surveyed maps,* more detailed and accurate, *topographical maps* that show contours of hills and land levels, *aerial photographic maps,* and *maps for specific purposes,* such as road maps, city maps, or maps of the historical background of an area.

Every map should have a section that tells about that particular map. This is called the *legend,* and contains information about the map: the name of the map (what it covers), the scale of the map (how much distance one inch covers on the map), a direction arrow (indicating where North is on the map, so it can be oriented), any special signs used in

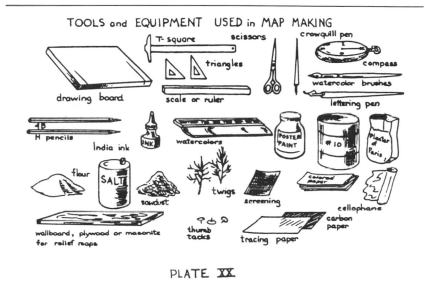

PLATE XX

making the map (called map signs), the date, and the maker's name. Even the simplest maps must have these items so that the person looking at the map can use it accurately (Figure XX-1).

In making any map, plan the size the map is to be; block it in on paper for center position; plan a place for the legend. Sketch map in pencil; then finish with India ink or permanent felt tip markers (see Chapter VIII on Sketching and Painting).

PICTORIAL MAPS

Pictorial maps are maps drawn to scale, but with the map signs and symbols enlarged and out of proportion to the scale, highlighting such features. In making a camp map, the tents, buildings, campfire site, waterfront, and trails will stand out from the map to show the general layout. Front and side view of buildings are generally better than top views, though the general appearance is of a view from the air. This type of map is used for camp booklets and folders, for postcards, and for wall decorations. The method calls for free-hand sketching, with much imagination in the use of the traditional camp symbols and background.

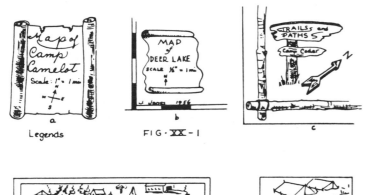

Legends   FIG·XX-1

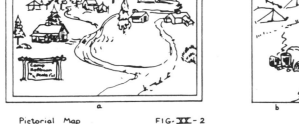

Pictorial Map   FIG·XX-2

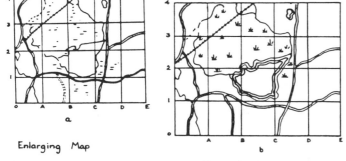

Enlarging Map

FIG·XX-3

ENLARGING SECTIONS OF MAPS

When a specific part of a larger map is wanted, one area can be enlarged or blown up by the *grid system*. A road map or a topographical map or a handmade map may be used as the base.

Equipment and materials needed: drawing board; T-square and triangle; pencil and ruler; paper for map.

Steps

1. With a T-square and triangle, mark off the area to be enlarged on original map. Mark this area into grids or squares (Figure XX-3 *a*) horizontally and vertically.

    On paper for enlarged map, plan position of map, with legend, and in pencil draw line for bottom edge of map. Mark off places for squares, the same number as are on the area marked on original map, but in proportion desired. That is, if squares on original map are one inch, squares on enlarged map may be two inches, four inches, etc.
3. Draw the left vertical line on enlargement, and mark squares in similar fashion. Finish off the other two sides, and mark the grids on enlargement. (Measure and mark carefully.) Mark the grids on both maps with letters across the top and numbers on the sides (Figure XX-3).
4. Sketch the features of the original map on the enlargement, being guided by the lines within the smaller grids (Figure XX-3 *b*).
5. Ink in the features on the enlarged map, and when ink is dry, erase pencil marks.
6. Finish map with legend.

TRACING A MAP

Another way to reproduce a map, in part or as a whole, is to trace it. A road map, topographical map, or aerial photography may be used. This is often the basis for a pictorial map.

Equipment and materials needed: drawing board; T-square, ruler, triangle; masking tape; H and 4B pencils (hard and very soft); tracing paper; paper for map; map to be traced; carbon paper.

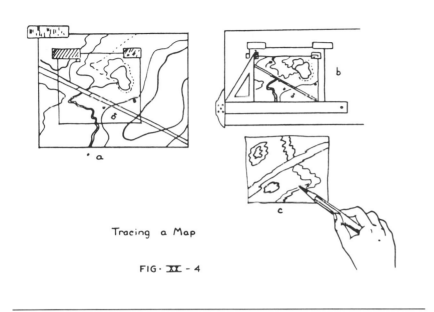

Tracing a Map

FIG· XX - 4

Steps

1. Fasten map or photograph to be traced to drawing board with masking tape. Mark off area to be traced, if whole map is not to be used.
2. Fasten tracing paper over map or photograph with masking tape (Figure XX-4 a).
3. With hard pencil, trace the features that will appear on the new map, such as rivers, trails, places of interest (Figure XX-4 a).
4. Remove tracing paper and check to be sure all features are recorded clearly. Replace carefully and add, if necessary.
5. Remove original map, and place tracing paper on drawing board. With T-square and triangle, draw the boundaries of the map (Figure XX-4 b).
6. Turn tracing paper over, and with *soft* pencil shade over the lines that will be placed on new map. It is not necessary to cover the areas that are blank (Figure XX-4 c).
7. Hold tracing paper up to light, to see if all lines have been covered. Add, if necessary.
8. Fasten map paper to drawing board, and fasten tracing paper in place on map paper, being careful to arrange margins, centering, place for legend, etc.
9. With well-sharpened *hard* pencil, go over all lines on tracing paper, using even pressure. (Keep pencil sharp.)
10. Remove masking tape at two corners, and look to see if all lines have been traced. If not, complete tracing.
11. Remove tracing paper and go over the lines on new map with India ink and pen. Draw in any buildings, map signs, etc., that are desired, and put in legend. (See pictorial maps, above.)
12. Carbon paper may be used instead of steps 6 and 7; the carbon paper is slipped under the tracing paper and the tracing is done as above.

Suggestions for reproduction: if the map is to be reproduced by photostat or other processes, ink the tracing. Blueprints may be made from the tracing, also, but the black lines will appear white on the print.

If the map is to be reproduced by mimeographing, ink the tracing, or go over the lines with a soft pencil, then slip the tracing under the mimeograph stencil for a second tracing on the stencil. If map is to be photocopied, use India ink or tracing paper.

THREE-DIMENSIONAL MAPS

A three-dimensional map may be used as an exhibit on a table, or on a wall. The basic map is flat on paper, wall-board, or wood; and the buildings and other symbols are made of paper, cardboard, or other materials in three dimensions, and fastened at the proper spots.

If the background of the map is to be predominantly one color, such as green for grass, cover the foundation with green paper, paint, or cloth. Make waters—brooks, lakes, etc.—of blue paper or cellophane. Make sand and fields of brown paper.

Make buildings, tents, etc., as in dioramas (see Chapter XV on Correlation with Nature, and Chapter XVII on Favors and Decorations). Sponges dyed green make good trees; small twigs of evergreens may be used for temporary maps. Small lumps of clay may be used to make trees, frames, cranes, etc., stand up.

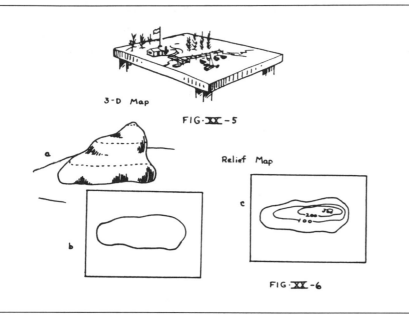

3-D Map

FIG·XX-5

Relief Map

FIG·XX-6

RELIEF MAPS

Relief maps are more accurate representations of the terrain than flat or three-dimensional maps. Relief maps show contours of the land, with hills and valleys. This is a fine project for a group of campers to make, either for acquainting new campers with the trails and areas on the camp site, or for in-town promotion activities.

To make a relief map, it is necessary to use and understand a topographical map. These maps are made by the U.S. Geological Survey and may be obtained from local Survey offices or from the Superintendent of Documents, Washington, D.C. 20010. Hikers and trippers should be familiar with the topographical map sections for the area around the camp or in the trip country. On these maps the height of land above sea level is indicated by brown lines with numbers on them. Thus by looking at the lines it is possible to tell if the land rises at all, and if the rise is gradual or sharp. By symbols, the maps indicate swamps, geological formations, rivers, roads, some buildings, and so forth.

To help campers understand the lines indicating contour, cut a potato in half and lay it on a paper (Figure XX-6 *a*). This will represent a hill. Draw around the base with a pencil (Figure XX-6 *b*). Remove potato, and the contour line of the paper looks like the base of the hill at sea level on the map. If the hill were 300 feet high, and the lines on the map were 100-foot divisions, this hill would have three different contour lines. Cut the potato into three horizontal slices, the same thickness. Place the second slice in the first drawing and draw around it. Then place the third or smallest slice in the center of the second drawing, and draw around it (Figure XX-6 *c*). In making a relief map, layers of cardboard or wood are nailed or glued together in the same way that the potato slices would be put back together to make the hill.

To Make a Relief Map

Work from a topographical map, or an enlargement of a section of one map, planning the total size of the table or base, which should be strong enough not to warp.

Work out the elevations and contours with pieces of wood or cardboard, and cover the whole base with plaster of Paris or papier-mache or similar mixture (see below) to make the map more nearly resemble the land. After the map is dry, paint with opaque water colors (poster paints) to simulate the landscape colors (Figure XX-7).

Buildings, trees, etc., may be added as desired. Be sure to keep them in scale, otherwise the map will be misleading. The buildings and other symbols will probably be very small; they may be modeled from clay or plasticene and painted with the poster paint.

A legend should be added either on the map, or on an easel nearby.

To Make the Base Mixture

—*Papier-mache:* shred newsprint paper into small strips. In a bowl or basin put one pint flour paste (see below) with one tablespoon glue. Thin with water to syrupy consistency. Mix newsprint into paste, and squeeze until mass is pulp-like. Spread over the foundation, molding the terrain to look like the original. Place in warm, sunny place to dry.

—*Flour paste:* mix three-fourths cup cold water and one cup flour in double boiler top. Stir and cook, adding one cup hot water gradually. Add a little powdered clove to discourage mildew. When smooth, it is

Relief Model   FIG·XX-7

Mounted Map

FIG·XX-8

ready to use.

—*Paste and sawdust:* mix three-fourths cup flour with two cups water, and cook to make paste as thick as white sauce. Add sawdust gradually, as much as the mixture will take. Spread over the contours, as above. Let dry in sunny, airy place.

—Plaster of Paris: *see Chapter IV on Ceramics.*

MOUNTING MAPS FOR CARRYING ON TRIPS

Paper maps become worn and tear easily when folded and unfolded, so hikers and trippers often mount them on linen or muslin.

Adhere the map to the piece of cloth with diluted Sobo glue, pressing out any bubbles of air and leaving the map pressed between papers under a heavy weight overnight. The backing may then be trimmed, and the map rolled to go in a pack.

If the map is to be folded and carried in the pack, it is best to cut the map in sections. Paste the sections in order, on a piece of cloth, being sure there is a small space left between the edges, for the fold. Press firmly.

Maps to be used for hiking should be sprayed with clear plastic to keep them clean and easy-to-read.

Photography

Photography is allied to sketching and painting because the result of the activity is a picture. Good photography is based on the composition of the picture taken, on the originality of the subject matter, and on the skill with which lights and shadows are combined. In general, the same rules of composition which have been given for sketching and painting hold true for photography.

A large majority of campers have cameras. Many will have instruments of their own for the first time, and they will need guidance to gain satisfaction from their photographic efforts and to know the possibilities of their particular cameras, no matter how simple the instruments may be. They will need to learn how to get satisfactory pictures that tell the desired story, and that lead the young photographers along the fascinating trail of photography in general. Experienced photographers who know their cameras will be ready for activities in a darkroom, and for projects that make use of their picture-taking skills, such as a series of pictures for the camp log or a movie for camp promotion.

This chapter is not designed to give instruction in how to take photographs, but rather to give help to counselors in guiding this activity as part of a creative craft program. There are always some counselors who have an interest in photography, and they can help with informal activities in the tent or cabin groups, or in special groups of interested campers. Some camps have a special counselor in charge of photographic activities, especially if the camp has an extensive photography program.

In photography activities, it is very important that the counselor be aware of the need to help the camper with the simplest camera, and to

SUGGESTIONS FOR AN EXHIBIT ON _____
HOW TO TAKE GOOD PICTURES

keep fingers away from lens opening

Hold camera steady

Shoot so that sun does not shine on camera lens

Take a deep breath Slowly _squeeze_ shutter button

Look in your finder to see the picture

PICTURES OF PEOPLE SHOULD _____

have a center of interest

have contrast

show action (but not too fast)

group—not too many

PICTURES OF SCENES SHOULD _____

lead eye into center of interest

have good background

be framed

NOT cut across center

FIG. XXI-1

gear activities to include him. Much can be done with simple cameras, and first enjoyment in photography will come with successful picture taking, no matter how elementary. Campers with more elaborate cameras will need opportunities to learn how to use the various features of their cameras to best advantage.

A CAMP PHOTOGRAPHY PROGRAM

Here are some suggestions for activities that might be included in a camp program:

—*A interest group or club* may be formed by counselors and campers for those who are interested in learning about picture taking. This group may meet several times a week, or occasionally, as on a Sunday afternoon. It may be a clinic to which campers bring their problems in loading film or in which there is discussion of what makes a picture good. Informal talks, demonstrations of various types of equipment, evaluations of pictures, and similar topics may be included in the activities.

—*A day-by-day camera group* may be conducted by a designated counselor, in the form of a course.

—*A special bulletin board* may help point out good practices, and may be a place for exhibiting a selection of pictures taken by campers (Figure XXI-1).

—*A darkroom* may be part of the camp equipment; the simplest equipment would include that for printing negatives, the rolls being developed outside the camp. Or the equipment may be extensive enough to include developing paraphernalia. An enlarger is a fine addition, and presents many possibilities for experienced campers.

—*Exhibits and contests* may be held, especially in camps where the campers are registered for a period long enough to see pictures they have taken in finished form. This is seldom possible in a short-term camp. From such an exhibit, appropriate pictures may be printed by a group of older campers, to be used as banquet favors or to sell at the camp store.

—*A nature file* of photographs of nature subjects found on the site may grow from year to year, this being a combined effort with the nature department. Nature prints, similar to blueprints, but

HOW DO <u>YOUR</u> PICTURES LOOK?

HINTS ABOUT WHAT TO DO ✓ WHAT NOT TO DO

Shooting a pal?

Too far away — get up closer!

Too close! Look in your finder

Better. Get him doing something

Look at what else is in the picture

Too much scenery

New hat?

Too much background

Have a <u>highlight</u> — include people for contrast

FIG. XXI-2

made on photographic paper in a darkroom, may be made as part of such a file. (See Chapter VII on Printing and Stenciling).

—*A picture story of camp* may be developed by campers for use in the camp booklet or folder, or as promotional material.

—*A movie or set of colored slides* may be planned, staged, and photographed by an advanced group.

—*Step-by-step or how-to-do* series may be worked out in slides or black and white pictures, to use in teaching basic skills such as fire building and cooking.

—*Craft projects,* such as lashed or bark frames for photographs, albums with leather, paper, or wood covers, and cases for cameras and gear may be developed by individuals or by groups (see Chapter X on Woodworking, Chapter V on Leatherwork, etc.).

—*Photography with floodlights* may be part of rainy-day or camp-fire activities, if such equipment is available.

Resources

We have not attempted to list resources at the end of each chapter, as in the first edition, because books today become unavailable so quickly. Most camps or groups have libraries of their own or access to city or county libraries who may lend books for a longer period for use by craft programs. Local bookstores usually have a wide range of books in the arts and crafts. Listed below are some books currently available.

The American Camping Association Bookstore has an annual catalog of books including a section on arts and crafts. A copy of the catalog is free on request. Write to ACA Bookstore, American Camping Association, Bradford Woods, 5000 State Road 67 North, Martinsville, IN 46151-7902.

Alkema, Chester J. *Crafting with Nature's Materials*. NY: Sterling Press, 1972.

Ashley, Clifford W. *The Ashley Book of Knots*. NY: Doubleday, 1944.

Barnes, Charles Barnes and Blake, David P. *Creative Macrame Projects*. NY: Dover Publications, 1972.

Bridgewater, *Easy-to-Make Decorative Kites*. NY: Dover Publications, 1974.

Broadwater, Elaine. *Claycraft at Home*. Radnor, PA: Chilton Book Company, 1978.

Crawford, Marguerite C. and Fuller, Marietta C. *Cornshuck Crafts*. NY: Exporelian Press, 1967.

Day, JoAnne. *The Complete Book of Stencilcraft*. NY: Dover Publications, 1987.

Egge, Ruth Stearns. *How to Make Something for Nothing*. NY: Coward: McCann, 1968.

Elliott, Geoffrey. *Sketching for Beginners*. London: Watron-Giptell Publishers, 1970.

Endicott, Robert F. *Wood Fun for Kids*. NY: Association Press, 1961.

Grangier, Stuart E. *Creative Papercraft*. London: Stuart Press, 1979.

Grater. *Complete Book of Paper Mask Making*. NY: Dover Publications, 1978.

Groneman, Chris H. *Leathercraft*. Peoria, IL: Charles A. Bennett Company, 1963.

Hammett, Catherine T. *The Campcraft Book*. Martinsville, IN: American Camping Association, 1987.

Held, Shirley E. *Weaving, A Handbook for Fiber Craftsmen*. NY: Holt, Rhinehart, and Winston, 1972.

Ickes, Marguerite and Esh, Reba Selden. *The Book of Arts and Crafts*. NY: Dover, 1954.

Johnson, Mary Elizabeth and Pearson, Katherine. *Nature Crafts*. Birmingham, England: Oxmoor House, Inc., 1980.

Johnson and Coker. *Complete Book of Straw Craft*. NY: Dover Publications, 1974.

Kuykendall, Karen. *Design in Papier-Mache*. NY: Hearthside Press, 1968.

Lindbeck, John R. et al. *Basic Crafts*. Peoria, IL: Charles A. Bennett Publishers, 1969.

Linsley, Leslie. *Wildcrafts*. NY: Doubleday and Company, 1977.

Leeming, Joseph. *Fun With Clay*. NY: J. B. Lippencott Company, 1944.

Meilach, Dona Z. *Contemporary Leather*. Chicago IL: Henry Regnery Company, 1971.

Meilach, Dona Z. *Macrame: Creative Design in Knotting*. NY: Crown Publishers, 1971.

Meilach, Dona and Snow, L. E. *Weaving Off Loom*. Chicago, IL: Henry Regnery Company, 1973.

Melen, Lisa. *Knotting and Netting*. NY: Van Nostrand Reinhold, 1971.

Miller, Lenore H. *The Nature Specialist*. Martinsville, IN: American Camping Association, 1986.

Pearse, Jack and Taylor, Bryce. *High Above the Thundercloud*. Huntsville, Ontario: Camp Tawingo Publications, 1986.

Peduzzi, Anthony and Judy. *Making Action Toys in Wood*. NY: Sterling Publishing Company, 1985.

Petersen, Grete. *Creative Leathercraft*. NY: Sterling Publishers, 1960.

Petersen, Grete. *Making Toys with Plywood*. NY: Reinhold Book Company, 1971.

Pitz, Henry. *Sketching with Felt Tip Pens*. London: Studio Publishers, 1961.

Self, Charles R. *Making Birdhouses and Feeders*. NY: Sterling Publishing Company, 1985.

Shaw, G. Russel. *Knots: Use and Organization*. NY: Macmillan, 1972.

Tangerman, E. J. *Basic Whittling and Woodcarving*. NY: Sterling Publishing Company, 1984.

Trevor, Henry, *Pottery Step-by-Step*. NY: Watson-Guptill/Ballantine Books, 1966.

Upton, John. *The Woodcarver's Primer*. NY: Stover Press, 1982.

Villasenor, David and Jean. *Indian Designs*. Happy Camp, CA: Naturegraph Publishers, 1983.

Wilson, Eva. *North American Indian Designs*. NY: Dover Publications, 1987.

General Index

Index to Projects by Craft